The English Face

BY DAVID PIPER

With 145 illustrations in photogravure

THAMES AND HUDSON

FOR ANNE HORATIA

'Be careful of your face, my dear.'
(Evelyn to his wife, 22 February 1652)

ALL RIGHTS RESERVED 1957
TEXT PRINTED IN GREAT BRITAIN BY
HAZELL WATSON AND VINEY LTD AYLESBURY
PHOTOGRAVURE BY VANDYCK PRINTERS BRISTOL

CONTENTS

ILLUSTRATIONS

The author is deeply grateful to Her Majesty the Queen for gracious permission to reproduce portraits in the Royal Collection; and to Her Majesty Queen Elizabeth the Queen Mother. He is also greatly indebted to the generosity of all private owners, and to those in charge of public collections, for permission to reproduce objects in their care; the names of owners are given in the entry for each illustration.

chalk and Indian ink, on pink paper, $12\frac{1}{2} \times 9\frac{1}{2}$ in. Probably in her late twenties; she was beheaded, 19th May 1536, to make room for Henry's third queen, Jane Seymour. *The late Earl of Bradford.* page 42

17 JANE SEYMOUR; by Hans Holbein, 1536 (?). Detail, from the three-quarter-length painting on wood (about half life-size). Aged about 27. *Kunsthistorisches Museum, Vienna.* page 47

18 HENRY VIII; by Hans Holbein, 1536 (?). Detail, from the almost miniature ($11 \times 7\frac{1}{2}$ in.) half-length painting on wood; some-times said, but doubtfully, to have formed a diptych with the 'Jane Seymour' now in the Mauritshuis, The Hague. *Baron Thyssen-Bornemisza, Lugano.* page 48

19 THOMAS CRANMER; by Gerlach Flicke, c. 1546. Detail, from the almost life-size three-quarter-length painting on wood. Aged 57. *National Portrait Gallery, London.* page 61

20 ELIZABETH I; artist unknown, c. 1546. Detail, from the life-size three-quarter-length painting on wood. As Princess, aged about 13. *Windsor Castle; by gracious permission of Her Majesty the Queen.* page 62

21 ELIZABETH I; by Nicholas Hilliard, 1572. Detail, enlarged, from the miniature. Aged about 39. *National Portrait Gallery, London* (no. 108). page 62

22 ELIZABETH I; artist unknown, c. 1575/80. Detail, from the life-size three-quarter-length painting on panel. Aged about 45. *National Portrait Gallery, London* (no. 2082). page 63

23 ELIZABETH I; artist unknown, c. 1588. Detail, from a life-size three-quarter-length painting on panel (a variant of the Armada portrait at Woburn Abbey). Aged about 55. *National Portrait Gallery, London* (no. 541). page 63

24 ELIZABETH I; by William Rogers, 1589. Engraving, $9\frac{3}{4} \times 6\frac{1}{4}$ in. *British Museum.* page 62

25 ELIZABETH I; by Isaac Oliver, c. 1600. Detail, enlarged, from the unfinished miniature. Aged about 67. *Victoria and Albert Museum, London (Crown Copyright).* page 63

26 ELIZABETH I; by Nicholas Hilliard, c. 1590/1600. Detail, en-larged, from the miniature. In her sixties. *Victoria and Albert Museum, London (Crown Copyright).* page 63

Museum, taken before the statue was restored to its site after the war.) *Whitehall, London.* page 105

38 CHARLES I; by Nicholas Hilliard, c. 1608/9. Miniature, slightly enlarged. As Duke of York, aged about 8. *Victoria and Albert Museum, London (Crown Copyright).* page 106

39 CHARLES I; by Sir Peter Lely, 1647. Detail, from the life-size painting of Charles I and his son James II painted for the 10th Duke cf Northumberland when Charles was held at Hampton Court; known as the "Clouded Majesty" portrait, from the poem about it by Lely's friend, Lovelace. Aged 47. *The Duke of Northumberland.* page 106

40 CHARLES I; studio of Daniel Mytens, 1631. Detail, from the life-size whole-length painting (one of several versions between 1629 and 1631). Aged about 30. *National Portrait Gallery, London (no. 1246).* page 107

41 CHARLES I; by John Hoskins, c. 1642. Miniature, actual size. Aged about 42. *Windsor Castle; by gracious permission of Her Majesty the Queen.* page 106

42 CHARLES I; by Edward Bower, 1649. Detail, from the life-size three-quarter-length painting based on studies made at the trial of Charles. Aged 49. *By gracious permission of Her Majesty Queen Elizabeth the Queen Mother.* page 106

43 CHARLES I; mezzotint engraving by J. Simon (early 18th century) from a painting by E. Bower, 1649. Detail, showing how the later engraver has barbered Charles' beard to "Van Dyck" trim; the engraving is from the version at Jesus College, Oxford, in which the face is as in no. 42 above. *National Portrait Gallery, London.* page 107

44 CHARLES I; by Sir Anthony van Dyck, 1635. Detail, from the half-length life-size canvas, painted as a model to send to Bernini in Italy that he might make a bust from it. Aged 35. *Windsor Castle; by gracious permission of Her Majesty the Queen.* page 108

45 CHARLES I; by Nicholas Briot, 1630. Medal. Issued in assertion of Charles' claims to the Dominion of the Sea. *British Museum.* page 108

46 CHARLES I; by Nicholas Briot, 1639. Medal. Revised version of the 1630 medal (no. 45). *British Museum.* page 108

47 CHARLES I; engraving, after a lost bust by Gian Lorenzo Bernini, 1636, based on a painting by Van Dyck, 1635. See no. 44. *British Museum.*   page 108

48 JOHN, 1ST BARON BYRON (d. 1652); by William Dobson, c. 1644. Detail, from the life-size three-quarter-length painting. *Lt.-Colonel J. Leicester-Warren.*   page 113

49 'THE BROTHERS'; by Sir Anthony van Dyck, c. 1635/40. Life-size (87 × 50½ in.). Two young courtiers (their identities are lost). *National Gallery, London.*   page 114

50 ELIZABETH, COUNTESS OF CASTLEHAVEN (1580–1647); by Sir Anthony van Dyck, c. 1635–7. Detail, from the life-size three-quarter-length painting. Aged about 55. *The Earl of Pembroke.* page 119

51 OLIVER CROMWELL; by Samuel Cooper, c. 1650/3. Miniature, enlarged from 3⅛ × 2½ in. Probably the original unfinished sketch from the life, kept by the artist as a pattern; finished versions are not known with dates earlier than 1656, but Cooper was working for Cromwell by 1650, and this sketch may date from c. 1650/3. See also no. 52. *The Duke of Buccleuch.*   page 120

52 OLIVER CROMWELL; by Sir Peter Lely, c. 1654. Detail, from the life-size bust painting; Lely seems to have produced several versions of this design after Cromwell's appointment as Protector (16th Dec. 1653), probably as official "presentation portraits"; two were done for the Portuguese and Dutch ambassadors. Lely's portrait seems to be based mainly on Cooper's; see no. 51. *City Museum and Art Gallery, Birmingham.*   page 121

53 THOMAS HOBBES (1588–1679); by Samuel Cooper. Miniature, enlarged from 2⅝ × 2¼ in. Drawn in the sixteen-sixties, this is a "pattern" sketch from the life. Aged in his seventies. *Edward B. Greene Collection, the Cleveland Museum of Art, Ohio.*   page 121

54 BARBARA VILLIERS, DUCHESS OF CLEVELAND (1641– 1709); by Samuel Cooper, c. 1660. Miniature, reduced by approximately a quarter. A "pattern sketch", unfinished. Aged about 20: "a woman of great beauty, but enormously vicious and ravenous; foolish but imperious, very uneasy to the King, and always carrying on intrigues with

other men". *Windsor Castle; by gracious permission of Her Majesty the Queen.* page 121

55 DOROTHY OSBORNE (Lady Temple); by Sir Peter Lely, 1653 (?). Detail, from the life-size bust painting. Aged about 25. *The Countess Mountbatten of Burma.* page 122

56 CHARLES II; by H. Pellé, 1684. Marble bust, life-size. Aged about 55 (in the year that he died). *Victoria and Albert Museum, London (Crown Copyright).* page 127

57 NELL GWYN (1650–87); by Sir Peter Lely, c. 1670. Detail, from the life-size nude, perhaps the 'Madam Gwynn's picture naked, with a Cupid' that belonged to James II; the identification is not however quite certain, and this portrait has been called Barbara Villiers (see no. 54). *Denys Bower, Esq.* page 128

58 SAMUEL PEPYS (1632–1703); by John Hayls, 1666. Life-size (29½ × 24½ in.), holding a poem starting "Beauty, retire . . .," set to music by himself. Aged 34. *National Portrait Gallery, London.* page 137

59 JOHN, 1ST DUKE OF LAUDERDALE (1616–82) and ELIZA-BETH, DUCHESS OF LAUDERDALE; by Sir Peter Lely. Detail, from the life-size three-quarter-length, perhaps of about the time of their marriage, 1672. She is aged about 44. *Ham House (Victoria and Albert Museum, London; Crown Copyright).* page 138

60 DUKE OF LAUDERDALE; by Benedetto Gennari, c. 1674. Detail, from the life-size three-quarter-length painting in Garter robes. Aged about 58. *Lord Tollemache.* page 138

61 DUKE OF LAUDERDALE; by John Riley, c. 1680. Detail, from the life-size bust painting. Aged about 65. *The Duke of Northumberland.* page 138

62 MRS. ANNE SOTHEBY; by Sir Godfrey Kneller, 1692. Detail, from the life-size three-quarter-length. A typically Augustan beauty. *The late Major-General F. E. Sotheby.* page 143

63 JOSEPH ADDISON (1672–1719); by Sir Godfrey Kneller, c. 1705. Life-size (36 × 28 in.); one of Kneller's portraits of members of the Whig club, the Kit-Cat. *National Portrait Gallery, London (no. 3193).* page 144

men, Sheppard was hanged at Tyburn, 16th November 1724, aged 21. *British Museum.* page 166

75 SARAH MALCOLM; by William Hogarth, 1733. Approximately original size; detail, from the painting showing her in her cell not long before her execution, for murder, in Fleet Street, March 1733; aged about 25. *National Gallery of Scotland, Edinburgh.* page 166

76 WILLIAM HOGARTH (1697–1764); by L. F. Roubiliac, c. 1740 (?). Detail, from the life-size terracotta bust. Aged about 43, or younger. *National Portrait Gallery, London.* page 171

77 COLLEY CIBBER (1671–1757); by L. F. Roubiliac. Detail, from the life-size coloured plaster bust (the eyes are glass, and the turban detachable). Actor, dramatist, and Poet Laureate; here apparently aged about 70; probably of the seventeen-forties. *National Portrait Gallery, London.* page 172

78 'THE SHRIMP GIRL'; by William Hogarth (? c. 1750; it is not exactly datable). Oil sketch, life-size (25 × 20¾ in.). *National Gallery, London.* page 177

79 Detail, about actual size, from no. IV of 'MARRIAGE À LA MODE ('LA TOILETTE'); by William Hogarth, c. 1743. The faces of the musicians at least may be English only by immigration. *National Gallery, London.* page 178

80 'HOGARTH'S SERVANTS'; by William Hogarth, c. 1750/60 (?). 24½ × 29¼ in. The title is traditional and may well be correct; the old man is perhaps Ben Ives. *National Gallery, London.* page 179

81 JOSEPH HIGHMORE (1692–1780) and (right) an old SCHOOL-MASTER; by Joseph Highmore, c. 1750. Detail, from the life-size group of 'Mr. Oldham and his Guests' over a bowl of punch. *Tate Gallery, London.* page 180

82 MARY MONCKTON, COUNTESS OF CORK (1746–1840); by Sir Joshua Reynolds, 1777/8. Detail, from the life-size whole-length; a well-known and somewhat eccentric blue-stocking, here aged 31. *National Gallery, London.* page 185

83 CHARLES JAMES FOX (1749–1806); by Joseph Nollekens, c. 1802. Marble bust, life-size. Aged about 53 (his "black and bristly person" aged fast from sheer relentless living). *Victoria and Albert Museum, London (Crown Copyright).* page 186

14

small-scale whole-length. A "romantic" view of the poet, aged 21, of which he said: "It does not *flatter* me . . . but the subject is a bad one and I must even do as [my valet] does over his Greek wines, make a face and hope for a better." *By gracious permission of Her Majesty the Queen.* page 228 by H. Collen, 1829. Miniature (reduced from $4\frac{3}{4} \times 3\frac{1}{2}$ in.). Lawyer, Master of the Rolls; aged 46. *National Portrait Gallery, London.* page 259

114 JANE MORRIS, posed by D. G. Rossetti for an unknown photographer in 1865. *Dr. H. Gernsheim.* page 260

115 ELIZABETH SIDDAL (1834–62); by D. G. Rossetti, c. 1863. Detail, from 'Beata Beatrix', a posthumous memorial by Rossetti of his wife; she died, from an overdose of laudanum, aged 28. *Tate Gallery, London.* page 260

116 'THE FRONT ROW AT THE OPERA'; by William Holyoake. Detail, from the less than life-size painting of the 'seventies (?). *Glasgow Art Gallery.* page 261

117 EMMA, MRS. MADOX BROWN; by Ford Madox Brown, c. 1852. Detail, black chalk ($6\frac{1}{2} \times 7$ in.). Study for the head of the depressed woman emigrant in the 'Last of England'; she is aged about 20. *City Museum and Art Gallery, Birmingham.* page 261

118 CHARLOTTE BRONTË (1816–55); by her brother P. B. Brontë, 1835. Detail, from the group (rather less than life-size) of the Brontë sisters. Aged about 20. *National Portrait Gallery, London.* page 262

119 CHARLOTTE BRONTË; by George Richmond, 1850. Detail, chalk drawing, about life-size. Aged 34. *National Portrait Gallery, London.* page 262

120 GEORGINA TREHERNE (later Mrs. Weldon); by G. F. Watts, 1858. Panel, 21×17 in. A well-known beauty, painted at Little Holland House. *The Viscount Wimborne.* page 271

121 ALFRED, LORD TENNYSON (1809–92); by Julia Margaret Cameron, c. 1867. Detail, from the photograph ($9\frac{3}{4} \times 12$ in.). *Dr. H. Gernsheim.* page 272

122 ALFRED, LORD TENNYSON; by G. F. Watts 1863/4. Detail, from the life-size bust painting. Aged about 54. *National Portrait Gallery, London.* page 273

123 CARDINAL HENRY EDWARD MANNING (1802–92); by G. F. Watts, 1882. Detail, from the life-size three-quarter-length. *National Portrait Gallery, London.* page 274

124 'ARRANGEMENT IN GREY AND BLACK' (Carlyle); by

Life-size (89½ × 45 in.). Artist and author; aged 29. *Tate Gallery, London.* page 297

137 'VERNON LEE' (Violet Paget, 1856–1935); by J. S. Sargent, 1881. Detail, from the life-size bust painting. Essayist; aged 25. *Tate Gallery, London.* page 298

138 GEORGE MOORE (1852–1933); by W. R. Sickert, c. 1891. Detail, from the bust painting. *Tate Gallery, London.* page 299

139 FREDERICK GUSTAVUS BURNABY (1842–85); by J. G. Tissot, 1870. Painting (panel), 19½ × 23½ in. Soldier, traveller, journalist, politician and balloonist. *National Portrait Gallery, London.* page 300

140 'THE PRIVATE VIEW, ROYAL ACADEMY, 1881'; by W. P. Frith, 1881/2. Detail, showing OSCAR WILDE (with top-hat, and flower in his coat) "as a well-known apostle of the beautiful, with a herd of eager worshippers surrounding him. . . . A group of well-known artists are watching the scene". They, including G. A. Sale and H. S. Marks, are on the right, top-hatted; over Wilde's left shoulder are the heads of Ellen Terry and Irving. *A. C. R. Pope, Esq.* page 305

141 SIR SYDNEY WATERLOW, BART. (1822–1906); by F. A. Taubman, 1900. Life-size bronze statue; merchant, Lord Mayor of London and public benefactor. (Photograph: The Topical Press.) *Waterlow Park, Highgate, London.* page 306

142 WILLIAM EWART GLADSTONE (1809–98); by Sir J. E. Millais, 1879. Life-size (49 × 36 in.). Aged 70. *National Portrait Gallery, London.* page 306

143 SIR GEORGE GROVE (1820–1900); by Sir Alfred Gilbert, 1896. Bronze bust, life-size. Aged 76. *Royal College of Music, London.* page 306

144 SIR CHARLES JAMES NAPIER (1782–1853); by Smart, c. 1850 (?). The conqueror of Sind; aged about 60. *National Portrait Gallery, London.* page 311

145 EDWARD HARRISON, Governor of Madras, perhaps by a member of the Chinqua family, c. 1715, who were producing similar portraits in Madras. Coloured plaster (?) statuette. *Mrs. Sybil Cleaver.* page 312

Chapter 1

STONE EFFIGY TO
RENAISSANCE PORTRAIT

THE BRITISH people were slow to show their faces. Towards the end of the twelfth century their bodies begin to take substance, uniformed in the costume of their calling, robe or armour, knights or priests, but each effigy on the tomb-slab nevertheless a tough memorial of the individual who lies dissolved in dust beneath it. The vast majority of them have no faces; they have been rubbed out by time, by image-breakers or by those who sign desecration by their initials. The faces were probably never very individual, to begin with; perhaps contemporaries could read them as individual likenesses, but to us, even when they are in good condition, they are but a general indication of human features.

During the thirteenth and fourteenth centuries the rendering becomes more subtle, and more examples are in fair condition; very often they are individual faces in as much as they are distinguishable one from another. But they are difficult to judge as portraits of living people: half-submerged in the dark aisles and chapels of their churches, they are so intimately involved with death. The monuments of which they are part, tombs sometimes canopied, fretted, carved, into virtual chapels, are not attempts to preserve the joys of life, to catch and picture the individual soul in an open eye; they are statements of what has been, the accomplishment in rank and wealth and piety. For all the hands in prayer, meekly joined upon their breasts, the effigies are also symbols of earthly pride, and official; they proclaim that their originals have upheld an inherited name or estate, or that they have founded them.

A tomb with effigy was a luxury of the great, and generally it demonstrated greatness, one's place in the hierarchy of the world. The king wears his crown, the bishop his mitre and his robes, the knight his armour, all of it, a glimpse of his face only in the opening of his helm, the long moustaches escaping over the chain-mail bib. The faces are less eloquent than the clothes; very few of these effigies are likely to make you catch your breath, as you stoop over them, in a sudden premonition that they will blink their eyes; yet gradually they are becoming livelier, not only on the tombs, but on the roof-bosses and the corbels. Soon the faces will wake.

Interest in the description of the human being is an essential characteristic of the Renaissance. The word "Renaissance" has become suspect, and many scholars are now more concerned to trace the continuity, the gradual evolution of style, and perhaps tend to underplay the revolutionary side of the four-teenth and fifteenth centuries. The movement was not of course a volte-face overnight; it spread over centuries; nevertheless there was a change, a radical one. In art, one aspect of this change was that the individual, temporal history of the human being becomes a major theme. For the artists of the Middle Ages, the body was but the ephemeral lineament that the soul takes on for a second of eternity; its quirks and characteristics, its displacement of time and space, its differences from other human bodies, were of no interest. Like Plato's prisoners, they saw the bodies of the passers-by as frail coloured shadows of a hidden reality cast upon a wall. The reversal of this process is clear already in Dante; the vivid and subtly differentiated characters that people Hell, Purgatory and Paradise are essentially projections upon infinity of earthly originals. Dante himself is one of the first men of the Late Middle Ages of whom a reasonably individual likeness has come down to us.[1]

Plate 1 In England it comes later; only in Chaucer does the anony-mous crowd of pilgrims fully resolve into its component individuals. Chaucer's own portrait, in Occleve's manuscript in the British Museum, is the earliest portrait, in the modern

Chaucer c.1410 (?) anon.

2 *Richard II* c.14
anon.

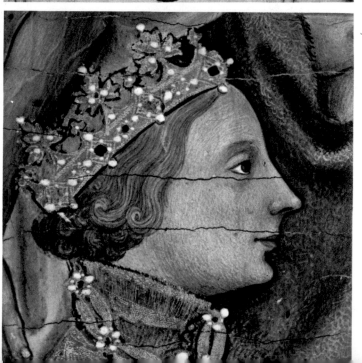

3 *Richard II* c.1.
anon.

Richard II 1394/6
Broker and G. Prest

5   *Richard, Earl of Warwick*   c.1449   *John Massingham*

sense, of an English poet: his face would not surprise you on top of a shooting jacket in the 1880's. You might even glimpse it today, beard and all, at an Academy private view. It is a posthumous portrait, but Occleve makes his intentions in including it plain: "that in order to remind other men of his personal appearance I have had his likeness made here to the end, in truth, that those who have least thought and memory of him may recall him by this painting."[2] But individual faces are distinguishable rather earlier perhaps than Chaucer's, and it is easiest to trace their emergence in the funeral effigies at Westminster Abbey.

The first detailed account of a king's burial that is relevant is probably that of Henry II, who died on the 6th July 1189, at Chinon. The following day he was carried to be buried "clothed in royal apparel, wearing a golden crown on his head, and having gloves on his hands and a golden ring on his finger, a sceptre in his hand, footgear woven with gold, and spurs on his feet, girt with a sword, he lay *having his face uncovered*".

Almost exactly thus Henry's tomb effigy still lies, in that strange English shrine at Fontevrault, in the vaulted and empty silence of the abbey church that is, or was, surrounded by a political prison for collaborators. (Close by him lies Richard I, or Cœur de Lion, who died ten years later of wounds at Chaluz. Their faces, though doubtless originally idealised and now restored, are clearly differentiated, at least in as much as Henry, who is recorded as a very stout man, is much fatter in the face than Richard.) The habit seems to have been to expose the dead king, vested with all the regalia of kingship, with his face uncovered. This last would be of grave political importance (and still may be, as in Stalin's case), in order to demonstrate that the king really was dead, and his successor justly entitled to his place. The face of the dead man was shewn that it might be recognised.

27

The relation of the tomb-effigy to the burial is probably simply explained; the box-like tomb represents the coffin, the effigy the dead man displayed on top of it. The function of the funeral effigy, not to be confused with the tomb-effigy, was, as it were, transitional between the king's body and his enduring image, the tomb-effigy. As funeral ceremonial became more elaborate and so more protracted, it became impracticable, for reasons of putrefaction (in spite of embalming), to display the king's body. A facsimile became necessary. Documentary evidence suggests that such a facsimile may have been used for Henry III's funeral in 1272, but the first royal funeral in which beyond doubt one was used was that of Edward II, in 1327, when 40 shillings was paid for a wooden image of him to set on the coffin: a likeness (*ymaginem de ligno ad similitudinem dicti domini E[dvardi] deffuncti*).

Significantly, three months elapsed between the king's death and his burial at Gloucester. It would be natural for the sculptor of the alabaster effigy at Gloucester to work from the temporary wooden funeral effigy, but though there is probably some element of portraiture in that serene and saint-like face, it is much idealised. Its function is no longer the same; it is primarily memorial, hagiographical.

The wooden funeral image used in 1377 for his successor, Edward III, survives still in Westminster Abbey. Though it has long since lost its beard and wig, and most of the coloured gesso which built up the features, it agrees well enough in shape with what little is visible of Edward's face behind the venerable whiskers of the gilt-bronze effigy in Westminster Abbey. Recently a considered (but not unanimously accepted) opinion has suggested that the face of the funeral image is based closely on a death-mask, and that it shows, on its left cheek, the physical effect of the stroke from which the king died.[3] Richard II renounced the throne before he died, and so a king's funeral was not to be his lot. He died in obscure circumstances in 1400; as his renunciation might be held by his partisans to have been made under duress, and the finality of his extinction was extremely desirable to his usurper, his body was "embalmed and seared and covered with lead all save his face (to the extent that all men might perceive that he was departed out of this mortal lyfe)", and so accoutred, Richard was borne openly from Pontefract to London.[4]

It seems likely that the funeral effigies of the fourteenth century were made as likenesses, with the deliberate intention that they should be recognisable. It is not impossible, indeed, that they were almost facsimiles, modelled upon masks taken from the face of the dead. Their function, however, was probably in the first place a political one, and they do not necessarily indicate a wider interest in realistic portraiture; their purpose was to show that their subject was dead. With Richard II, although no funeral image was made for him, the case alters, for he is the classic point of demonstration that the English portrait has, at last, arrived, at the turn of the fourteenth to the fifteenth century. There are three major portraits of Richard. The copper tomb-effigy in Westminster Abbey was ordered from Nicholas Broker and Godfrey Prest, citizens and coppersmiths of London, in 1395, that is, five years *before* Richard died. The contract allowed Broker and Prest two years for their work, and the suspicion seems legitimate that Richard took a personal interest in his own image; one would expect a portrait. The resulting face is stylised to a degree but seems recognisably individual with a most unusual nose, tipped like an arrow-head.[5]

Plate 4

The date of the other two portraits is more problematic. They are both paintings, the colossal throned whole-length "in majesty", in Westminster Abbey, and the famous Wilton Diptych. The Westminster Abbey painting, it has been suggested, was painted to commemorate Richard's visit to

Plate 2
Plate 3

Westminster on the translation of Edward the Confessor, 15th October 1390, but there is nothing much either for or against this suggestion. From the stylistic evidence, one might expect the painting to be rather later. The Wilton Diptych, as to date and authorship, French or English, remains a field for unresolved scholarly tilting.[6] But all authorities agree in placing these two paintings, if not within Richard's lifetime at least within living memory of him; in both of them the king has a more youthful appearance than in the effigy.

The full-face view of the Westminster picture confirms the full-face view of the effigy, and the profile in the Wilton Diptych, as Richard, sponsored by his patron saints, kneels in adoration to the Virgin and Child, is even more decisive, with precisely that sharp point of nose. Here are three portraits clearly representing the same man, but each one leaving the impression of a distinct and individual view of him. They approach very closely to realistic portraiture, detailing and perhaps even dwelling on the physical characteristics by which his contemporaries recognised him.

The portraits of Richard do not however mean that realistic portraiture is becoming commonplace, an everyday occurrence. What is known of his character suggests that his tastes were sophisticated and in advance of his time, and his portraits may be a reflection of his taste rather than that of his contemporaries. Art certainly was becoming more realistic in the way it strove to present an imitation, an illusion, of the surface of the world. The representation of a tree must look like a tree that has grown from the earth, with boughs in which the wind moves and on which birds sit, but not a particular tree; so too a man's face must be credible, have the tincture of flesh and blood and show the wearing of time and of experience. But the number of cases in which the lively and individual faces of the fifteenth century can be said with confidence to be the faithful portrait of this or that man or woman, are remarkably few in comparison with the wealth of portraiture that the Italians and the followers of Jan van Eyck in the Netherlands were dispensing on the Continent.

In 1442 Henry VI was wondering whether to marry one of the daughters of the Count of Armagnac, and if so, which; he gave his envoys very specific instructions, to "portraie the iii daughters in their kertelles simple and their visages like as ye see their stature and their beaulte and color of skynne and their countenances with al maner of fetures".[7] But here there was a specific function for the portraits, though a warmer one than in the case of the funeral effigies. Many of the late thirteenth-century and fourteenth-century tomb-effigies are vivid in their realism; faces like those of the Canynges in St. Mary Redcliffe, Bristol, of many of the knights, their heads now no longer boxed in their helms, and clean-shaven.

Surely the astute, authoritative face of William of Wykeham (d. 1404) in Winchester Cathedral, the intent aspiration of Sir Robert Harcourt (1471) at Stanton Harcourt, the whole-some features of "Mrs. Oteswich" in St. Helen's, London— surely these are portraits? Sometimes, as in fact with William of Wykeham, it is possible to check them against other repre-sentations of the same person; but more often it is impossible to confirm that they are portraits.

A well-known example, and one of the finest, most striking, of English fifteenth-century effigy-heads, is that of Richard Beauchamp, Earl of Warwick, in St. Mary, Warwick. He *Plate 5* wears his hair trimmed, like a fitted cap, his mouth is drawn down towards the corners, his eyes are wide open under the raised eyebrows, looking up in perhaps not entirely con-fident anticipation; his hands are raised on his breast, not together, but apart, as if caught in an involuntary exclamation of incredulous amazement. It is, it would seem, a portrait modelled with the most remarkable humanity. But Warwick died in 1437, and his tomb was not started till 1453 and completed in 1456, almost twenty years after his death; the contract, which was drawn up in 1453 and which survives, gives no hint that this is a portrait, rather the contrary:

the said Will Austin doth covenant to cast and make *an image of a man armed,* of fine latten garnished with certain ornaments, viz.—with sword and dagger; with a garter; with a helme and crest under his head, and at his feet a bear musled, and a griffon, perfectly made of the finest latten, according to patterns, and to be layd on the tombe, at the perill of the said Austin, for the sum of xl/li.[8]

Did the "patterns" include a portrait of Warwick, or were they only for the perhaps more important detail of armour and of heraldry, the labels of rank and of blood? Was the image intended to be more than merely that "of a man armed"? It was noted by the antiquary Leland in the sixteenth century— "entombed right *princely* and porturyd with an image of copper" —but exactly what Leland meant by "porturyd" is as uncertain as the nature of the "patterns" used by Will Austin.

The fifteenth century was an age of uncertainty. The humanistic conception of portraiture was slowly filtering in from the Continent, together with the technique of the Van Eycks, the science of perspective, the desire to leave a more permanent, unfading facsimile of one's flesh and blood behind. But England was not yet a prepared soil in which such refinements would flourish. The internal disturbances, the Wars of the Roses, have, as direct causes of the meagreness of English fifteenth-century art, been exaggerated. The major causes were probably the immaturity of the country and its relative poverty, as compared, for example, with Italy; the poverty was intensified by war, but Italy too at this time was not precisely a peaceful country. In England the minds of great men seem to have concentrated on the struggle for power to the exclusion of most considerations of art; when they were dead, their family might consolidate their pride and achievement in an expensive

Edward Grimston   1446   Petrus Christus

7 Henry VII 1505
Michiel Sittow (?)

8 Henry VII 1512/18
Pietro Torrigiani

9 Henry VII 15
anon.

tomb, but while they were alive they had little time for the refinements of painting and sculpture.

For posterity such negligence is sad; one has only to see what we lack, to think of the Van Eycks, of Van der Weyden, of Memlinc in the Netherlands; of Fouquet in France; and of the astonishing profusion in Italy: the medals of Pisanello, and the portraits of the Venetian and Florentine schools. A very few Englishmen of the time were painted abroad, and have their resulting monuments in the canon of European art, from the huge posthumous equestrian portrait of Sir John Hawkwood—*Ioannes Acutus Eques Britannicus*—painted by Uccello in the Duomo at Florence in 1436, to the minutely particular Edward Grimston, painted by Petrus Christus. *Plate 6* Hawkwood is indistinguishable in general appearance from any other Italian condottiere, Grimston from any equally well-to-do Fleming.[9]

Between 1471 and 1483, under Edward IV, the country began to prosper, and the king himself died a very rich man; this prosperity was not gravely shaken by Richard III, and Henry VII, from the field of Bosworth in 1485, was able to proceed upon a consolidation of the Tudor dynasty and of England, a combination that was to survive through fair weather and foul, for the next century. It is the century of the first full flowering of the English face, and the faces of the Tudors themselves are amongst the most rare and curious specimens.

Chapter II

HOLBEIN—PAINTER AT COURT

HENRY VII, first of the Tudors, was not a very lavish patron of the arts; that rôle he left to his son. He himself is in fact the only person of his reign whom one can assess from a variety of surviving images, none of them probably (and certainly not the most revealing ones) commissioned by himself. They are of great interest.

Henry was the first king of England since the Norman Conquest to have predominantly British blood—specifically, Welsh blood (the Tudors were succeeded in England by Scottish kings, and the Scottish by Hanoverians). His family was of obscure but certainly Welsh origin; his great-grandfather was steward to the Bishop of Bangor; his grandfather was a clerk of the wardrobe to Henry V's queen, Catherine of France, but, astonishingly (probably) married her after Henry's death; their son, Henry's father, married Lady Margaret Beaufort. In Henry's veins there ran then the royal blood of France, and, through the rich and various strain of the Beauforts, the royal blood of England. He might be claimed, in mixture, as a typical Britisher of the ruling classes of the period, though with a pronounced Welsh and unusually royal flavour.

What did he look like? There seems to have been a standard portrait of him that was, with variations, in circulation during his reign; a pale and impersonal image, somewhat, I would guess, of a token image (painted in what was probably the current native style, of which the Countess of Salisbury is a fine example). Several examples still exist, notably two belonging to the Society of Antiquaries, but they are not impressive when compared with the three that I have to discuss.

In 1505 there came to England, upon an embassy of marriage, one Hermann Rinck; with him came a painter who

Plate 10

36

has been plausibly identified as Michel Sittow, a court-painter who worked for Isabella the Catholic and Margaret of Austria. The portrait that Sittow painted of Henry VII for Rinck on that occasion is now in the National Portrait Gallery. It is a very popular portrait, and its popularity must rest on the trenchant vividness, hitherto unparalleled in painting in this country, with which it conveys the impression of a living character; it is completely *vraisemblable*. Conceived in the Northern tradition that derives from the Van Eycks, it is less than life-size, but surely studied from the life. The design, with one hand as though resting on the frame, was already a stock one, used by painters such as Memlinc, and the portrait was also conditioned to an extent by political considerations; it was destined to delect a woman whom he might wish to marry, a woman moreover who was a daughter of Maximilian, King of the Romans and in line for the Emperorship of the Holy Roman Empire. Hence no doubt the red rose in his hand, for love and friendship (and also for Lancaster), and hence the Order of the Golden Fleece about his neck rather than the insignia of the Order of the Garter, for the Fleece would carry greater weight abroad than the Garter.

Plate 7

But the face is naked, and it is not a face that most people now would care to send as a bid for marriage, although, for Maximilian, if not for the daughter, the flesh would be the least part of the bargain. It is the face of an elderly man, though sprightly, though very much alive. It is a fascinating face but not a sympathetic one; most people find it sly; the thin lips in a line that borders on the smirk, the almost sharp nose and the bead-bright eyes calculating under the utterly untrustworthy angle of the eyelids. He has the air, in his little niche, with the Golden Fleece round his neck, of a far too worldly saint, a mean St. Money-Bags.

It is perhaps unfortunate for Henry's reputation that this portrait should hang, in the Portrait Gallery, close to that of

Richard III, in which Richard's admirers (oblivious of the fact that the portrait is not contemporary, but a later copy, and of extremely doubtful value as evidence) are inclined to find a frank, manly and open countenance, so unlike that of his usurper. A more favourable advocate for Henry is the bronze

Plate 8

tomb-effigy in Westminster Abbey, modelled by an Italian sculptor of the High Renaissance, Pietro Torrigiani, who is likely also to have been responsible for the admirable coloured bust of Henry in the Victoria and Albert Museum. This is a posthumous portrait, contracted for in 1512, over three years after Henry's death, and the features have been idealised, the expression deleted from lips and eyes. It is the image of a Renaissance prince, of immense dignity, but as a factual account of Henry's face, most people, I think, would guess it to be further away than is Michel Sittow's painting.

Plate 9

This is not borne out by the third portrait of Henry; we turn again to the funeral effigies in Westminster Abbey, where the head of Henry's image survives. It is the most remarkable of the early funeral effigies, and recently attention has been drawn to very plausible technical evidence that the face is a death-mask, a cast, that is, taken from a mould on the king's face after his death, and then worked up in some degree, notably in the eyes. Here, then, must be the actual lineaments and proportions of Henry's face, and Torrigiani's idealised portrait approaches them more accurately than does the apparently extremely naturalistic rendering by Sittow. (Torrigiani almost certainly knew the funeral effigy and no doubt based the face of his tomb-effigy largely on it.) The face of the funeral effigy, stripped of its datable frame of hair, and clothes, has a timeless quality in spite of the mutilation of his nose; it might be the face of a Roman, it might be the face of an outstandingly capable business magnate of today.[10]

I have dwelt on the face of Henry VII in greater detail than I shall be able to allow for most, because in it are clear

Margaret Pole, Countess of Salisbury   c.1535   anon.

11

13

12

14

11 *Henry VIII 1525/6 Luke Horenbout (?)*

12 *Henry VIII 1525/6 Luke Horenbout (?)*

13 *Henry VIII c.1540 Hans Holbein*

14 *Henry VIII 1544 Cornelis Matsys*

15 *Henry VIII c.1537 after Holbein*

· SVA

16 *Ann Boleyn* c.1536 (?) *Hans Holbein*

already several of the fundamental problems that concern the relationship of the face to its portrait. All portraits can be related to two extremes: on the one hand, the accurate facsimile of the individual, and, on the other, the contemporary conception of what the individual ought to look like. One extreme is represented by the death- or life-mask, actually moulded on the person; the other, on its highest level, by the ideal portrait, on its lowest by the fashion-plate. One tendency is to particularise the subject, to distinguish him from all other men; the other is to merge him in the type.

To see how difficult it is to achieve the facsimile, one need only look at the funeral effigy of Henry; the mask itself is timeless, I have suggested. Yet is it? Is a face of flesh and blood, even though dead, ever so final in its modelling? Nor can one ignore the extensions of the face, which are not cast, but modelled; the hair has gone, but the neck remains. When the effigy was seriously investigated for the first time, in 1907, the experts, not yet claiming the face as a death-mask, came to the conclusion that it was probably Italian work; apart from technical considerations, the superb, princely carriage of the head on the elongated neck may have influenced this conclusion. If the hair were shown, the face would of course be set more firmly in its time; few things place a man—and even more, a woman—in time than the way they wear their hair. Few things, as any designer of costume for stage or film knows, are harder to imitate. In theory, the face is naked; in practice it is subject to innumerable ephemeral whims of fashion; it may even be covered with paint (a consideration that we shall have to take into account at a later stage), but even if untouched by cosmetic, its whole character and expression is acutely sensitive to the slightest change in the variable frame of hair and whiskers, of hat and neckwear. It is even more subject to the artist who paints or sculpts it, and to his style.

43

And here the curious fact must be stressed, that from the time of Henry VII onwards, for two and a quarter centuries till about 1735, the most influential portrait-painters who shape the British face will be foreigners. Holbein, Eworth, the Dutch and Flemish immigrants at the end of the sixteenth century, Mytens, Van Dyck, Lely, Kneller. Even for those little interested in the arts, the names of Holbein, Van Dyck, Lely and Kneller may summon up each one an aspect of English history.

There are, of course, English portrait-painters of great ability, perhaps of genius, but even with due acknowledge-ment granted to William Dobson and Samuel Cooper, the only true exception to this foreign predominance, the only English painter who was the most important, the most charac-teristic of his age in this country, was Nicholas Hilliard. On the whole (and this is true, though to a lesser degree, of the sculptors) for over two hundred years we see the British face through the eyes of foreigners, or through the eyes of British painters who are, in more or less degree, imitating the foreigners.

In the perennial contest between artist and sitter, this, though it is a factor which must always be borne in mind, does not mean, of course, that the artist had it all his own way. Given the time and the sensibility to acclimatise himself, the artist will adapt himself and modulate his style, but when he comes on a short visit, as did Sittow and Torrigiani, he will tend to express his new sitters in terms of his accustomed style, to turn Henry VII into an intriguing Burgundian royalty or into an Italian magnifico of the Renaissance. Henry VII himself would probably have been more sympathetic to the former view (Sittow's). But Henry VIII, who commissioned Torrigiani's effigy after his father was dead, was more interested in the Italian way of life.

From Henry VII's portraits also it is clear how the purpose

for which a portrait is made may affect it; the overture of wooing in the Sittow portrait, the funeral tradition of an exact likeness in the death-mask, the idealised formality of the tomb-effigy. Every portrait arose out of a specific occasion; there was no idea yet in England that they might be simply desirable house furniture; that was only to begin in the reign of Henry VIII.

Henry VIII came to the throne young and handsome, in many ways the exact opposite of his father—extravagant, cultured, a good scholar, a wily theologian, a musician—above all, from our point of view, a generous patron of the arts. To begin with, his delight in visual splendour took a more extrovert form than the reduplication of his own person in the mirror of portraits; his coronation was of considerable splendour, and he took great delight in less formal revels, in masques newly introduced from Italy, in pageantry that was to reach its peak at the Field of Cloth of Gold in 1520. His court rapidly began to rank as one of the foremost in Europe, and to it came the artists from abroad. Torrigiani already by 1511; a Neapolitan, Volpe, by 1512. Some stayed only a short time; others, like Toto del Nonziata, the future Serjeant-Painter who came about 1519, settled for life. With these foreigners came a new conception of the human form.

Henry's form, in the early part of his reign, was the subject of universal admiration:

the handsomest potentate I ever set eyes on; above the usual height, with an extremely fine calf to his leg; his complexion fair and bright, with auburn hair combed straight and short in the French fashion, and a round face so very beautiful that it would become a pretty woman, his throat being rather long and thick.

This was not a biased report, but from a foreigner reporting home; so too, a little later, in 1519, another wrote that he was the handsomest sovereign in Europe: "a great deal handsomer

45

than the King of France." Henry would have liked that, for Francis I was his great rival, and Henry had just grown a red-gold beard to rival Francis'. "He is", goes on the writer,

extremely fond of tennis, at which game it is the prettiest thing in the world to see him play, his fair skin glowing through a shirt of the finest texture.

In fact, he enchanted and attracted his contemporaries, and in 1520, face to face with Francis I at the Field of Cloth of Gold, he emerged well from the comparison. One witness said that though Francis was taller, Henry had the more handsome and feminine face.[11]

This last comment will surprise those whose image of Henry is that supplied by Holbein. But apart from some pale and conventional icon-like images that reveal little and are almost interchangeable with similar paintings of earlier kings, there is no portrait of Henry VIII as he was during the first fifteen years of his reign, until 1525. Then there came two *Plates 11, 12* very competent and unjustly neglected miniatures, both dating, according to inscriptions on them, from his thirty-fifth year, though one shows him beardless and the other bearded. The plumpness that had been commented on at the Field of Cloth of Gold is notable, especially in the shaven jowl, but neither of them are yet aweful images. Their painter has not been really satisfactorily identified. But they are wholly in a tradition first fully manifested about 1520 in some miniatures attributed to Clouet in a manuscript in France, full-bodied and remarkably realistic. The miniature work of Holbein grows naturally out of this tradition.

There follow in time a number of portraits, life-size, of Henry VIII, in which we see him thickening, the jowl growing weightier, until at last, about 1536, he is ripe for Holbein: he had divorced Catherine of Aragon, challenged the Pope and the whole of Catholic Europe, and had set up his

Jane Seymour   1536 (?)   *Hans Holbein*

18   *Henry VIII   1536 (?)   Hans Holbein*

own Church with himself as its Supreme Head; he had begotten Queen Elizabeth and executed her mother; he was marrying for the third time and to achieve the security of an heir.

So it was that Holbein saw him for the first time in paint, and he painted him half-length, less than life-size. It was apparently in celebration of his marriage, and there was a companion portrait of Jane Seymour: they are now split, but in 1547 were still together. "Item a table like a book with the picture of kynge Henry theight and Quene Jane." But, even though they once folded on a hinge face to face in darkness, neither are friendly faces. Earlier in his career, Holbein, as in his painting of his wife and children, had been capable of imaginative masterpieces of the greatest tenderness, intimacy and compassion; by 1536, however, he had become Court-painter, and it was no longer his business to woo the subtler, spiritual undertones from the visible surface, though he could still do so. His business was to paint the surface with accuracy, losing none of the splendour of fur and brocade and jewel; his enduring success arises not merely from his technique in doing this, but in the artistry with which he could preserve the physical weight of personality of his sitters, and in the case of Henry VIII, his power, his magnificence, his ruthlessness. *Plates 17, 18*

Soon after the marriage portrait, Holbein painted Henry VIII as he faced him, four-square; one hand on hip, one hand on the dagger, the shoulders wide, the legs straddled like those of Atlas, but to bear his own weight, his own Church, his own kingdom. So Holbein painted him in the Privy Chamber at Whitehall; at the end of the century people still shivered when they saw that picture, and it is difficult to conceive any other image that Sir Walter Raleigh could have had in mind when he wrote, about 1614: *Plate 15*

for King Henry the Eighth, if all the Pictures and Patterns of a merci-less Prince were lost in the World, they might all again be painted to the Life, out of the Story of this King.[12]

49

The Whitehall painting was more than a portrait of Henry VIII; it was one of those dynastic visual decrees in which the Tudors, from Henry VII's planning of his chapel in West-minster Abbey onwards, took such delight. It showed Henry and Jane Seymour (mother of his male heir), and, behind them, Henry VII and Queen Elizabeth of York. Of Henry VIII's own portrait, the face is but a small proportion of the whole, the Tudor majesty of which Henry is but the tenant. The life-size standing whole-length, as a pictorial formula, had been used already by lesser painters in Germany and Austria, and, most superbly, by Titian for his Charles V (now in the Prado) in 1533. It was a formula reserved by both Titian and Holbein for their most important clients; only one whole-length of a subject Englishman by Holbein is recorded.

In Holbein's state-portraits the full conception of the Renaissance theory of portraiture is first realised in practice in England. Holbein, of course, was a German-Swiss, but no narrow provincial; he had travelled in Northern Italy and in France, he knew the work of Raphael and da Vinci, and he came to England bearing a passport from his intimate friend, perhaps the greatest and most articulate of the northern humanists, Erasmus, to Thomas More.

Holbein knew the artistic theory of his time. This theory, particularly in as much as it concerned portraiture, was codified in explicit detail by Lomazzo later in the century. Italian critics were agreed that a literal copy of nature was not the be-all and end-all of painting: behind the super-ficial phenomenon lay, as for Plato, the Idea. The artist's concern was with both. Lomazzo therefore praises "i ritratti intellettuali"—intellectual portraits, expounded by the artist "in natural form expressing the concept of his mind or idea". This ideal approach cannot but condition portraiture. Lomazzo recommended, amongst other things, that only those people should be portrayed who were worthy of recording. They

must be shown in suitable apparel, and their rank and splendour might decorously be stressed by attributes such as armour,
regalia, laurels and batons.

Emperors above all other Kings and Princes should be endowed with
majesty, and have a noble and grave air which conforms to their station
in life . . . *even though they be not naturally so in life*.[13]

In Holbein's state-portrait of Henry, without the assistance   *Plate 13*
even of permissible attributes such as crowns and robes, the
painter has confirmed the king surely in imperial rank.
Majesty in his port, sheer omnipotence in his bulk, and in his
face power, pride and gravity, and some, at least, of the
qualities that might be admitted as pertaining to nobility. Yet
it is far from obvious that, to achieve this, Holbein has flattered
Henry or departed from the truth. Something of the king's
titanic width may be padding, but that was doubtless there
already, in the clothes; in the face, feature by feature, though it be
not lovely, as in those small eyes whose very existence is threatened
by the encroaching flesh, seems scrupulously recorded. This
is the account that posterity has accepted as Henry.

Other views however are legitimate. The engraving by
Cornelis Matsys of 1544 is taken from another angle. The   *Plate 14*
artist might easily now be accused of a satirical or at least
ironic intention, but probably unjustly. This is an essay in that
tradition of portraiture of which Sittow's Henry VII is one
example: a tradition already old-fashioned when this plate was
engraved. Matsys worked in Antwerp, and there is no record
of his being in England; yet, however this portrait came into
being, whether from the life or at second-hand, it suggests very
vividly an aspect of Henry's closing years that would not be
guessed either from Holbein's account or (for Holbein's is
perhaps seven years earlier than Matsys') from the Holbeinesque
portraits of about 1544 as at St. Bartholomew's Hospital.
Towards the end, Henry's legs could no longer sustain their

unwieldy burden, and he had to be moved by some form of conveyance, even from one room to the next.

People of slightly less exalted rank also began to be interested in the perpetuation of their own faces. The first group of private citizens whom we find acting as patron of a portrait-painter is the group that centres round Thomas More; from them Holbein probably received most of such encouragement as he did get on his first visit to England in 1526: the Mores, the Ropers, William Warham, Brian Tuke. On his second visit, when More had already fallen, Holbein was patronised mainly by German steelyard merchants, and only in 1536 did he become the king's painter; thereafter he seems to have painted mainly courtiers.

Outside the limited circles that patronised Holbein there were a few prosperous merchants, whose interests straddled the Channel and whose portraits have an international flavour: the Withypols (painted by Antonio da Solario, who may have been in England in the second decade of the century),[14] the Kytsons, the Greshams. But the majority, perhaps, of the faces that we know now of Henry VIII's reign were recorded for us by Holbein.

In the whole history of art there is perhaps no painter through whom one could hope to know a sitter's face better. "Holbein", wrote Evelyn to Pepys in 1689, "really painted to the life beyond any man this day living": the same might have been said at any time since. *To the life:* Holbein's style is not merely as crystal, through which his sitters' faces are seen naked, but it carries for many people a feeling of revelation, a sensation like seeing someone you know stripped of their habitual spectacles. In almost all later portraits, fashion, whether artistic or sartorial, obscures the face, shaping the features and affecting the glance. Holbein's people, massive, unquestioning and unquestionable in the illusion of their flesh, still stand after four centuries from their dust.

It has been suggested, very plausibly, that he used some mechanical contrivance to take the initial drawings from the life; but, if so, it was an aid entirely subservient to his genius. Though it might be thought to account in part for a certain rigidity in some of his later work, that at times verges upon the uncanny and improper silence of wax-works, it is nevertheless precisely in his preparatory drawings, as in the great series at Windsor, that the individual genius of his style is most easily grasped. Almost all are but ghosts of what they once were—rubbed, retouched by the hands of succeeding centuries—but through almost all of them the quality of Holbein's line still tells in its acute, selective economy, and his sitters live as creatures of his own imagination. By his drawing of Anne Boleyn alone he makes Henry's passion comprehensible, rebuking with his entranced eye the cold conclusions of the Venetian envoy—

Plate 16

not one of the handsomest women in the world . . . Of middling stature, swarthy complexion, long neck, wide mouth, bosom not much raised, and in fact has nothing but the King's great appetite, and her eyes, which are black and beautiful.[15]

In the drawings, Holbein seems often to catch and hold, on a rectangle of rose-tinted paper, the evanescence of life, to indicate the imponderables and the infinite possibilities of movement. When, from a drawing, he built up a painting, these tangential extensions, into other dimensions, of time and of human society, almost vanish; against a flat and static background, perhaps of an empyrean blue, the sitter bulks in a definition that is final and monumental. He is assessed, as though in an inventory for posterity, item by item; that this sum total is more than an inventory he owes to the skill, never surpassed, by which Holbein held the compromise between his love of detail and his power of modulating the broad movement of volume, and of contour upon contour.

His sitters do add up; one might almost invent an instrument by which their displacement or their specific gravity could be measured. That this apparent naturalism is in fact achieved by the most sophisticated artifice, needs stressing, and yet it is true that in Holbein's paintings, in the best of them, the claims of sitter and artist are balanced as perhaps they have never been balanced since. Charles V has succumbed to Titian, Philip IV to Velazquez, even Charles I to Van Dyck; between Holbein and Henry VIII (unless this be an illusion natural to English eyes) the match is drawn.

In comparison with Holbein, every taker of portraits who has worked in Britain seems mannered, and only Holbein seems to have that purity of style through which a sitter appears to tell his own story, with a clarity that is a distillation of the truth. He worked for not more than twelve years in England, and he has left us at the most a few dozen faces of Henry VIII's subjects. Quantitatively, in the vast flood of portraits that gradually spreads after him, it is nothing; his importance for this book is over-riding, for no one ever surpassed him in reconciling the obstinate individuality of a given face with the claims of a great work of art.

He was aided by a variety of chances, of which not the least was that he was the first major artist in the English field. He was helped, as far as the face is concerned, by the costume of his time; rarely have neck and hair been so little fussed. With the women, indeed, the hair was almost invisible, rolled under the hood, or glimpsed, smooth, centrally parted, and flat, under its gable or curve, so that the face appears as though in naked high relief from its frame. In his time the clean-shaven page-boy-bobbed faces of the men gave way to the close-cropped hair and the beard of the last years of Henry's reign, from 1536 onwards. The beard seems to have been worn relatively straight, at least in comparison with the Elizabethan extravagances which were to come. Although one finds writers like Horman in his *Vulgaria* stating as early as 1519 that women "whyte theyr face, necke and pappis with ceruse", cosmetics had clearly not yet the importance that they were to have at the close of the century; there is no evidence either of eye-brow or hair plucking in Holbein's portraits. His sitters, moreover, had in artistic matters no doubt a certain unin-hibited naïveté, that left their faces wide open to the painter. After Holbein, both painters and sitters became more and more subject to precedent and to fashion.

Chapter III

THE ELIZABETHANS –
A ROCK AGAINST TIME

HOLBEIN, dying of the plague in 1543, left no school of painters developing directly out of his own style. He had, however, helped largely to condition the English to certain habits, one of which was the desirability of perpetuating in paint an accurate reflection of one's face. Indications of the two trends that were to run parallel through later Tudor portraiture are distinguishable in his work. On the one hand, the more naturalistic tendency, often German or Dutch in flavour, and on the other, notably in his use of flat arabesque design, that delight in more abstract formal values which was to be characteristic of the Mannerists.

Although the painters who succeeded him immediately show at least an awareness of his work, and occasionally almost quote from him, they nearly all have their roots in Northern European movements which had developed parallel to Holbein rather than out of him. Edward VI employed Scrots (or Streetes), a Netherlander who came to England about 1545 from service with Queen Mary of Hungary, the Regent of the Netherlands, and who was well aware of fashionable court portraiture as practised on the Continent. Edward also employed Hans Eworth, an Antwerp painter, who was established here by 1549, and who was to paint also Mary and Elizabeth.[16] There was also the Westphalian painter, Gerlach Flicke, active in England between 1547, or earlier, and his death in 1558.

Of these Scrots is notable especially for his whole-length portraits: of Edward VI in a pose adapted, probably partly for political reasons, from Holbein's Henry VIII, and the Earl of Surrey. The Edward VI is very similar to Clouet in feeling:

the Surrey much more Italianate, but in each the rendering of the face is both less sensitive in detail, and weaker in grasp of structure, than with Holbein, though still, especially in the Surrey, very naturalistic.

Flicke, the German, a painter of the most accomplished though somewhat strident ability, is closer in sentiment to Holbein, yet how inferior in subtlety is evident from his Cranmer. Remarkable a portrait though it is, it is not remark‐ *Plate 19* able enough to convey that complex character, timid and subtle and ultimately more stubborn than the fire into which he thrust the right hand that had offended by recanting; it seems rather to me the face of ecclesiastical power politics.

But the artist in whose work the effect of the movement of style upon the face can be traced, during the transitional phase between Holbein's death in 1543 up to about 1570, is Hans Eworth. He was a Flemish painter from Antwerp, of great technical skill, but not an artist of the first rank: not an original genius, like Holbein, able to create a style, but one very sensitive to fashion and adapting himself to it, sensitive to his patron's wishes, and sensitive, too, to their faces. A most able portrait painter, he was trained in the Antwerp school; that is, not as a court‐painter, but as one who had to provide likenesses that had no nonsense, and at the same time a certain fashionable trimming of nonsense, sometimes an allegorical scene in the Mannerist style, an intrusion of naked smooth‐limbed deities, labelled here and there with explanatory verses:

More than the rock amidst the raging sea, the constant heart no danger dread nor fears.

Such is Eworth's portrait of Sir John Luttrell, 1550, his realistic bearded head consorting strangely with his pale body waist‐deep in a tempestuous sea, and, more strangely, with the elegant figure of Peace, who, from a crowded Heaven of uncertain stability, takes him by the arm. But also, in the composition of some of his portraits, he draws heavily on Holbein, and later on Sir Anthony Mor who was in England in 1554 long enough at least to paint Queen Mary Tudor. Eworth worked on most scales, except perhaps that of the smallest miniature. He painted portraits not unlike the little pieces of Corneille de Lyon; he painted them on all scales upwards to life-size. But constant among his variations is his concern for the individual character of the face. (If he had not had the forethought to sign many of his works, we might well have made at least three separate masters out of him on stylistic grounds.) From about 1554 onwards (when he was estab-lished as a court-painter) there is traceable in his faces a more schematised rendering of the features, in line with an increasing insistence on a flatter pattern of background and on the detail of dress; he is developing towards what is generally known, though unjustly, as the late Elizabethan costume piece.

Plate 30

But throughout all his work his interest in the individuality of his sitters' faces remains; as in his double portrait, small in scale but superbly incisive in character, of the thirty-six years old Duchess of Suffolk, and her twenty-one year old Master of the Horse, Adrian Stoke, whom she married after the Duke had been executed. The modelling, though softer than Holbein's, is scrupulous; the flesh has a curious transparency, plumply taut, sometimes almost ballooned.

Eworth's work can be considered as a sort of microcosm, in which almost all the trends that will develop in painted portraiture to the end of the sixteenth century are visible, with the chief exception of the miniature in which Hilliard was to develop his own original genre. The characteristic composition of the portrait between 1550 and 1580 shows the subject three-quarter-length, the body cut off at mid-thigh, standing, turned three-quarters to left or right, the hands tranquil, one of them perhaps resting on the sword-hilt or holding a pair of gloves. The general impression is cold, of a proud and aloof dignity; one seems to see them from below their own level.

Magnificent exemplars of this design were supplied by Titian, and in the North, most successfully, Mor drew heavily upon them, chilling and glazing Titian's rich and broken colour, stiffening the pose. This same coldness and surface glaze, combined with a careful imitation of minute detail, from the wiry curl of the individual hair to the tiniest facets of complex jewellery, is common to all North European portraiture of the period. It occurs in England, sometimes on a life-size scale, sometimes on a smaller scale; sometimes Flemish or Dutch in atmosphere, sometimes approximating to the German harshness of Tom Ring. Even most of the head-and-shoulders portraits might be, as it were, truncated three-quarter-lengths.

A little before 1580, whole-lengths—rare since about 1555 —come into fashion again; the three-quarter-lengths are extended, though the desired impression of detached magnificence is not necessarily thereby increased, for once the feet appear they have to be harnessed to the common ground. Paradoxically, it is the whole-lengths on a miniature scale that are most impressive.

To some degree, all these portraits are state portraits, even when their sitters had but the most tenuous connections with the court, if any at all. They are visual demonstrations of a code of manners, corresponding very closely with that laid down in Castiglione's *Book of the Courtier*, known in England soon after its first appearance in 1528, and very widely known after the translation by Sir Thomas Hobie of 1561. An emphasis on sobriety of clothes and bearing, and a certain calm magnificence of spirit, best indicated by Castiglione's account of Francis I:

and it seemed to me that besides the grace of his person and the beauty of his face, he had in his aspect such loftiness, joined however with a certain gracious humanity, that the realm of France must always seem too small for him.

It is vain therefore to hope for much intimacy with these portraits: intimacy was not their object, indeed it was contrary to their object. The idea of a portrait is still closely linked with that of the tomb-effigy. After an inconclusive flirtation with the purely Italian Renaissance style in the first half of the century, the Gothic tradition, in the effigies themselves if not so firmly in their settings, prevailed. Stiff, flat on their backs, hands together, they lie, formally clothed according to their degree in life.

The painted portrait was but a domesticated tomb-effigy; its object to fix and perpetuate the mortal achievements, the rank, wealth and lineage of its subject; to demonstrate him in his own long gallery, by his own hearth, perhaps as the founder of his line, as Sir William Petre at Ingatestone, or to set him in context with the other great men of his time and of the past, as in the enormous portrait galleries of the Earl of Leicester, of the Fitzalans, Earls of Arundel (later Lord Lumley's) and of the Archbishop of Canterbury, which began to build up in the fifteen-sixties. Sometimes, portraits were re-duplicated almost in mass, and distributed perhaps almost as political propaganda. There are many portraits of Leicester, while Burghley seems to have been represented, to judge by our scanty knowledge of contemporary inventories, in almost every house that boasted a collection of pictures.

There may be complaints that I am neglecting the face, but the neglect is inevitable. For this sort of portraiture the face was far from enough. Apart from the fact that the face of flesh grows, shrivels over the toothless mouth, decays, betraying the splendid face of paint, there is the intolerable fact that other people have faces as good, perhaps better, than yours, whatever their standing. The face is naked, and nakedness is a great

Thomas Cranmer   c.1546   Gerlach Flicke

20

21

ELIZA. TRIVMPHANS

24

20 Elizabeth I c.154
anon.

21 Elizabeth I 1572
Nicholas Hilliard

22 Elizabeth I c.157
anon.

23 Elizabeth I c.158
anon.

24 Elizabeth I 1589
William Rogers

25 Elizabeth I c.16c
Isaac Oliver

26 Elizabeth I c.159c
Nicholas Hilliard

23

26

27   Mrs. Mole   c.1605   Nicholas Hilliard

leveller, as the numerous though apparently ignored sumptuary laws tacitly admitted. How might a king be known from a lord, a lord from a knight, a gentleman from a serf, but by their clothes? Therefore it was laid down, who might wear fur and who golden chains.

In their portraits the Elizabethans insist on their rank through their clothes. Size was soon proved vain; Holbein might seem to reserve whole-lengths for royalty, but in the year after his death the rich young Mercer, Thomas Gresham, had a magnificent whole-length painted when he got married. A precise indication by clothes proved to have its drawbacks. Castiglione had observed that the "principle and true profession" of a man of rank was that "of arms"; hence the tendency of everyone entitled to armour to appear in it. Sir Philip Sidney—courtier, poet, patron and all other talents, *Plate 28* chose to be painted as a soldier in armour; but so too Sir William Petre on his tomb lies encased in steel, though if ever a man was a Secretary by nature and by calling, it was he. Something still more precise was needed.

At this point, in order to learn to read the painted images of themselves that the Elizabethans have left us, it is necessary to consider the crucial case of the Queen herself.[17] The first sight we have of Elizabeth is in her twelfth or thirteenth year, *Plate 20* about 1546: a three-quarter-length painting at Windsor. It is near enough to Holbein to have attracted his name within a century (it is listed as by him in Charles I's catalogue); it was however painted after his death, is at once softer and more elegantly mannered than his work, subscribing already to the standard international three-quarter-length design. It is evoked adequately by the entry in the Royal Inventory of 1546/47: *item a table with the picture of the ladye Elizabeth her grace with a booke in her hande her gowne like crimson cloth of golde withe workes.* A portrait of an extraordinary adolescent sobriety, her face of a delicate clarity in which only the shadowy depths of the eyes have refused definition. It is in harmony, except for the mystery of the eyes, with Roger Ascham's schoolmasterish report of her made not long afterwards: "in adornment she is elegant rather than showy" . . . a scholar already fluent in French, Italian and Latin and perhaps grounded well enough in Greek. He goes on to describe her literary style which she liked

to grow out of the subject, chaste in its appropriateness, beautiful in clarity. She admires above all, modest metaphors and comparisons of contraries well put together and contrasting felicitously with one another.

Here are already the seeds of her later style and her later appearance, though they were to grow away from modesty and restraint into a fantastic complexity of profusion. But it is Elizabeth herself who discloses the plot of her future portraiture. Writing to her brother Edward VI in her late teens, when sending a portrait (now lost) of herself to him, she said: "for the face, I grant, I may well blush to offer, but the mind I shall never be ashamed to present."

Nothing satisfactory or relevant to our purposes has yet come to light of Elizabeth in her twenties. She succeeded to the throne in 1558, and seems almost at once to have had trouble with her portraits, for in 1563 Cecil, that supreme Elizabethan public relations officer, was drafting a decree to attempt some sort of control over the publishing of her image. The draft complains of the daily proliferation of unsatisfactory likenesses of the queen ("errors and deformities"), and records a demand that she

be content that some special cunning painter might be permitted by access to her Majesty to take the natural representation of her Majesty whereof she hath always been of her own will and disposition very unwilling, but also to prohibit all manner of other persons to draw paint grave or portrait her Majesty's personage or visage for a time until by some perfect pattern and example the same may be by others followed.

Whether this draft was put into execution is unknown, although at the end of her reign there was certainly an official holocaust of portraits of her judged unseemly and improper "to the great offence of that beautiful and magnanimous Majesty wherewith God hath blessed her". But it is clear that Elizabeth disliked sitting for her portrait and at the same time had strong views about the way in which she should be portrayed. These views she elaborated in a famous interview recorded by Hilliard "when first I came in her Highnes presence to drawe". That is presumably in or before 1572, the date of his earliest extant miniature of her, in the National Portrait Gallery, that seems to be a likeness drawn from the life. This is Hilliard's report:

This makes me to remember the wourds also and reasoning of her Majestie when first I came in her Highnes presence to drawe, who after showing me howe shee noted great difference of shadowing in the works and diversity of drawers of sundry nations, and that the Italians, who had the name to be cunningest and to drawe best, shadowed not, requiring of me the reason of it, seeing that best to showe onesself nedeth no shadow of place but rather the oppen light; to which I graunted, and afirmed that shadowes in pictures were indeed caused by the shadow of the place or coming in of the light as only one waye into the place at some small or high windowe, which many workmen covet to worke in for ease to their sight, and to give unto them a grosser lyne and a more aparant lyne to be deserned, and maketh the worke imborse well, and shewe very wel afar off, which to liming work nedeth not, because it is to be viewed of necessity in hand neare unto the eye. Here her Majestie conceived the reason, and therfore chose her place to sit in for that purpose in the open alley of a goodly garden, where no tree was neere, nor any shadow at all, save that as the heaven is lighter than the earthe so must that little shadow that was from the earthe. This Her Majestie's curious demaund hath greatly bettered my judgment, besides divers other like questions in art by her most excellent Majestie, which to speak or write of were fitter for some better clerk. . . .[18]

The close similarity between the Queen's views on painting

and those of the Italian mannerists has been clearly demonstrated by Mr. John Pope-Hennessy: the insistence on the
avoidance of shadow, and on "the depiction of form through
the scarcely perceptible gradations of tone, which Zuccari
likens to the receding surface of a column".[19] The Queen
herself hints that chiaroscuro, the use of light-and-shade in
the modelling, might serve to conceal imperfections in the
sitter, but that it was too gross a method for a portrayal of
flawless beauty. She might have been asking for a crystalline
naturalism in the rendering of her own features, and although
Plate 21   Hilliard's own miniature of 1572 is an admirable and credibly
unflattering likeness of a woman of 39, it is one of the last
portraits of her to suggest such candour. In the painting
Plate 22   known as the Cobham portrait, perhaps of 1575-80, we have
probably in fact the last authorised approach to a naturalistic
rendering of the Queen; an admirable and inexpressive face,
yet a little haggard and worn, the face of a much-tried woman
in her early forties. And by then the dilemma was already
upon her.

Elizabeth was of course far more than a mere woman. She
was Queen, she was the Virgin Queen; she was the figurehead
not only of State but of Church, so that a poet might exhort his
readers to sing "Vivat Eliza for an Ave Maria"; she was the
centre of an extraordinary court cult, constantly re-defined
from an inexhaustible symbolism—she was the rose, the Rosa
Electa, at once that esoteric rose that burns at the heart of Jean
de Meung's *Roman de la Rose* and the rose that is the Virgin
Mary; she was Pandora, Astraea; she was the pearl, the
phoenix, the pelican in its piety suckling her country on her own
blood. Yet she remained, in spite of all, a mere woman, ageing.

But a decaying face was incompatible with a votive deity,
and so, from about 1580 onwards, she, no longer blushing,
offers her face, but substitutes an exposition of some aspect of
her mind. Her face, in the portraits, is rendered by an opaque

and unblemished mask; her identity is portrayed by the regal splendour of costume, by a richer cloth, by more jewels than any subject could display, and, more specifically, by crown, sceptre and orb. Particular qualities of her identity are displayed emblematically, by such symbols as the sheathed sword, the pelican, the phoenix, the olive branch; by a rainbow held bodily in the hand, or, as in the Ditchley portrait, by a whole sonnet let into the picture, and by her passage through storm and sunshine, recalling Sir John Harington's account:

when she smiled it was a pure sunshine, that everyone did chuse to baske in, if they could: but anon came a storm from a sudden gathering of clouds, and the thunder fell in wondrous manner on all alike.

In painting, this method answered at least one temper of the Elizabethan imagination: the piling together of images, the heaping of inflated unanatomical limbs, regalia, gems, the entire disdain of naturalistic illusion. Eventually it escapes altogether from the orthodox canons of European art: it is vain to judge it by its plastic values, for it is a hybrid of costume, of calligraphy, of flat repetitive design; of literature and of emblematic love.

It is perhaps easiest read if considered almost as heraldry. Each part has its significance; pose, costume and attributes establish the subject precisely in its rank, in its lineage, and in the centre its final individuality is differenced, as by a heraldic label, by the pale mask of the face. A later French theorist, Henri Estienne, though speaking specifically of emblematic devices, indicates the claim that can be made for emblematic portraiture, surpassing

not only all other Arts, but also Painting, since this only representeth the body and exquisite features of the face, where as a Device exposeth the rare conceipts and gallant resolutions of its author far more perspicuously, and with more certainty than Physiognomy can by the proportions and lineaments of the face.[20]

When she was sixty, Elizabeth on one of her progresses stayed with Cecil at Theobald's; the usual pageant opened with a Hermit. "I behold you," said the Hermit,

the self-same Queene, in the same esteate of person, strength and beautie, in which so many yeares past I beheld you, finding no alteration but in admiration, in so much as I am persuaded that Time, which catcheth everyebody, leeves only you untouched.

Time, in fact, as in the poet's imagination, has stopped. Age cannot wither her. Hilliard used one unwrinkled mask for her in all his miniatures of her last fifteen years. But, alas, age of course had caught her, at least in the unblinkered eyes of unprejudiced observers like the French ambassador, who describes the great reddish wig, and then:

as for her face, it is and appears to be very aged, and her teeth are very yellow and unequal compared with what they were formerly, and on the left side less than the right.[21]

Elizabeth herself no doubt clung to the abstract notion of her feminine charm, consolidating the abstract by paint as much on her person as in the images of it, but the tragedy of Essex must have brought home to her, as perhaps no other defection could have done, the vulnerability of her myth of agelessness. "Her delight", wrote an observer, "is to sit in the dark and sometimes with shedding tears to bewail Essex." Her reluctance to see herself truly mirrored is rumoured by several sources, most graphically—with almost a touch of King Lear—by Ben Jonson to Drummond of Hawthornden: she "never saw herself after she became old in a true glass; they painted her, and sometymes would vermilion her nose."[22]

Plate 26

Hilliard's mask of the Queen has the effect of broadening her brow—"her fore-head large and faire, a seemly seat for Princely grace"—of plumping the cavities of the cheeks and shortening the face. It is repeated in certain life-size portraits

in the Hilliard style, such as the Armada portrait at Woburn *Plate 23*
and the Rainbow portrait of Hatfield. Not all her late portraits
of course are quite so idealised; the face in paintings generally
associated with the Anglo-Flemish manner of Gheeraedts, like
the Ditchley whole-length and that at Hardwick, is long and
gaunt with indubitable age, although smoothed out no doubt
by the painter's brush.

The Hilliard mask is probably the best exemplar of the
ideal Elizabethan female beauty, and it corresponds to the
descriptions of the poets. The colour scheme was red and
white, "roses in a bed of lilies shed", as Spenser described
Belphoebe, with hair "like golden wires", the face should be
round and ruddy, with a broad brow; delicate, very slight
"pensild" eyebrows; grey eyes set wide, lips like the inevitable
cherry, and the neck like an ivory column. Thus Elizabeth
herself, without too gross a departure from fact, might be
rendered by her painters, and all ladies of rank modelled themselves upon it, though not all were blessed with golden hair.
Hence, in part, the reason that so many portraits of unknown
Elizabethan women have been wrongly re-baptised with the
Queen's name. Not even the greatest of couturiers have dictated
fashion and beauty culture to the extent that Elizabeth did.
From portrait after portrait the smooth pale unshadowed faces
gleam out, the contrasting red of their cheeks generally now
faded by time or dimmed by old varnish.

The perfection of these masks was contrived with perhaps
even more trouble than is the case today; they were guarded,
outdoors, by masks from the grave threat of roughening or of
tan and particularly from the ultimate hideousness of freckling.
Lotions were brewed from roses and cherries; ass's milk was
commended as a cleansing agent. For blemishes, extraordinary
concoctions, like that of turpentine, rosin, beeswax, hog lard
and honey, were made up. These were mainly prophylactic;

71

for accenting beauty, there were cosmetics. Painting the feminine face was now an established habit, not confined to the court, and there is a considerable contemporary literature on the subject, for the most part abusive. The agonised search for new cosmetics already foreshadows the beauty pages of modern women's magazines; eyes were sharpened with kohl, and no doubt, in the words of a recent fashion editress, if "made up with discretion would last their owners all evening and dominate their face".

There was already trouble with non-permanent red for the lips, and numerous recipes for mouth-washes suggest difficulty over one aspect of personal hygiene. Sir Walter Raleigh, opening up the distant wonders of Guiana, was interested enough to note

divers berries, that die a most perfect crimson and Carnation; And for painting, all France, Italy, or the east Indies, yeild none such: For the more the skyn is washed, the fayrer the cullour appeareth . . .

Egg-white seems to have been a popular base, in extremes, for "renewing old riueld faces", but primarily for a glaze, a fine shine and polish to the skin, which then, unlike now, was fashionable.

This votive mask was poised generally upon a stiff froth of lace and canopied by an artifice of hair. The lace is the ruff, which appears in the 'forties and 'fifties as a simple frill on the collar, but which by 1560 envelopes the throat, clustering like an elaborate cake-frill, tight to the ears. It was to remain, in various shapes and sizes, more or less in fashion for the next seventy years. About 1580 it expands into the cartwheel ruff, on which the head sits like John the Baptist's on a platter, but by 1590 it has opened in front to show the throat, and from 1600 it is decadent, in an extreme diversity of forms. Above it the hair, which until about 1575 is contained generally modestly under a hood with a falling veil, tends to puff in a matching profusion of tight curls "and least it should fall down, it is under propped with forks, wyers & I cannot tel what, rather like grim sterne monsters, than chaste christian matrones". Curled with irons, anointed with pomades and perfume, the hair had often been dyed to the fashionable blonde—"to make haire as yellowe as gold. Take the rine or scrapings of Rubarbe, and stiepe it in white wine or in cleare lie . . ." If there was not enough hair, it was supplemented by false; on top, and amidst and amongst, was the display-ground for lavish jewellery, while from one ear, but rarely both, would dangle a large pearl.[23]

The men, in their outward appearance, were not of course so regimented as the women—rather, the reverse. In 1559 the Lower House had urged upon the Queen the wisdom of marriage, and in reply she drew off her coronation ring:

yea, to satisfie you, I have already ioyned myselfe in marriage to an husbande, namely, the Kingdome of *England*. And beholde the pledge of this my wedlocke and marriage with my Kingdome.

That this pledge was to be fulfilled became apparent only in the 'seventies, after many alarms and excursions, and it was sealed by the final breakdown of negotiations with the Duke of Anjou in the 'eighties.

With the abstraction of Elizabeth from the practical marriage market (she was fifty when it happened) her court became even more like a male, but platonic, harem; now that the wooing of her was but play, her courtiers had to play with all the greater concentration to maintain the suspension of disbelief. Sartorially, they reacted with frantic splendour and unparalleled variety, each a bird of different species sprouting its mating plumage before a common queen. And it is as birds of display that their portraitists delineate them, with something of the meticulous and stiff precision that Gould was later to exercise on the plates for his ornithological books:

peacocks, popinjays and birds of paradise. Only the older men, like Burghley, Heneage and Walsingham, retain the official sobriety of bureaucracy, but even against their sombre gowns may dangle a gleaming token of their devotion, a cameo of Elizabeth's head.

The details of the variations of dress, huge Spanish slops or Danish codpiece, peascod belly and mandilion capes, that lace surcoat knit of pearls worn by Essex over his black armour —these do not concern us, except where they are the immediate frame for the face. The fashion for ruffs applied to men exactly as to women, reaching its full bloom in the cartwheels of the 'eighties; but simultaneously with that monstrous flower there was a more informal neck‑wear which consisted of a simple, though generally lace‑edged, turn‑down shirt collar.

Hats appear relatively rarely in the portraits, but range from the tall black sugar‑loaf with curly brim—the copintank, as it were a cross between a top‑hat and a bowler—and the flat velvet cap; on these, generally, jewellery was worn or at least a feather, while the Earl of Cumberland displayed in his a jewelled glove of Elizabeth's. The hair, since Henry VIII had his own head "polled" in 1536, continued short, usually cropped very close, but from the 'seventies was subjected by most courtiers to a carefully calculated dishevelment, combed forward on brow and temples in obligatory curls, with an effect that looks forward to the dandies of the Regency.

In the middle of the century most men wore beards—elderly men apparently always—a curious two‑pronged form remaining fashionable until about 1580, although what is thought of as the characteristic Elizabethan beard, short and pointed, is found throughout the reign. Hilliard's own self‑portrait of 1577 is a perfect exemplar of the presentation of a man about court, although he lacks the single ear‑ring that some of them wore. In the 'eighties beards went out of fashion with some for a brief spell, until Essex grew a fine reddish spade-shaped specimen during his excursion to Cadiz, and with it set a fashion on his return.

But this variety was controlled by the painters, the same painters who were transubstantiating Elizabeth into icon. They produced, with two exceptions, no major innovations in their pictorial designs, which remained basically variations on the static three-quarter-length court-portrait theme: polite, aloof, polished and rigid, still the two-dimensional counter-part of the tomb-effigy. Beneath the jewelled doublets and the ruffs, the bodies are but lay-figures, posed; on top of them, expressionless, the mask, hirsute or clean-shaven. They are more individualised than the Queen's, but the same heraldic quality of the whole is rarely absent. The technique, at its extreme, gives the impression of flesh like translucent wax stretched on the skull; usually the paint is thin, and sometimes even the "bones" of the underlying pencil drawing on the ground can be discerned through it. On a life-size scale, the result, in the hands of those who worked in the manner of Hilliard, like Segar, and to a less extent George Gower, is often vacant and dead; in Hilliard's own hands, in the com-pression of the miniature, its justification can be breathtaking.

The majority of Hilliard's miniatures show little more than *Plates 27, 29* the head. He was one of the exceptions to the rule, a great formal innovator, the master of the oval miniature in locket-shape. Trained as a goldsmith, his portraits are also jewellery; whereas the life-size portrait was house-furniture, his were furniture for the person, and a new intimacy is endemic if only in their size and purpose—small enough to be held in the palm of the hand, they could be private; they might be dis-played publicly, worn on a long chain, or even, as Elizabeth wore Cecil, on a shoe; but they might also be worn under the dress, over the heart or kept close in a lidded locket. Sometimes they are inscribed with a motto or tag, haunting and now inexplicably relevant as a refrain; or some symbolic allusion

75

may be incorporated in the design, as in the famous miniature of the dark man in his shirt, posed against a background of leaping flame.

But here at last it is the face that is the thing, and much of Hilliard's fascination lies in the tension between his masterly sense for design and his respect for the individuality of his sitter. In a passage, for the requotation of which no apology is necessary, he wrote:

so hard a matter the artist hath in hand, calling these graces one by one to their due place, noting how in smiling the eye changeth and narrow-eth, how the mouth a little extendeth both ends of the line upwards, the cheeks raise themselves to the eyewards, the nostrils play and are more open, the neck commonly erecteth itself and the forehead casteth itself into a plane as it were for peace and love to walk upon.[24]

Plate 29

At one extreme of his work are the stylised portraits of Elizabeth, and much of this stylisation appears also in his court-portraits, where the formal interest is perhaps not entirely fused with the human one. So with his Raleigh—the dark pointed head set on the dazzling lace-dish of the ruff; it is admirable, Raleigh the wit, the dandy, but it does not imply the whole man as we know him. Aubrey (although, writing long afterwards, about 1680, he is suspect) adds with words almost another visual dimension:

He was a handsome, and bold man. . . . His beard turned up naturally. . . . He had a most remarkable aspect, an exceedingly high forehead, long-faced, and sour eie-lidded, a kind of pigge-eie.

Hilliard is perhaps most exciting to the modern eye in those portraits that have lost their identity or bear an obscure name that has left no reverberations in history, faces which can be confronted with no previously-conceived image of what they ought to look like, and each of which is as fraught with mystery and as unanswerable and still demanding as the tomb of the Unknown Warrior.

Such are the portraits of Mr. and Mrs. Mole; he was an obscure official and tutor who is said to have been made against his will (he was a devout Protestant) to travel in Italy, where he was trapped by the Inquisition and imprisoned for life. The miniature of his wife was with him, and returned to his family by a visitor who was allowed to see him. The accretion of some such legend, if the story be not truth, seems almost inevitable about these two faces, while one of our most austere and restrained scholars, John Pope-Hennessy, has been moved to divine *angst* in them.

Plate 27

Hilliard, as we have seen earlier, subscribed to the Queen's artistic views, and so in practice did almost all the painters who portrayed the court. It would, however, be wrong to suggest that all Elizabethan portraits are so dominated by extreme artistic theory that there was no concern for naturalism. There seems to have been always a demand for a lively and likely likeness, but the artists who could have supplied them were mainly subordinate to the court fashion. In 1569 the Mercers rejected a statue of Sir Thomas Gresham because it differed "from his trewe image and picture".[25] At the close of the century the tide began to turn; about 1596, Essex, with his fresh red Cadiz beard, sat to Isaac Oliver, and not to Hilliard, who had previously painted him.

Oliver, Hilliard's former pupil, retained his master's love of delicate and rich detail, but his approach was basically different, and his art more naturalistic; unlike Hilliard, he built his people up by light out of shadow, and the results are fleshier, more palpable. In his work, English portraiture begins to come back into line with the main North European tradition; although it was not to fall fully into line until more than thirty years later, the Elizabethan experiment gradually gives way from this date onwards.

It must be confessed that the Elizabethan face that survives is inadequate; inadequate as image or mirror of the age.

77

Hilliard might have left us a Benedick, even perhaps a Mercu-
tio, he could scarcely hint at Hamlet, and Lear is beyond his
horizon. His miniature of Drake, though agreeing admirably
with Stow's description—"round headed, browne hayre, full
bearded, his eyes round, large and clear, well favoured, fayre
and of a cheerefull countenance"—is simply too small. There
is hardly a hint in Elizabethan portraiture at the largeness so
characteristic of the age, at its incredible intellectual variety and
curiosity; there is a positive contradiction of its essential movement, of that swift, robust and dangerous vitality that
circled the world and explored the heaven and hell of
Shakespearian tragedy.

Yet the main reason for this inadequacy is itself part of the
Elizabethan character; they were not interested in the visual
arts as such. Nowhere, apart from Hilliard and a handful of
artists, is there evidence of any awareness of the nature and
importance of, for example, the Venetian painting of the time,
which was that of Titian, Tintoretto and Veronese. Sidney,
in Venice, sat to Veronese, at someone else's behest, but shows
in his letters no comprehension of, and little interest in, the
prodigies of genius unfolding about him in that city. It is
probably not unfair to cite Robert Dallington's opinion of the
Italians as characteristic of that of the English to the visual
arts: conceding that Italy excelled in architecture (the reason
being obvious, that marble was to hand), and in painting and
poetry "and no marvaile, when all their time is spent in
Amours and all their churches deckt with colours".[26] The
English had other things to do.

Although the habit of portraiture had spread, the clientele
was still limited. It seems to have been practised hardly at all in
Ireland and Wales, and relatively very little in Scotland. It
was popular in court circles, and is reasonably inclusive. We
know, for example, what almost all the Knights of the Garter
about 1580 looked like. Outside the court, the habit was still

restricted. Bishops showed a worldly interest in perpetuating their mortal images, leaving behind them a series of gaunt wooden and unfriendly faces; to a lesser extent aldermen, mayors and merchants were interested, but they usually employed inferior artists, and were anyway perhaps more inclined, like country squires, to entrust memory of themselves to robed stone effigies on their tombs. The College of Physicians allowed their fellows a curious privilege on payment of a small fee; that of displaying their own portraits in the College, presumably as memorial but apparently also possibly as advertisement.[27] An exception was the great family of the Greshams, who employed, amongst others, Mor and Cornelius Ketel. But apart from the lower ranks of society, whole professions remain almost unrepresented; the most aggravating gap is amongst the poets. Peele, Kyd, Greene, Marlowe, Webster, even Spenser: nothing remains of them. For Shakespeare himself we are perhaps lucky; on the evidence of his social standing, there is no valid reason for expecting anything. We have in fact two portraits which probably have some tenuous connection with the reality of his person, though both are posthumous: the sad scratch that Droeshout engraved for the First Folio, 1623, and Gerard Johnson's bust at Stratford, memento of a *Plate 32* sober citizen of some standing. The irrelevance, the impertinence of both, is painful, but historically we have no right to expect more.

Sir Philip Sidney, paragon of Elizabethan virtues, is a disappointment of almost the same order. There are two portraits only, of each of which several versions exist: both are well authenticated, but they might well represent two different people (the Veronese is lost). One, probably painted in the *Plate 28* Low Countries in 1577, shows him posed according to etiquette as a conventional soldier, wearing a gorget; the other, of about 1585, with his head on a circular ruff, as a conventional courtier. Neither sheds any light on the discrepancy

between Ben Jonson's account—"no pleasant man in countenance, his face being spoiled with pimples and of high blood
and long"—result of measles and small pox, as confirmed by
Moffet's contemporary *Life*, and the passionate eulogies
poured forth at the time of his death, of which this is but one
sample:

> When he descended downe the mount
> His personage seemed most divine,
> A thousand graces one might count,
> Upon his lovely cheereful eine . . .

If, in some catastrophe, all vestiges of Elizabethan civilisa-
tion had been swept away, save only their life-size painted
images, we should scarcely be able even to guess at its unparalleled richness and variety. It would seem, rather, like some era
of decadence, inhabited by a remote race of beings, gaudy in
their vanity yet veiled with their pride; men and women of
stiff bodies, stiff habits, stiff minds, their imaginations blinkered
and confined like mill-horses within the well-worn orbit of a
dead mythology—an illusion that many of them, presenting
faces like rocks against time, seem to have wished to perpetuate
even in their features, the "windows of their souls".

A curious comment sometimes offered, as if in explanation
of one aspect of the Elizabethan character, is that it was young.
It is too often forgotten that England was already old, and it is
on the age and pedigree of race that so many portraits insist.
Certainly this was an uneasy period of social resettlement and
expansion, and the insistence on antiquity reflects men's unease when values were shifting so rapidly and incalculably.
They liked, those who could, to dwell for their own comfort
and peace of mind on at least the legitimacy of their blood
and state.

So their portraits have a heraldic quality, often made more
precise by the presence of a many-quartered coat of arms,
and so their faces are set in rigid moulds that will give as

Sir Philip Sidney 1577 anon.

29   *Sir Walter Raleigh*
     c.1585 Nicholas Hilliard

30   *Duchess of Suffolk and Adrian Stoke   1559   Hans Eworth*

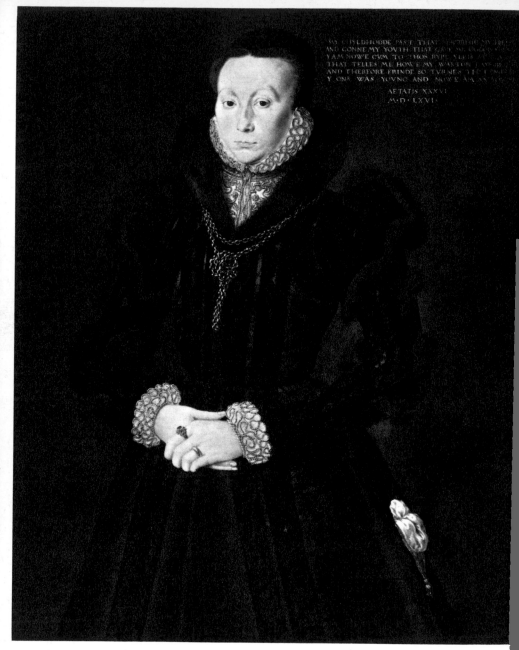

WE CHYLDHOODE PAST THAT . . . .
AND GONNE MY YOVTH THAT . . . .
YAM NOWE CVM TO THOS RYPE YERE . . . .
THAT TELLES ME HOWE MY WANTON . . . . . .
AND THERFORE FRINDE SO TVRNES THE . . . .
Y ONS WAS YOVNG AND NOW . . . .

AETATIS XXXVI
M·D·LXVI·

31   *Mrs Joan Wakeman*   1566   *Hans Eworth*

little as possible away. This pride is expressed vividly in an explosion of Richard Bertie to Burghley, after a Fitzalan had impugned his ancestry:

my lord of A[rundel] (as I am informed, more of his accustomed good nature than of my desert) told the Queen I was no gentleman, which perhaps being otherwise unwilling, somewhat stayeth, but if that respect had stayed her ancestors in the time of Fitzalan, bailiff of London, my lord should have lacked his lordship thus to embroil others. As I have no cause, so I am no whit ashamed of my parents, being free English, neither villeins nor traitors. And if I would after the manner of the world bring forth old abbey scrolls for matter of record, I am sure I can I can [sic] reach as far backward as a Fitzalan.[28]

But they had too a well-developed corporate arrogance; already in 1497 Trevisano had noted that the "English are great lovers of themselves . . . and whenever they see a handsome foreigner, they say that 'he looks like an English-man', and that 'it is a great pity that he should not be an Englishman'". (Trevisano commented that Scotsmen, how-ever, were said to be handsomer.)[29] This trait was remarked by others in the sixteenth century, and it is still sometimes sensible in the tone of voice with which, say, a Frenchman from Nor-mandy may be appraised: "you'd think he was an Englishman."

Yet against this arrogance is often to be set a religious humility; each portrait is but another vain attempt to fix a moment, an ephemeral phenomenon, on the retina of time; and the vanity is often openly admitted by a motto or by a skull. Mrs. Joan Wakeman stands, composed and resigned, in black, her hands folded, in the year 1566:

Plate 31

> My chyldhodde past that bewtifiid my flesshe
> And gonne my youth that gave me color fresshe
> Y am now cum to thus rype yeris at last
> That telles me howe my wanton days be past
> And therfore frinde so turnes the tyme [with?] me
> Y ons was young and nowe am as you see.

85

It is a resignation that few women of her age would submit to today; she was only thirty-six, and still very much alive, with thirty-two more years of old age to endure.

Many of the Elizabethan faces of course still come alive through no virtue of their painters. Give them a name—and what names: Elizabeth herself; Cecil, Walsingham; Frobisher, Grenville, Raleigh or Drake; Sidney; Leicester or Essex—and their stiff faces light up like transparent masks lit by a brilliant candle within. And sometimes the cool, clear-cut technique of the painters succeeds in detaching an image of the most pristine quality like a spring flower against a clear blue sky. Such are not only the best of Hilliard's miniatures, but even occasionally the life-size portraits, as Hieronymus Custodis' exquisite rendering of the young Elizabeth Bruges at Woburn Abbey.

Chapter IV

JACOBEAN MELANCHOLY

THE RECENTLY-COINED expression "Jacobethan" can be applied with equal aptness to the human frontispieces of the period as to those of architecture. The mixture of style continues; in some portraits, till as late as 1620, the Elizabethan court-manner persists, by now degenerated into true fashion plates, inflated whole-length costumes standing in a display-niche draped with metallic curtains the texture of which prophesies plastic. At Redlynch Park, two ladies are represented by identical portraits, only the heads being different.

But simultaneously the naturalistic tendency announced by Oliver's miniatures is gathering strength; by 1620 three painters of considerable ability from the Netherlands were working in London; Paul van Somer, Abraham van Blijen-berch and Daniel Mytens, and though they brought no radical originality, their sitters emerge in a more human probability. Oliver himself was working until his death in 1617 (as also Hilliard, a paling and ageing shadow of his former self), and before he died one Cornelius Johnson had begun a career that was to outlast the as yet unheralded Van Dyck, painting, to begin with, close in manner to Oliver's miniatures, but on a life-size scale.

But on the whole, at the court, the faces read as a prolonga-tion of the Elizabethan masks. James' large and "rowling" eyes, his thin beard, are composed near enough to dignity not to disgrace majesty, and his tongue, "too large for his mouth", constrained behind his lips; Queen Anne's high nose is in the true Elizabethan tradition, and about them are ranged the courtiers, more densely bearded now, shapeless and perhaps even often stodgy in bolstered breeches.

A few of them emerge with startling clarity; Lord Herbert of Cherbury, whose vanity, elsewhere so pyrotechnically

displayed in his autobiography, laid itself out in an icono-
graphy of astonishing variety. We see him solemn in robes of
the Bath; melancholic, prostrate in a landscape by a stream,
while his charger stands by; lovelorn in his lacey shirt or in
medallic profile like a new emperor, and, finally, his bodiless
and staring head, floating amongst clouds.[30] Francis Bacon,
in his formal painted portraits, is muted by a top-hat and
chancellor's gown, but in his seated effigy head on hand, in
the church at Verulam, the tireless mind may seem to have
but dozed off, the better to take up, after a few seconds or
millennia, its train of thought; death is no reason to lie down.
In Oliver's profile of that meteor, Henry Prince of Wales,
there is comprehensible something of the ardour, tough and
sensitive as a ship's prow, that so struck his contemporaries.
Although, in the same artist's miniature of Donne, the poet's
personality seems trimmed with his beard to an almost
suburban spruce, it escapes still in that fantastic gesture to

Plate 33   death and to posterity, his monument in St. Paul's; of the
"sitting" for this Walton has left his unforgettable account:

> Several charcoal fires being first made in his large study, he brought
> with him into that place his winding-sheet in his hand, and having put
> off all his clothes, had this sheet put on him, and so tied with knots at
> his head and feet, and his hands so placed as dead bodies are usually
> fitted, to be shrowded and put into their coffin, or grave. Upon [an urn]
> he thus stood with his eyes shut, and with so much of the sheet turned
> aside as might shew his lean, pale and death-like face, which was pur-
> posely turned towards the East, from whence he expected the second-
> coming of his and our Saviour Jesus . . .[31]

Plate 34   Yet in its more prosaic way, the massive belligerent head
of Ben Jonson, painted probably by van Blijenberch about
1617/20, has a more immediate, because less contrived,
impact. A face at once brutal and subtle, burning and
melancholic, the face of "a great lover and praiser of himself,
a contemner and scorner of others, given rather to losse a

88

friend, than a Jest, jealous of every word and action of those about him (especiallie after drink which is one of the Ele- ments in which he liveth) a dissembler of ill parts which raigne in him, a bragger of some good that he wanteth, thinketh nothing well bot he himself, or some of his friends and Countrymen hath said or done . . . passionately kynde and angry, careless either to gaine or keep, Vindicative, but if he be well answered, at himself ". It is the face of the author of *Volpone*, as of *The Alchemist*, as of *Drink to me only with thine eyes*; the face of a man who "heth consumed a whole night in lying looking to his great toe, about which hath seen tartars & turks Romans and Carthaginians fight in his imagination".[32] Even the bruising suffered over three centuries by the paint that records his image seems not inappropriate.

In these cases, all men outstanding, not only in their genera- tion, for the quality of their imagination, the sitter seems to burst the conventions of the art of the day. Van Blijenberch's head and shoulders of Jonson is an orthodox composition from which Jonson insists like a momentarily mild bull from too small a cattle-van. But gradually the technique and the scope of the painter's art develops. Daniel Mytens, precursor and to some extent the herald of Van Dyck, softens up the tight conventions of society portraiture, though his effects are gained by his skill and dignity in the handling of the whole composition, rather than by a noticeably much freer handling of the face.

Plate 34

More significant is the work of Cornelius Johnson, who, after the rather wooden portraits of his earlier years, began in the late sixteen-twenties to harvest a rich crop of sitters in which all critics agree in finding a specifically English atmosphere of character. Johnson was not a great painter; he steered a demure course through the various distractions that beset the taker of portraits. His modesty was such that stronger personalities could invade and possess his own, and his paintings are some-

Plate 35

times all but indistinguishable from those by the purely Dutch
Miereveldt, and at other times from those by Mytens, while
in his final English period, between 1632 and 1643, he can be
no more than a muted echo of Van Dyck. Yet his work as
a whole is quite distinctive. Most of his sitters give the impression of belonging to a well-to-do, well-mannered and
unostentatious level of society.

Johnson worked for the court, but his clientele extended far
wider than that, to the country squires, and, with rare exceptions, it is not as courtiers that his sitters appear. His characteristic design is a half-length, to the waist, the hands not
showing, set against a plain background, the costume sober
for the time, uncomplicated by draperies. The rhetoric in which
both Mytens and Van Dyck, in their different ways, were
masters, was foreign to him; he might ape it, but he could
produce no original development of it. Glancing round his
sitters, it is rather as though one were at a luncheon-party of
local gentry that Dorothy Osborne might later write-up. They
are polite, their hands are underneath the table; they are
reserved, sitting a little back behind the picture-surface, yet at
ease, unself-conscious, inhabitants of a common culture in
which decorum, the facts of life and also poetry all have their
importance. They are formal, and yet they have that warm
elusive intimacy that can be distilled from the felicitous inter-
play, by masters, of social conventions. This effect is that of
the whole portrait; to the painting of the faces in particular he
brought no new technique, but a sympathy for the individuality
of the sitter perhaps more sensitive, on a life-size scale, than
that of Isaac and Peter Oliver in the miniature.

Johnson is, from the point of view of the social historian, of
great importance, for he records a new level of life. But for the
ostentatious world of high fashion he was simply not enough.
By 1620, a small but outstanding group at court had become
conscious that England was backward in her design for living.

The movement to leaven this provincialism was headed by the great connoisseur, patron and collector, Thomas Earl of Arundel; hard on his heels came first Henry Prince of Wales, then his brother, later Charles I, and the Duke of Buckingham. All these men—apart perhaps from Buckingham—seem to have been extremely sensitive in their purely aesthetic reactions, but for all of them, though probably least in the cases of the two princes, the works of art that they collected with such far-ranging energy were also very much furniture for their own personal grandeur.

Arundel himself was one of the greatest and in some ways most unsympathetic snobs (as in his behaviour to Strafford) in British history, yet one who might seem almost to justify it, apart from his great learning and his generous patronage, sheerly by his physical projection of his character; "Here comes", said the Earl of Carlisle, "the Earl of Arundel in his plain stuff and trunk hose, and his beard in his teeth, that looks more like a Noble Man than any of us". While reactionary in his attitude to costume (maintaining that the looser French fashions "would bring Majesty into contempt") he was very progressive in his choice of the painters who portrayed him. One of Mytens' earliest portraits, about 1618, shows him with his statuary deployed behind him; he seems to have been responsible for Van Dyck's first, though largely unprofitable, visit to England in 1620 and was then painted by him; in the 'twenties he sat at least twice to Rubens, in the 'thirties at least twice to Van Dyck again.

By 1620 the Baroque movement was well established throughout the main continent of Europe, liquidating the entangled conventions of Mannerism with a rush of movement, melting the artificiality with a new naturalism. With Rubens' return to Antwerp from Italy in 1608, the portraiture of at least the Catholic Northern Courts had succumbed to the Baroque vision, which managed to convey, as no portraits had yet done, a sense of naturalistic illusion, of the breathing and lively presence, and at the same time still to exalt the person, superhuman, to convey through him an ideal majesty no whit less impressive than that of the rigid effigies of Clouet or Sustermans.

It was to Rubens that Buckingham went in Paris in 1625: Rubens did not come to him. Although of course he did not travel specifically to sit to Rubens, he took good care not to miss the opportunity. Buckingham's earliest portrait, that of about 1616 by one of the most formal of the Jacobethan "Curtain-Masters", a whole-length in which the Garter Robes seem too loud for a smart yet insipid mask, and Rubens' equestrian apotheosis of him (probably posthumous, about 1628) are a world apart. In Rubens' head and shoulders

Plate 36

portrait, in the Pitti Palace, and in the drawing in the Albertina, there is at last discernible something of "one of the handsomest men in Europe", of that "enigma of the world" who flew, rather than grew, as Clarendon said, almost from gutter to Dukedom. Some may detect a certain brassiness, a vulgarity in the features, that has something of the "flash boy". Buckingham, as a collector of works of art, was certainly an accumulator for prestige purposes, in the early American millionaire tradition, rather than a connoisseur with the learning and discrimination that both Charles and Arundel commanded.

Charles himself did not go to Rubens: Rubens came to Charles in England, in 1629/30, not as a hired painter, but as an ambassador for Spain. Charles knighted him, and he painted Charles as St. George (he also painted Arundel). It is symptomatic of an entirely new relationship between sitter and artist in this country; at last the artist is recognised, if only by a small coterie, as an aristocrat—at least of the aristocracy of genius. It is also in its way symptomatic of the unreality of that small coterie to whom the arts meant so much; Charles was not, with a Baroque flourish of sword and of shining

33 John Donne 1631 Nicholas Stone

William Shakespeare c.1620
Gerard Johnson II

34   Ben Jonson   c.1617/20   A. van Blijenberch (?)

armour, to conquer the dragon; of Rubens' other two English patrons, Buckingham was already dead from an assassin's knife, and Arundel was to die in voluntary exile during the Civil Wars, in 1646.

Rubens himself would not be confined in England, and it was only in 1632 that the court managed to attract a satis⁄factory substitute, an artist also of major stature and former colleague of Rubens, an artist whose hand is often discernible, even after three centuries, in contemporary portraiture today: Anthony Van Dyck.[33]

Sartorially, it was as though England had been loosening up for the event for years. Men's clothes, especially breeches, had swollen to their elephantine climax under James I, but had been softening since before his death in 1624; the hair worn comparatively close since the end of Elizabeth's reign, or at the most bobbed over the ears, began, with the young courtiers, to grow, long but asymmetric, into the trailing love⁄lock, sometimes with curls that suggest the agency of tongs, and always falling on the left shoulder, a mode already practised by Henry Wriothesley in the first decade of the century. And about the year Van Dyck arrived, 1632, the lace collar for ever associated with his name was finally adopted by the king in place of the falling ruff, although the so⁄called Van Dyck beard had been in fashion since 1610 at least.

The full beard, however, became unfashionable except for older men, and in the 'thirties and onwards the *reductio ad absurdum* of the beard, a minute patch of hair immediately under the lower lip, was worn by many, always with a moustache. In women's clothes, the formidable cartwheel⁄topped skirts began to melt into softer falling lines, but the sleeves swelled into the 'twenties, until women's arms looked like the bulbous legs of Jacobean furniture; neck⁄wear varied from broad starched lace edgings cut usually low and square, to many variations of the obstinate ruff. After Buckingham's death in

1628, and Henrietta Maria's subsequent conciliation with Charles, the Queen's French taste began to exert its influence on costume, in a line of dress at once much simpler, much more elegant and surely much more comfortable.

The hair is worn low on the crown, with a fringe, and clustered thickly over the ears, also often with a love-lock; curls appear to have been imperative, and the Elizabethan preference for blondes has yielded considerably, no doubt in compliment to Henrietta Maria, to brunettes. The fantastic jewellery of the Elizabethans vanished almost completely, and a simple string of pearls, with often a pearl in the ear, seems to have been as *de rigueur* as it was on English twin-sets between the wars. Painting of the face appears to have fallen from favour, perhaps already in the reign of James, who, in spite of his own breeches, was harshly outspoken on what he considered immodest excesses in the appearance of his subjects. There is, however, evidence enough that it was still practised, perhaps with discretion at court, with the usual indiscretion amongst the women of professional sex, and not at all by the gentry and the middle-classes. The ideal of feminine beauty is plumper now, more roundly sensual; the colour scheme is no longer pink and white, but, as described by Herrick, more lushly claret and cream:

> Black and rowling is her eye,
> Double chinn'd, and forehead high:
> Lips she has, all Rubie red
> Cheeks like Creame Enclaritèd:
> And a nose that is the grace
> And Proscenium of her face.

("The face", as John Bulwer was to write in 1650, "must needs be plain that wants a nose.")

Van Dyck arrived in England at the height of his powers, and was greeted as royally as Rubens, with a knighthood, a pension, a golden chain and the lease of a house at Black-friars. Within a year he was fully established, incorporated even into the language; less than ten years later he was dead, and his activity actually in England was hardly more than eight years, but the impact he made was out of all proportion to the length of his stay. He was already a fully-formed painter, but still chameleon-like, as he had shown himself in Italy, in his sensitivity not only to local colour and atmosphere, but to national character, and it is fascinating to attempt to analyse how one knows that his English portraits are English, that they could have been painted nowhere else in the world.

With him he brought of course the whole panoply of the Continental Baroque style, and, willy-nilly, he swept the rigid upstanding Englishmen into its rhythm; the picture-space, that had been a tight box, or effigy-niche, opens on his strongly-stressed diagonals into infinity, as if burst open by a sudden wind, in which curtains and draperies leap into life. His portraits are conceived as a whole, not as figures with objects. This too he had done in Genoa and in Antwerp, but now his colour is keyed higher, silvery in tone, shimmering with an English light. And there is, too, against the Baroque move-ment of his paint, a still restraint. The figures themselves do not move, but are caught as it were in an exquisite poise of balance. When he attempted to transfer something of the sweetly-aspiring saintliness of his Genoese religious manner on to his English sitters, the result tends to the ludicrous; he did it rarely, but the spectacle of the stout Rachel, Countess of Southampton, on a cloud upborne with a glistening globe (as Fortune), is curious rather than convincing. But in most of his English portraits there is this certain reticence combined with a certain somehow disdainful elegance of posture.

Van Dyck's name, like Holbein's, immediately conjures up in the mind a lost society. He is responsible for the visual glamour of the Cavaliers, though his picture answers most obviously to only a part of the truth. His sitters, with very few exceptions, come from the closed circle of the court, and he painted them as it were in masque-ing mood; in their very last, most exaggerated clothes, sometimes hopelessly involved, for practical purposes, with drapery, at other times as shepherds or shepherdesses in an unlikely Arcadia, as warriors in armour already obsolescent.

Yet behind the make-believe, generations now have sensed something more, a melancholy, a bitter-sweet vernal acknow-ledgement of transience such as that that Herrick sang. It may be that one exaggerates Van Dyck's melancholic temper in foreknowledge of the doom that was soon to overtake the society that he painted, but the strength of the myth that he created remains almost untouched in the popular imagination by the realistic probings of modern scientific historians. The myth focuses of course on one man: Charles I.[34]

Charles' appearance can be plotted almost year by year from when he was eight until he was forty-two; only three portraits of any significance are known from the last war-harassed seven years of his life. The earliest likeness of him extant is a tiny *Plate 38* miniature by Hilliard of about 1608/9, in the full Elizabethan tradition; it shows an expressionless boy's face, the hair brushed up into a quiff, with a tall, bulging forehead. A medical diagnosis of this image has suggested rickets,[35] and certainly Charles was an awkward boy, weak in the legs and with an impediment in his speech. The Hilliard is rather characterless, and portraits of Charles at this period, and indeed until as late as 1616, tend to be confused with those of his brother Henry, in whose shadow his first twelve years were so palely and obscurely drawn out.

This image gradually takes on a more characteristic shape, most markedly in Isaac Oliver's miniature of 1614, and then in the National Portrait Gallery whole-length perhaps by Van Blijenberch. It is, however, only about 1620 that the face we

Englishwoman   1633   Cornelius Johnson

36   *Duke of Buckingham   1625   P. P. Rubens*

know from Van Dyck begins to cohere, in a series of portraits   *Plate 40*
by Mytens. First the moustache appears, then, about the time
of his accession, the beard, at first wispy, then consolidated into
a rather Dutch pointed sobriety. In his face so far there is
dignity and decorum, but nothing discernible as melancholy,
and it is indeed extremely hard to state wherein lies the melan‐
choly of Van Dyck's interpretation. The face of the man in his
thirties has by now shed its puppy fat, and set, a little long,
heavy‐lidded; the love‐lock falls elegantly on to his left shoulder,
a little distrait; the beard has its crisp individuality.

The melancholy seems a matter of overtones; and yet was not
Bernini, according to a story of very respectable antiquity,
profoundly moved by the doom written in those features,
though twelve years had yet to run before Charles went to the
scaffold? But Bernini's own interpretation, carved from Van   *Plate 44*
Dyck's triple portrait without any first‐hand knowledge of the
sitter, seems to me to project a typically Bernini robustness,
almost swash‐buckling, on to Charles. Charles' essential
character seems to evade all questions, not only those of the
historians who return again and again to it, but also those of
his contemporaries, two of them men of genius, who tried to
find it in his face. Le Sueur's version of Charles, the famous   *Plate 37*
equestrian portrait at Charing Cross, is, as Miss C. V. Wedg‐
wood has pointed out elsewhere, almost jaunty if you consider
it with an honest eye; yet it inspired Lionel Johnson to write a
poem scarcely less well known than the statue itself: "Never
was face so stern with sweet austerity." But many people will
still agree with Northcote, who early last century admired
Van Dyck's head of Charles so much: "it might", he said,
"almost serve as model to paint the Saviour from." Van Dyck
seems to have painted Charles the Martyr long before the
event.

Moreover, it is certainly Van Dyck's view of him that persists
in the mind's eye; the interpretations of Mytens in the 'twenties

Plate 41

Plate 42

Plate 43

(even though he sometimes showed Charles with eyes nearer to brown than to light grey) are respectable. So too are those of Hoskins in 1642 and of Lely in 1647, showing Charles with a lip-tuft instead of a beard. Finally, at his trial, the beard spread rather roughly over his jawbone and lower cheeks, and so he was painted by Edward Bower. Yet an early eighteenth century engraver, J. Simon, when he reproduced Bower's painting, tidied and trimmed the beard back to the canon sanctified by Van Dyck.

It is, of course, Van Dyck's head that inspires all the nineteenth-century representations of the king; it was also to a Van Dyck of Charles that Madame Dubarry pointed when lecturing Louis XV on the probable consequences of his behaviour whenever he "seemed inclined to listen to the suggestions of his natural goodness of heart" and act with clemency towards his subjects. Van Dyck succeeded, of course, in concealing the infirmity of the king's legs, and, by intro-ducing no factors that might give a scale of comparison, his small stature. But others did that too; it was not difficult. Charles has been estimated to have been about 5 feet 4 inches in height, but the directions to Le Sueur for his equestrian statue were to make a "Horsse in Brasse bigger than a greate Horsse by a foot, and the figure of his Maj. King Charles proportionable full six foot". What then did Van Dyck do for Charles that no other artist could do?

He excelled in the first place by sheer quantity. It is im-possible to estimate precisely how many sets of sittings Charles gave him between 1632 and 1641; not more than ten, and perhaps considerably less. But from that meagre contact Van Dyck embroidered the theme, re-duplicating his variations in the shadow-factory of his studio; he painted Charles as the paternal monarch amidst his family, he painted him with his horse in a landscape as the country land-owner; in armour in many variants, some heroically equestrian; he painted him in

full coronation regalia and as a Knight of the Garter, and for *Plate 44*
Bernini he painted him three in one.

He excelled again in sheer quality; the construction and design of his portraits are professionally magnificent, even though he had not, particularly in his groups of more than two, the organic surety of composition of his master, Rubens, and this soundness of structure tells even in the countless copies whence the finer subtleties have evaporated. There is an old story that Rubens encouraged Van Dyck in portrait-painting because he feared his abilities in a wider field, but it is more probable that he recognised in Van Dyck what is perhaps the specific quality of a great portrait-painter, the ability to preserve the individuality of a sitter and yet at the same time to enhance it, by absorbing it into a grand pictorial design. It is a quality that generally implies a weakness in its owner, a certain lack of essential urgency, as though the painter needed the extraneous response and opposition of his subject to impel him; in Rubens himself it was drowned in his own strength, to which too the individuality of his sitters succumbs.

In the midst of the parade and pomp of the most grandi-loquent portrait by Van Dyck, there remains a hard core, an individual human face, observed and recorded with the most scrupulous and subtle skill. The faces, in the liquid cascades, silks and satins of the women's clothes or above the peacock male foppery of the men, are often outshone, withdrawn behind the fashionable mask, a smooth oval; but, if isolated, almost all the faces that Van Dyck painted are miracles of sensitive apprehension. In skill he had no rival in England, and it was the skill that dazzled the majority of his sitters, unlearned in aesthetics; the same magic, illusionism, that has enchanted the public since Apelles. His sitters found themselves, their spit and living image, but somehow a little larger than life, and more glamorous.

Whether he positively flattered, and if so, how, remains

largely open to speculation. In Charles' case there are two portraits that may indicate a hint of the answer; these are not by Van Dyck himself, but by the medallist Briot. One medal was struck in 1630, the year before Van Dyck arrived; the other in 1639, when Van Dyck's reign was all but over. The medals are by the same artist (in this case a Frenchman) of the same man; in ten years, between thirty and forty, a man may change, but the difference in this case postulates an impossible change of bone-structure: the physical proportions have altered, the face is longer. No one can say whether Briot, in his second medal, was seeing through Van Dyck's eyes, but the image certainly corresponds very nearly to the Van Dyck image of Charles; it may be that the characteristic effect of his style on the English face was a lengthening, and a long face is proverbially the face of melancholy.

Plate 45
Plate 46

A long face can be found again and again in Van Dyck's male portraits of the Caroline court; his men tend to the indifferent proud in expression, heavy-lidded, with long noses somewhat equine, aloof and perhaps somehow a little blind, if only to the extent of an utter unconcern for defeat. Generalised, it is a cast of feature that is repeated in Lely's and in Kneller's sitters, and right through to Reynolds and Gainsborough. One might suggest that Van Dyck invented the English gentleman, but such generalisations can always be contradicted by the subtle individuality of the faces that he painted, and sometimes, as in his astonishing portraits of Strafford, "Black Tom", by the eruption of titanic character.

The convention of manners is expressed in the bearing rather than in the face, but it is marvellous how Van Dyck can marry the convention to the most unlikely face without the face being swamped. His Archbishop Laud, for example, the Anglican prelate at his most worldly, a little stout perhaps, but inhabiting his gracious voluminous lawn rochet with an

Charles I   1633   Hubert Le Sueur

38

39

41

42

40

43

38 Charles I   c.1608/9
   Nicholas Hilliard

39 Charles I   1647
   Sir Peter Lely

40 Charles I   1631
   D. Mytens

41 Charles I   c.1642
   J. Hoskins

42 Charles I   1649
   E. Bower

43 Charles I   *after Bower*

44   *Charles I* 1635   *Anthony van Dyck*

45   *Charles I*   1630   *N. Briot*   47   *Charles I*   (1636)   *after G. L. Bernini*
46   *Charles I*   1639   *N. Briot*   *after Van Dyck*

aristocratic poise; and yet, once one's eye has been caught by
Simonds d'Ewes' maliciously concise account of Laud—"a little,
low, red-faced man, of mean parentage"—one questions Van
Dyck's version, only to find that there is nothing in the face that
contradicts Simonds d'Ewes, though he was a hostile witness.

With women, perhaps, he flattered more blatantly; Mytens'
sober version of Henrietta Maria is quite incompatible with
Van Dyck's, and the dismay of Henrietta's niece, when she
saw her aunt in the flesh for the first time after knowing her
only through Van Dyck's portraits, is well known: she found
the teeth stuck out like defence-works. But the evidence is
contradictory; here is the Countess of Sussex, very mortified on
seeing her own portrait (now, unfortunately, lost) for the first
time:

> very ill-favourede, makes me quite out of love with myselfe, the face is
> so bige and so fate that it pleases me not at all. It lokes lyke on of the
> windes puffinge—but [she adds ruefully] truly I think tis lyke the
> originale.[36]

The portrait of Lady Castlehaven is probably as good evidence   *Plate 50*
of Van Dyck's integrity as any, her face conforming to the
smooth fashionable oval outline, yet distinguished from all other
faces with the most troubling skill. She is clearly a woman of
rank, fashion and beauty. She is also recorded in history
as a woman of passion sometimes amounting to promiscuity;
she also brought about the death of her (admittedly undesirable)
husband, and was described, albeit by a most hostile witness,
as "the wickedest woman in the world". Van Dyck has not
labelled her face with these singular achievements, but he has
left us the living image of a character vivid enough to contain
them, and much more, even the spectator's charity.

Van Dyck's picture, however, is of the Caroline court, and
he painted most of the men who, a year after his death, were to
form the vanguard of the Royalist cause in action. The

opposing faction had no social ceremonial to match the court's; for a courtier, one may guess, to sit to Van Dyck was something that one did, like going to Ascot. Outside the court, to have one's portrait painted was far more haphazard, and the quality of the portraiture far inferior.

Van Dyck had no rival. Few people fundamentally out of sympathy with Charles were painted by Van Dyck: the Earl of Warwick perhaps was one, and also a few of those whose loyalties were later to prove ambivalent, men like Goring and Holland (who began an ardent Royalist, toyed and clinched with the Parliament, but was at last executed as a Royalist)— but none of the great names of the Parliamentary cause were personified by Van Dyck. Of Eliot there is but a sickly ghost-like reflection, of Hampden no certain portrait at all survives, and hardly anything even of Essex. Pym and Fairfax were painted by a former assistant of Van Dyck's, Edward Bower, but the only considerable portrait Bower ever painted was of Charles I at his trial, and the virtues of that portrait arise from the drama of the occasion, not from the intrinsic merit of a work of art.

The body of professional painters serving the public at large was of mediocre ability, sometimes thrusting their clients, gawky as rustics, into Van Dyckian postures, sometimes, with a more modest and often charming naïveté, content to record their heads and shoulders frankly and unassumingly, as often did Cornelius Johnson, until he withdrew from the noise of war to Holland in 1643. It is in his portraits that there can be sensed that steady placid continuity of life: they are family-portraits, dining-room portraits, whereas the great set-pieces of Van Dyck demand the setting of the state-room, as, *in excelsis*, in Inigo Jones' great double-cube room at Wilton. Many of Johnson's portraits have now lost their names; most of them were of people not in the centre of the stage, unused to limelight, content with local and domestic virtues; yet some of them no doubt were "village Hampdens", and one of them was certainly John Milton, containing that immense sonorous genius almost primly within an utterly unremarkable surface presentation.[37] He might have sat to Van Dyck, but it is somehow unthink/able; he might, on the other hand, have sat to Poussin.

To Van Dyck at court succeeded William Dobson, an English painter. His reign lasted only four years until his premature death in 1646, when only thirty/six years old. His beginnings are mysterious, and still to be investigated; hardly anything certain from his hand is known before 1642, but during the four years that he was active in London and at Oxford he recorded a picture of the Caroline court essentially different from that of Van Dyck. He is the painter not of the peacetime court, but of the embattled Royalists, of the Cavaliers.

It is, to generalise very broadly, as though Van Dyck painted his sitters as members of the Dramatic Society, while Dobson showed them (sometimes the same sitters as Van Dyck's) as members of the Rugby Club. He was a painter of great technical ability, but coarser and often clumsier in his handling than Van Dyck, with a broken richness of texture that is barbaric in comparison. He worked closer to his sitter than Van Dyck, so that his people are more burly, sometimes seeming a little larger than life; yet they are of life in a way that Van Dyck's never are, high in colour, wearing their flesh, at once gross and enjoyable, and, alas, sad, with the same parade as their turbulent satin and lace. Their characteristic weapons are not swords, but firearms (a great rarity in Van Dyck). They will go into battle; it will be no stage/skirmish, and in it they will sweat, and kill or be killed. Yet they are often also men of culture and of breeding, sometimes insisted upon by the introduction of a classical bust or bas/relief. The detail here *Plate 48* reproduced is from the portrait of John, 1st Lord Byron, a more purely martial portrait, dangerous, even a little Satanic with his scar, the eyes very slightly hooded; a face proclaiming, better than could medals, the man of action, who fought in the Low Countries, and at Powick Bridge, Edgehill, Roundway Down, Newbury and Marston Moor.

Many of the Cavaliers seem to have found time between battles to sit to Dobson; the Parliamentarians seem to have thought, possibly with reason, that they had better things to do. Also they had no painter to hand of the calibre of Dobson. Only when they had consolidated their position, and had become the government, did they have to face the problem of official portraiture.

Portraits were wanted, not only by their loyal followers but by foreign potentates. Though it would be disingenuously naïve to expect barbarian portraits of Roundheads, the extent to which the new rulers succumbed to tradition is startling, and its manner macabre. For their appointed painter was Van Dyck, the chosen painter of the apotheosis of autocratic monarchy. They did not, of course, resurrect him from St. Paul's, but they employed to take their portraits one Robert Walker, who openly avowed that as far as he could find Van Dyck had been the greatest master of poses, and that if he could find a better one, he would borrow from him.

Walker was not merely influenced by Van Dyck; he painted Van Dyck's portraits all over again, with different heads. On the body of Sir Edmund Verney, who had died heroically at Edgehill defending the royal standard, was set now Cromwell's head, now Ireton's, now Haselrigg's. On to the body of the Royalist High Admiral, Percy, went the head of the Parliamentary naval commander, Richard Deane. Other artists besides Walker did the same trick. P. Lombart's engraving of Van Dyck's equestrian portrait of Charles I (now at Windsor) was altered mercilessly and on the decapitated shoulders grew Cromwell's head; while Van Dyck's body of the Duke of Hamilton (beheaded in 1649) also was found suitable for Cromwell.

Lord Byron c.1644 *William Dobson*

Lord John and Lord Bernard Stuart, afterwards Duke of Lenox.

49 'The Br
c.1635/.
Anthony va

Walker unfortunately lacked the skill of Van Dyck, when it came to recording the features; he was a smooth and dull painter. I have already lingered at some length on the face of Charles I; it is as well to consider in detail the face of his great antagonist, not only for balance but because here is the face of a man who is of the essence of the English genius.[38] One of the anecdotes let in to enliven most textbooks of English history is that of Cromwell's instructions to his painter:

Mr. Lilly I desire you would use all your skill to paint my picture truly like me & not flatter me at all but [pointing to his own face] remark all these ruffness, pimples, warts & everything as you see me; otherwise I never will pay a farthing for it.

It is a story of compelling antiquity, said to have been told by the second Duke of Buckingham to Captain Wind and by him to George Vertue, who wrote it down about 1720.[39]

It was certainly not said by Cromwell to Walker (as is sometimes wrongly stated), to judge by the warts, which Walker glossed over; but was it said to "Lilly", Sir Peter Lely? Lely *Plate 52* painted Cromwell, and there are many copies of his portrait of him, but there is also a very similar portrait on a miniature scale by Samuel Cooper. Cooper's and Lely's portraits are so *Plate 51* close that one must depend on the other; no two painters could arrive at so identical an image from different sittings from the life; that it is Cooper's miniature that is the original is, I think, reasonably proved by a simple count of warts. Lely has left one cut, in the corner of Cromwell's right eye by his nose, or, if not left it out, glossed it into a polite bump.

There are of course other images of Cromwell; the idealised profiles by Simon on the coinage constitute one of the finest achievements in English medallic art, while at the other extreme there are a whole series of death-masks, and one mask, at Chequers Court, said to be modelled on the life. The death-masks are an exact transfer of the flesh, yet personally I find they

Plate 106

leave the mind unstirred, as any survey of the locked stable after the horse has fled; even the life-mask will not kindle—it has none of the sensitive magic that certain later life-masks can communicate, such as those of Blake or Keats. Practically, on technical grounds, there is no reason to challenge its authenticity; I object to it on psychological grounds—I find it impossible to imagine Cromwell having his face daubed with pomatum, and covered with wet plaster, possibly even with straws stuck up his nostrils. (The process is described by Pepys and others.)

It is to Cooper's portrait that I return again and again, and it is an image in the light of which all accounts of Cromwell should be read. It ennobles Warwick's account of him speaking in Parliament, in a plain ill-cut cloth suit:

his linen plain and not very clean . . . a speck or two of blood upon his little band . . . his countenance swollen and reddish, his voice sharp and untunable and his eloquence full of fervour.

It cancels the grudgingness in Clarendon's great assessment, and exposes Evelyn's description as peevish partisanship. Evelyn found in "the Lines of his ambiguous and double Face . . . Characters of the greatest Dissimulation, Boldness, Cruelty, Ambition in every touch and stroak."[40] And from it most of Carlyle's rhetoric falls away into silence. It is for me one of the most moving, one of the greatest of British portraits.

It should therefore follow, if one is to play that particular game, that Cooper is one of the greatest British portraitists. For me, this is so; indeed as a face-painter I would claim that he has no rival in Europe in the seventeenth century; this is not of course to set him above the great imaginative geniuses of the century, who included Rembrandt and Rubens, Vermeer and Poussin and Hals—and Velazquez. Cooper's masterpieces are not his "finished" works, brilliant though many of them are, but that handful of studies from the life, painted a little larger than his normal miniature scale, and apparently retained by the painter as patterns from which he could produce replicas as and when required. One of the reasons why he is so under- rated, or perhaps rather so infrequently rated, is the difficulty of writing about him.

One can point to the artist's fantastic manual skill, one can even demonstrate his habits of presenting his sitters, his forced lighting, his characteristic treatment of the eyelids, but the artist himself nevertheless remains unrevealed. The style is the man, the style is Rembrandt or Delacroix, Hilliard or Cosway, but with Cooper the style is the man he is portraying, and he annihilates himself in his sitter, in this still, yet almost breathing image. Nothing could be farther from the debased naturalistic illusionism of, for example, certain painters of the late nine- teenth century, whose works, as you look at them, disintegrate into an inventory of detail. Behind Cromwell's warts (each casting its own private shadow, a shadow that could belong to no other wart) there lies again, as with Holbein, that sure summary of the essential volume and displacement of the head, though unlike Holbein, Cooper achieved this largely by the contrast of light and shade.

On 10th January 1662, Evelyn saw him setting about it:

being call'd into his Majesties Closet, when Mr. Cooper (the rare limner) was crayoning of his face & head, to make the stamps by, for the new mill'd mony, now contriving, I had the honour to hold the Candle whilst it was doing; choosing to do this at night & by candle light, for the better finding out the shadows.

This of course was a special case, a drawing (probably that now at Windsor) for a low relief, and Cooper may not always have forced the light to that extent when building up his portraits, but Gainsborough, as we shall see, used much the same technique in his oil portraits.

In the entranced, minute observation of surface phenomena that Cooper reveals in these unfinished studies, he was very much of his time; with just that scrupulousness and curiosity did the early fellows of the Royal Society record all strange departures from the norm in the physical world, "warts and all". The nearest parallel is John Aubrey,[41] for whom Cooper was "the Prince of Limners". Isolated examples of attempts at verbal physical characterisation exist before Aubrey, but on nothing like such a scale, and whereas Cooper was restrained by his chosen medium to a study of the head and shoulders, Aubrey often tackled undismayed the whole-length portrait. In 1660

Plate 53 Aubrey persuaded Hobbes to sit to Cooper, and between Aubrey's description and Cooper's portrait one can still see Hobbes almost in the quick. Here is part of Aubrey's account:

In his youth unhealthy; of an ill yellowish complexion . . . he tooke colds, being wett in his feet (then were no hackney coaches to stand in the streetes), and trod both his shoes the same way. . . . From forty, or better, he grew healthier, and then he had a fresh, ruddy, complexion. . . . In his old age he was very bald (which claymed a veneration); yet within dore, he used to study, and sitt, bare-headed, and sayd he never tooke cold in his head, but that the greatest trouble was to keepe-off the flies from pitching on the baldness. His head was in compasse (I have the measure), and of a mallet-forme (approved by the physiologers).

His skin was soft and of that kind which my Lord Chancellor Bacon . . . calles a goose-skin, i.e. of a wide texture. *Face* not very great; ample forehead; whiskers yellowish-reddish, which naturally turned up— which is a signe of a brisque witt, e.g. James Howell, Henry Jacob of Merton. Belowe he was shaved close, except a little tip under his lip. Not but that nature could have afforded a venerable beard, but being normally naturally of a cheerfull and pleasant humour, he affected not at all austerity and gravity and to looke severe. He desired not the reputation of his wisdome to be taken from the cutt of his beard, but from his reason. He had a good eie, and that of a hazell colour, which was full of life and spirit, even to the last. When he was earnest in discourse,

50 *Lady Castlehaven* c.1635/37 *Anthony van Dyck*

51

51   *Cromwell c.1650/53 (?) Samuel Cooper*

52   *Cromwell c.1654 Sir Peter Lely*

53   *Thomas Hobbes c.1660/70 Samuel Cooper*

54   *Duchess of Cleveland c.1660 Samuel Cooper*

53

54

55   *Dorothy Osborne   1653 (?)   Sir Peter Lely*

there shone (as it were) a bright live-coale within it. He had two kind of looks; when he laugh't, was witty, and in a merry humour, one could scarce see his eies; by and by, when he was serious and positive, he open'd his round (i.e. his eie-lids). He had midling eies, not very big, nor very little. He was six foote high, and something better, and went indifferently erect, or rather, considering his great age, very erect. . . .

Aubrey tends of course to get lost in recording the warts and to forget the all; in his accumulated accounts, such as that of Hobbes, he carries a confused but vivid impression as of a number of film-shots, unedited. On other occasions, plumping his shots about his objective in a short salvo, he achieves extraordinary definition. Sir John Birkenhead of Cheshire:

He was exceedingly confident and witty, not very grateful to his bene-factors, would lie damnably. He was of middling stature, great goggli eies, not of a sweet aspect.

Or, simply, of Isaac Barrow:

He was a strong man but pale as the candle he studied by.

For neither Aubrey nor Cooper were their studies from the life objects of art. Aubrey's notes served as raw material for Anthony Wood's biographical dictionary of Oxford men, and were by Wood subdued into more polite formulae, though even so they brought a libel action upon him. Cooper, too, when making up the saleable article from his studies, subdued them diminuendo into the prim gold oval of the locket. In the finished versions of the Cromwell portrait (of which several exist), much of the freshness has inevitably vanished from the handling, while the sitter's shoulders are encased in the regulation armour. If a completed version of the Hobbes ever turns up, it is a fairly safe bet that his shoulders will be wrapped in the regulation loose black cloak.

Writing in 1641, Sir Kenelm Digby had compared life-size oil portraits with miniatures, saying that the former gave "pictures so like as some people think them even the worse for it. The best faces are seldom satisfied with Van Dyck; whereas not the very worst even complained of Hoskins." This is another tribute to Van Dyck's integrity in comparison with the prettifying performed by Hoskins (who was probably Cooper's first master) in his miniatures. By the time Cooper attained his maturity, the case was reversed; it is the miniaturist who now records every quirk and sally of the features, especially so in the case of his male sitters, but also to a remarkable pitch of honesty in the case of his women.

Cooper's rival in portraiture on a life-size scale was Peter Lely, whose career in England ran from about 1645 till his death in 1680; he was a most able painter, but his prime abilities lay in the composition of canvases sonorous in colour and rich in movement, and not in the recording and interpretation of his sitter's character. The contrast between his and Cooper's portrait of Cromwell is a little unfair to him, if, as I have suggested, his is based on Cooper's, but it is instructive, showing how the individuality of his sitter's features is general-

Plate 52

ised by the broad movement of the painter's style.

There is also, clearly visible in this case, that lengthening of the head that is demonstrable in the Elizabethans as in Van Dyck and which is a common principle of most fashionable painters and illustrators, down to the fashion-draughtsmen of the glossy magazines of today. Lely had taken Van Dyck's place as the leading portrait-painter in England by the late 'forties, and in common with most practising portrait-painters, his style depended very heavily on Van Dyck. In his more modest head and shoulders portraits before the Restoration, however, he has very much his own style, which lies somewhere between that of Van Dyck and Cornelius Johnson, harsher, more blatant than Johnson, with a sometimes posed elegance that is nearer Van Dyck, but often honest and forthright enough. He did not have the social or political affiliations that confined Van Dyck to one circle of society, but was well content to paint Charles I, then Cromwell, and then Charles II, to design a frontispiece for Lovelace's *Lucasta*, or to paint the regicide Sir Harry Vane.

Dorothy Osborne, writing to her lover about her portraits, gives a good picture of the prevarications and hesitations that must have beset the making of most portraits then as now. *Plate 55* In October 1653, she was

thinking of sending you my Picture till I could come my self, but a Picture is but dull company and that you need not, besyd's I cannot tell whither it bee very like mee or not, though tis the best I have ever had drawne for mee, and Mr Lilly will have it that hee never took more pain's to make a good one in his life, and that it was I think that spoiled it: he was condemned for makeing the first hee drew for mee a little worse than I, and in makeing this better hee has made it as unlike as tother. . . .

In June of the next year, 1654, she had apparently abandoned the Lelys as unsuitable, and was turning to Cooper:

I would have had (a picture) drawne since I cam, and consulted my glasse every morning when to begin, and to speak freely to you that are my friend, I could never find my face in a condition to admitt on't, & when I was not satisfied with it my selfe I had noe reason to hope that any body else should; but Ime afraid as you say that time will not mend it and therfore you shall have it as it is, as soone as Mr Cooper will vouchsafe to take the pain's to draw it for you. . . .[42]

Dorothy Osborne's comments make it clear that amongst the gentry of any standing, it had become a normal part of living to have one's portrait taken, for one's friends or for one's family; the habit had not yet spread much wider, and amongst those who could afford some likeness of themselves, religious scruples would sometimes intervene. Henry Newcome, a modest and soul-searching minister, for long refused the request of his family that he should be painted; he consented at length for his children's sake, but was disturbed when the portrait arrived:

I was but too much taken with my own shadow when it came home; but then I thought, a man should study both to be blameless and eminently active, that presumes to leave a picture behind him. If it put in mind of evil or of no good done by him, it is to little or bad purpose.[43]

The extreme Puritan would have rejected the idea of a portrait out of hand as a mortal vanity.

56 Charles II 1684 H. Pellé

57   Nell Gwyn   c.1670   Sir Peter Lely

Chapter V

RESTORATION BAROQUE

THE POPULAR impression of the transition from the Interregnum to the Restoration is perhaps much of an iron austerity yielding almost overnight to a gay ebullience, that might approach licence, but if so was still not unattractively human. In fact, in spite of Puritan restriction of such frivolities as the public performance of plays, the outward show of living had been brightening since about 1650. In May 1654, Evelyn wrote that "the Women beegan to paint themselves, formerly a most ignominious thing, and used onely by prostitutes", but Izaak Walton had commented on the use of "Artificial Paint or Patches in which [women] so much pride themselves in this age", over a year before.

Such evidence is very difficult to interpret; patches never appear in portraits and the amount of paint probably depended on the social status of the painter. Evelyn probably referred to the gentry; Pepys (rising middle-class) saw his wife wear black patches on 30th August 1660, and it was as late as 1667 that he wrote, not certainly of his wife: "I find her painted which makes me loath her." It is, however, fairly clear that a desire for a more vivid self-presentation was making itself apparent through the 'fifties; clothes were silkily voluminous in the skirt and loose in the sleeve; the dressing of the hair becomes steadily more elaborate.

For the men, the establishment in 1660 of a court interested in clothes did have an immediate and startling effect; the long hair waved into curls and flowed more thickly over the shoulders; the simple turn-down collar broke into a flat foam of lace covering half the shoulders and chest, while the sober black and white colour-scheme of suit and shirt exploded in an exuberance of white linen, many-coloured suits, ribbons and lace. Both the exuberance and the cut of fashion were stimulated by Louis XIV's court in France, a dependency that some Englishmen felt to be regrettable; a positive revolt, Charles II's attempt to rationalise men's clothing in a relatively severe black and white scheme once again, fell flat when Louis XIV put the lackeys in his court into identical uniform.

The tone in women's dress was no longer set by the Queen, as it had been in the society of Charles I; it was set by the King's mistresses. No coherent record of the rapidly changing detail in everyday dress survives; that provided by the portrait painters is of dishabille, the sweet disorder that so attracted Herrick. The shoulders are bare and in the case of the King's mistresses sometimes to the waist; but the dishabille, which is of the late supper table if not of the boudoir, is set in other contexts, Olympian or Arcadian landscapes, and the sitter provided with a shepherdess's spud or Minerva's helmet. The attribute of Nell Gwynn is not an orange, but a lamb. Barbara Palmer, later Duchess of Cleveland, appears as an erotic and unconvincingly repentant Magdalene in a wilderness, as St. Catherine or as her namesake St. Barbara, as well as Minerva. Her most outrageous posture, together with one of her bastards by Charles II, was sent by her later on, according to a story put about by Horace Walpole, to another of her children who was in a convent in France. It was there placed gratefully over an altar, until the nuns discovered that it was not, in fact, a representation of the Madonna and Child.[44]

The tone of portrait-painting was set by the mistresses, thus disguised as goddesses or shepherdesses; following them, more reputable ladies were disguised as royal mistresses, only slightly more buttoned-up, and so on down the social scale, the designs set by the most fashionable painters, especially Lely, being repeated verbatim except for the head; so, on 15th February 1666, John Hayls began to paint Mrs. Pepys "in the posture we saw one of my Lady Peters, like a St. Catharine".

The high priest of this transformation scene was Lely, of whom Dryden wrote: "he drew many graceful pictures, but few of them were like and this happen'd to him because he always studied himself more than those who sat to him." Pepys, when he saw the newly-painted Beauties which are now at Hampton Court, put it another way: "very good, but not like." Lely indeed rarely makes a profound statement upon the individual character of his sitters, but he betrays himself profoundly in every picture he painted, and, because he was so happily in tune with the visual display of the court he was called upon to portray, he tells us much in general about that limited circle of society. He was an opulent man, and his pictures reflect a tactile and baroque opulence of paint, of stuffs—gorgeous undulations of fine lawn, of silks and satins, whether the vestments of a bishop, the robes of a Knight of the Garter or the undress of a woman—and of flesh, a rich, plump, drowsy flesh, well-filled as upholstery.

His style, that early on could catch something of a morning mystery, as in his Dorothy Osborne, is, after the Restoration, of the blatant and sonorous afternoon, immensely able, often openly vulgar. The vulgarity, in the works which are by him rather than by his assistants, is redeemed by the pleasure of the paint. It is often so Dutch in temper that some of his pictures of this period can even by trained eyes be confused with those of Nicholas Maes or Jan Mytens. During his reign, which lasted from 1660 to 1680, almost the whole of Charles II's, there were of course other painters, but beside the miniaturist Cooper, only Michael Wright, and, very briefly, John Greenhill, preserved much individuality. The others aped Lely, but Wright in his dry way sometimes conveys, through a modest, slightly questioning reticence that recalls the characterisations of Cornelius Johnson, a person.

The fashionable face, examples of which can be found in the late work of Lely and his followers, especially of Wissing,

Plate 55

131

between about 1670 and 1685, is a horizontal one, a wide face. The tendency is visible in Lely's portraits of the 'sixties, but not so much in the faces, which still (even in the much-maligned Beauties at Hampton Court) have a fresh clarity. In his three-quarter-lengths of women, generally seated, the horizontal or shallowly diagonal stresses are very marked, in the movement of the arms, the slow swathe of silks; in the 'seventies this pictorial rhythm captures the faces too, now treated much more broadly, often more coarsely, indistin-

Plate 59

guishable one from the other. The eyes bulge from long slots in the flesh, the hair is built out at each side of the head, first with a wire support for dangling ringlets, and later con-solidated into a cluster of curls; mouths too are largely wide, full, with ripe and pouting underlip; the horizontal of the eyebrows is heavily marked, and the exaggerated top-lighting casts a shadow swagged about the chin, suggesting a second chin even when there is not one. Clearly, flesh is in fashion; the Elizabethan painters seem sometimes to be searching for "the skull beneath the skin"—for Lely, the skin sufficed.

Men's faces, too, yielded to a fat Baroque curvature, and in their case to a Baroque not only of a painter's style; they capitulated to the wig. The wig is a factor for which a modern observer can hardly make too great an allowance; it first caught hold generally on English male heads in the early sixteen-sixties, and it survived until over a century and half later. It was not of course an unknown phenomenon; wigs were fashionable in Assyria and in Egypt; later, the German tribes ran a profitable business exporting blonde hair to Rome, and the early Church Fathers denounced periodically the wearing of false hair. Throughout history women seem to have toyed with false hair (already in 1615, Barnaby Rich was denouncing the "lowsy commodity of periwigs" and "monstrous mop-poles of hair").

But the masculine fashion for wigs at this particular period is generally said to have its roots in France, in the sixteen-twenties, at the court of Louis XIII. Generally, it is fashionable for at least some hair to be worn; not to wear hair at all is to flout convention, which replies woundingly by ridicule; and when a profusion of hair is accounted a virtue, it is splendid to have more hair than anyone else. It happened, at Louis XIII's court, that long hair was fashionable for those of high rank, but unfortunately the highest-ranking of them all, the king, began to lose his hair prematurely. To begin with, he probably only supplemented what remained to him, but gradually the complete wig was adopted, and the court, by courtesy, followed suit; the extraordinary fashion was launched upon its long career, and for more than a century Europeans cropped their hair in order to wear someone else's. They seem to have been known in England during the 'fifties, and even earlier the Cavalier love-lock perhaps often had to be artificially produced; in 1655 the fifteen-year-old Francis Throckmorton was buying curling-tongs for his wig in Cambridge, but it was not until after the Restoration of 1660 that Charles II set the royal seal of approval on the fashion by going into a wig himself. He was turning grey.

The gradual yielding to the fashion is chronicled by Pepys. In 1662 his wife, short of ringlets, had taken to "a pair of perruques of hair, as the fashion now is"; in May 1663, he himself was toying at his barber's with two or three "borders" and periwigs—"yet I have no stomach for it, but that the pains of keeping my hair clean is so great". It took him six months to succumb, until on 30th October he bought a wig, but still hesitated before appearing publicly in it. On 2nd November he was encouraged by the Duke of York saying that he was going to wear one; on the third he took the decisive step, and had all his hair cut off—though, he admits, it went to his heart to part with it. On the fourth, apprehensively, he showed himself in public, wigged. To his relief there was no great comment, and even the severe scrutiny of the congregation at church next Sunday was not outraged. In 1665, he had second thoughts, grew his hair, but then cut it all off again because he found "the convenience of periwigs is so great". The fashion was in.

Opposition seems to have been very slight; the Anglican Church adopted it, after a little pamphleteering (the Archbishop of Canterbury, Sumner, still put on his wig to marry the Princess Royal in 1858, sixty years after it was generally abandoned); the left wing of the Church, the puritanically-minded and the Quakers resisted longer. John Mulliner, Quaker, in a pamphlet of 1677, *Against Peri-wigs and Peri-wig Making and Playing on Instruments of Music among Christians*, describes how he "was troubled and took a wig and burned it", but by 1717 even the Quakers, while deploring "extravagant" wigs, admitted those that could be described as "modest, decent, or necessary".

The chief arguments in favour of the wig were probably, as indicated by Pepys, those of cleanliness and, curiously, convenience. To wear short hair was unthinkable, as it immediately reduced a man visually to the rank of apprentice; facilities for washing were primitive, and the time expended on keeping long hair clean and groomed, before the wig, must have been considerable.

A man of any standing would have at least two wigs, so that one would always be ready. Other arguments put forward in its history on its behalf seem tendentious—the claim, for example, that a wig protected its wearer from colds: what happened in fact was that, on arriving home and removing the wig, one had to compensate for it by a turban-like cap or one did catch cold. To the eye it had considerable virtues; it lent maturity to the callow, and youth to the old, and it cancelled out baldness. Hogarth delighted to ridicule its excesses, but even he remarked that "the full-bottomed wig, like the lion's mane, hath something noble in it and adds not only dignity but sagacity to the countenance".[45]

Visually, it is of course just as much a manifestation of the Baroque style as is Lely's swirling paint, its sinuous and curling fall more satisfactorily linking an often obstinately rugged head to a posed and drapery-wreathed body than a mere neck. But for a full realisation of its stylistic possibilities one generally has to seek out the work of foreign artists, as in the Frenchman, Honoré Pellé's bust of Charles II. It is curious how precisely,   *Plate 56* with its massive emphasis on the head, the career of the wig coincides with the age generally known as that of Reason: all the great men of reason wore it: Locke, Newton, Addison and *Plates 66, 63* Pope: Lord Burlington, even Hume, even Dr. Johnson—and yet it is essentially such an unreasonable fashion, cutting off one's own hair in order to wear someone else's.

There were various sources for the hair of a wig; one could, like Pepys, have one's own hair shorn and made into a wig; some certainly had their wife's hair made into a wig for them-selves (and she, presumably, got someone else's); there was the hair of the dead, only not in times of plague; there were the fertile heads of the children of the poor, and probably, as in ancient Rome, some importing of Teutonic blonde hair. (In France there was a minor economic crisis when Colbert discovered how much gold was leaving the country to pay for golden hair coming in from Germany.) One could appear fair in the morning, and dark in the evening, to taste, but red hair was not used, for red is the colour of Judas.

The reign of the wig in its classic—that is, full-bottomed— form lasted some seventy years, from the sixteen-sixties into the seventeen-thirties. The wig as first worn by Charles II was tightly-curled, flat on top, falling below the shoulders; thence it developed (with variations) in fullness, the curls loosening, in length, and in height, growing above the head for some inches, sometimes into twin horns; it attained its maximum about 1700 and held it until about 1720. Lavater, the great apostle of the lore of physiognomy, was later to admit to some indecision about hair: "if it is not admitted to rank with the members of the human body, it is at least a part adherent to it." In the heyday of the full-bottomed wig, hair, though adjacent rather than strictly adherent, is of such splendour that the human face that it is intended to frame becomes, if not impossible to see, nevertheless impossible to assess in wig-less terms. Some have complained that Kneller's portraits of the members of the Kit-Cat Club, all painted when the wig was at its zenith, represent a lot of wigs with Whigs inside them; there is an element of justice in the accusation, and the modern eye often has considerable difficulty to make out what is going on inside.

The demand for portraits had increased at a remarkable rate during the second half of the seventeenth century, quite naturally as a result of a rising population and prosperity of the gentry. Building boomed, and a new standard of domestic display came in. In most houses of any standing, portraits were becoming usual furniture. A helpful work, *Polygraphice*, first published in 1675 but subsequently often re-issued, is in part a guide to social etiquette, and devotes a chapter to the Disposing of Pictures and Paintings: in the Dining Room the pictures of the King and Queen, or their Coat-of-Arms

forbearing to put any other Pictures of the life, as not being worthy to be their Companions, unless, at the lower end, two or three of the chief nobility, as attendants of their Royal Persons;

in the inward or withdrawing chambers, other portraits "of persons of Honour, intimate or special friends, and acquaintances, of Artists only". But the purely family portraits are for the bedchambers—

your own, your wives and childrens pictures, as only becoming the most private Room, and your Modesty: lest (if your wife be a beauty)

8 *Samuel Pepys* *1666* *John Hayls*

59

60

59 *Duke and Duchess of Lauder*
   c.1672 Sir Peter Lely

60 *Duke of Lauderdale c.1674*
   B. Gennari

61 *Duke of Lauderdale c.1680*
   John Riley

some wanton and libidinous guest should gaze too long on them and commend the work for her sake.

Such a discretion was certainly not generally observed, though it is curious to find Evelyn hanging the portrait of his extra-marital love Margaret Blagge—even though his most platonic and spiritual love—in his own and his wife's bedchamber. It aroused some comment from one of Mrs. Evelyn's friends and seems to have been moved fairly swiftly to the parlour.[46]

Modesty indeed is antithetical to the main-spring of por-traiture, which is vanity. All these people, increasing every year, who had themselves painted did not do so for reasons of self-effacement. They wished to put themselves on record in the light most becoming, not only to their physical charm but also to their social station. Hence Mrs. Pepys was painted in the pose and costume favoured by a lady of title. The progress of her husband's portraits is also interesting. In 1666 (when the Diary was in full spate) a middle-class urban civil servant with an unusual taste for the refinements of living (for that, rather than for the arts, as such), he sat to John Hayls. The *Plate 58* latter was an imitator of the most fashionable painter, Lely, but also of course much cheaper than Lely. Pepys did not conform to the extent that his wife did. He bought a loose drapery, a rich "Indian gown", specially for the occasion in order that he might be conventionally draped, but otherwise the portrait is unusual, and he gave Hayls a great deal of trouble.

Hayls painted a landscape background, and Pepys, after some hesitation, had it painted out; he holds a sheet of music on which is written a tune of his own composing. There was trouble before that was clearly legible, a trouble recorded in the Diary and also in an X-ray photograph of the painting, where further trouble is also disclosed with Pepys' right arm which does not show in the finished picture, but was originally held forward. The exaggerated turn of his neck was perhaps of his own choosing, too, though he complains that it gave him a violent crick in the neck.

Sorbière, the French traveller in England in the early sixteen-sixties, commented on the intolerable pride and haughtiness of the English nobility, and a reflection of this pride pervades the portraits of even gentlemen of the period. Yet it is curious to see how variously different painters may interpret the expression even of a proud aristocrat. The Duke of Lauderdale offers in his person an exceptional example:

haughty beyond expression, abject to those he saw he must stoop to, but imperious to all others [with] a violence of passion that carried him often to fits like madness.

He was in Scotland an able and extremely brutal adminis-trator; at Charles II's court, though one of the five great, the leaders of the Cabal, "He made a very ill appearance: He was very big: His hair red, hanging oddly about him: His tongue was too big for his mouth, which made him bedew all that he talked to: And his whole manner was rough and boisterous, and very unfit for a court." Another witness repeats the charge:

his head was towards that of a Saracen fiery face, and his tongue was too big for his mouth, and his pronunciation high Scotch, no high-lander like him. . . . This lord although not invited, ever intruded himself.

And yet all agree also on his extraordinary learning, "not only in Latin, in which he was a master, but in Greek and Hebrew", in divinity and in history.[47] He was often painted; the three reproduced here show him in his early fifties and early sixties; the first, by Lely, about 1673, contrives to impart an almost groomed, though slightly Dutch, chic; the second, of a few years later, is by the Italian Benedetto Gennari, nephew of Guercino, who produces in his hard, metallic light the full horror of the face—the bully, the thug, capable of a most

Plate 59

Plate 60

sinister joviality. The third, of about 1680, is by the English
painter, John Riley, in whose work critics discern a specifically
English temper, a melancholic, atmospheric feeling for his
sitter's character; and here indeed is a face of an elderly clubman,
irritable, with gout perhaps in some extremity, and intolerant,
but with some subtlety; the face of a man whose learning in
Greek and in divinity one might accept without surprise, and
a face that consorts oddly with the faces of the same man shown
by Lely and Gennari.

Plate 61

Chapter VI

THE POLITE MASK
OF THE AUGUSTAN AGE

LELY DIED in 1680; his close follower (also Dutch), Wissing, in 1686. Two years later came the Glorious Revolution, and with it a less ostentatious fashion in portraiture. To Lely succeeded Kneller. Sir Godfrey Kneller, German-born, trained in Holland and Italy, acknowledging in his style both Bol and Maratti, arrived in 1674. He saw at once what was wanted, and, to begin with, painted portraits that are sometimes so close to Lely's that they have been mistaken for them; but essentially his is a swifter and a leaner style than Lely's, vertical compared with what had hitherto been predominantly horizontal.

The seated women now sit up instead of reclining, and the men emerge in close-fitting velvet coats, as the billowing tide of draperies recedes. Faces stay plump (indeed a double chin now seems an essential of masculine and feminine beauty) but they lengthen, and noses are worn lofty and long; the narrowed elongated eyes remain and become even more of a formula. The mouth remains full, but now succinct, in the case of the woman, as a standard impression from a rubber-stamp charged with lip-stick. Feminine hair goes up, right up, leaving the face sometimes cruelly naked; a severe and forbidding style very often, and, particularly when elaborated by that strange towering structure of lace known as the *fontange*, no longer an allurement, but a defence mechanism. A long, well-fleshed face, framed in the voluminous but ordered foliage of the wig served men for some forty years between 1690 and 1730; with women the ideal seems to have been an unblemished long oval, set at an angle on the long smooth neck, reminiscent of the feminine beauty celebrated by Mannerist painters like Parmigianino.

142

Anne Sotheby   1692   Sir Godfrey Kneller

63 Joseph Addison c.1705 Sir Godfrey Kneller

It is generally a very summary portraiture; the niceties of character, and very often all character, escape it. Kneller himself, at his best a most subtle artist, could at his best catch the individuality beneath the wig, and better still when the wig was off, but almost all his women are insipid, and, now that the evanescent chic of fashion has long since evaporated, plain. Kneller was not of course the only painter, but he was during his long reign, right up almost to his death in 1723, the most fashionable one, and facially his rivals, Dahl, d'Agar, Richardson, Murray, Closterman, repeat the theme which is known as his. He was the chosen painter of the Whigs, and has left a splendid record of them in the portraits of the members of the Kit-Cat Club, but he also painted indiscriminately the rival party, including Harley and Bolingbroke; nor could anyone claim that those particularly under Harley's patronage, notably Dahl and Richardson, produced portraits in any way illuminating a specifically Tory *Lebensanschauung*. Kneller was also the most prolific painter of them all; teutonically industrious, he was also a master of business organisation, and his studio came far nearer to a factory than Van Dyck's or even Lely's: virtual mass-production explains a great deal of the standardisation of his products.

Yet part of this standardisation, this generalisation, is due to the temper of the age. Kneller formulated the Augustan face; a polite and urbane mask. His average presentation of his sitters (though not in the fully formal and official whole-lengths) is a "model of the middle style; on grave subjects not formal, on light occasions not grovelling, pure without scrupulosity, and exact without apparent elaboration; always equable, always easy. . . ." That, of course, was not written of Kneller, but is from Johnson's famous assessment of Addison's prose style. It applies equally, however, to Kneller's best middle style, as in the Kit-Cat portraits, as in his portrait of Addison himself— equable, easy; his shirt loose at his throat, he inhabits his wig

Plate 63

as inevitably as his sense his prose. But he is not familiar; sociable, but not intimate; he might smile agreeably, but already (in 1694) one of Congreve's characters, anticipating Lord Chesterfield, had laid it down that "there is nothing more un-becoming to a man of quality than to laugh". (How true to life this formally informal impression of Addison may be is another matter; it was Chesterfield himself who described him as "the most timid and awkward man in good company he ever saw".) The topography of his face is broadly treated, and rounded; the minute exploration of the terrain that Kneller's French contemporary, Rigaud, would have undertaken is not even attempted, while his clothes sit easy on him instead of crepitating with a Gallic, lacy vigour of their own.

Plate 62

In the painting of the face of Kneller's Anne Sotheby, of 1692, this generalisation is even more marked, as is usual in his portraits of women; the face becomes almost an abstract design (see the drawing of the eyebrow in one curve into the nose, the simplified eyes, the perfect rounding down cheek into chin and up again); she is fashionable youth. Yet, when stirred, Kneller could rise to heights far above even the pure middle style of the Addison; in his portrait of Sir Isaac Newton, for

Plate 66

example, as rare an interpretation as any genius could hope for. Seen from a distance, it is a stock head and shoulders portrait, a wigged man draped in the conventional meaningless drapery, set in the conventional painted oval within the rectangular canvas. Move closer, and the thing becomes alive with urgency. It is painted fast with the muscular vigour that may sometimes remind one that Kneller worked for a time under Bernini. It is also almost, in the modern sense, expressionistic, and uses distortion deliberately—the loaded iris of his right eye too great for the lids to contain it, and the wig not stuffy about his head, but lambent as an aura.

Kneller's average world, and that of all the society portrait painters of his time, is of the middle style, its inhabitants detached, each one scrutinised in his or her rôle as gentleman or gentlewoman. They never do anything extraneously in their pictures; to pose is full occupation. Towards the end of Kneller's long reign he painted Pope in the classic attitude of melancholy, visibly thinking, and before that painters like Jervas and Richardson had painted writers (Swift and Prior) actually with pen poised over paper. But that was the sign of a thaw in formal portraiture that was not to become general until the middle of the eighteenth century. Jacob Tonson, a late Kneller of 1717, is shown in an informal turban-cap instead of a wig (others in the Kit-Cat portraits are shown thus, but Tonson, surrounded by peers, knights and esquires, is the only one designated on his frame as "Mr."), clutching *Paradise Lost*, from which he made copious money; his expression however is not that of a contented tradesman, a publisher, but aweful, as though in communion with the spirit of Milton.

During the latter part of the seventeenth century the portrait-painters found their clients in a rapidly widening field. English country-houses, great and small, are full of ancestors of this period, of most callings, and mostly painted in the manner of Lely and then in the manner of Kneller; to be painted, they usually stripped themselves of any vestiges of their profession, and clad themselves in the uniform wig and loose cloak of the gentleman. Those, like Tompion with his clock, who admit to a mechanical skill, are rare, though those concerned with the liberal and humane arts and sciences may admit a book or an astrolabe; Kneller recorded himself with his grand new country house in the background.

Soldiers and sea-captains appear; Lely, in his fine series of admirals at Greenwich, gave them a rugged if somewhat Dutch individuality, but when Kneller and Dahl continued the series at the turn of the century, little smack of the sea was left clinging to them. Marlborough looks a little ill-at-ease in his breastplate, and the thunder of Blenheim did not shake the fabric of Kneller's canvases. At this time, too, the clergy, particularly bishops, began to sit with that unflagging assiduity in which they have persevered ever since; they are distinguished by their black gowns and plain bands, and, for the bishops, their splendid sweltering rochets of white lawn; but they, too, while differentiated by their costume, are gentlemen. The Anglican Church went into the wig with perhaps less questioning than did the Catholic, where there was even at one time a question of tonsured wigs. In expression they are benign, and on the whole, I think it is fair to say, plumper than the laity: Béat-Louis de Muralt, in 1695, was surprised to see in England "most of the clergy looking so healthy and prosperous and it is a pleasure to look at all these fat and rosy chaplains". The more radical wing of the religious movement, that of the Puritans and the Quakers, is of course very scantily recorded in portraiture, with the exception of Bunyan, whose blunt, brawny yet visionary enthusiasm still informs and transcends the mediocre painting of him by Thomas Sadleir.

The painted portrait was not the only way of preserving the face. The spark of genius seems to have deserted the miniaturists after Cooper's death in 1672, and did not kindle again for almost a century; a summary statement of character does not suit the scale, but this was what taste demanded, and so miniatures degenerated into little Knellers, Jervases and Hudsons, insipid and characterless. Between the sixteen-sixties and 1700 there was, however, a short fashion for miniature portrait-drawings in plumbago, or blacklead. The chief exponents of this art were David Loggan, born in Danzig and trained in Amsterdam, but of Scottish family; his pupil, Robert White, and T. Forster.[48] Loggan, both in his topographical work and his portraiture, was much influenced by Hollar, and he has a scrupulous eye for minute detail; his portraits offer a refreshing contrast with the schematised features of contemporary life-size portraits. He worked in Oxford and in London; he was not

Mrs. Harrison 1681
David Loggan

Beefeater 1713
Peter Angelis

66   *Sir Isaac Newton   1702   Sir Godfrey Kneller*

expensive though very popular, and the backbone of his clientele seem to have been the professional middle-classes, people of some book-learning, modest in their living, sometimes suspect of an agreeable, mild eccentricity, unspectacular but unflinching in their appearance—dons, doctors, clergymen, all ingenious men (including Aubrey, a drawing now, alas, lost), and almost for the first time in British portraiture, wives: not disguised as women of fashion, or as saints or goddesses, but fine and wonderful wives.

Loggan's approach was informal; he could even take his likenesses in a coffee-house. To represent his unpretentious but veracious work, the portrait of a certain Mrs. Harrison, *Plate 64* drawn in 1681, must serve—a homely wife, her face unshaped by fashion; posing of course, and frankly pleased to be doing so, but timeless: you could easily meet her in the porch after the Sunday morning service today. Robert White was less incisive in his modelling, but has preserved some remarkable people, not least amongst them Sir Thomas Browne and Titus Oates.

A similar veracity is hardly to be expected of the sculptural portraits. In John Bushnell[49] England had a baroque, Bernini-like sculptor of some talent, but his works are mostly sepulchral; straightforward portrait-busts for domestic purposes are very rare during the second half of the seventeenth century, and until about 1720.

The busts, made up from life-masks, which came into some sort of fashion in the sixteen-fifties, are known only by account (both Pepys and Huyghens sat for them and describe the process); with their glass eyes, they must have been very distressingly life-like, but they were made of plaster, and not one certain one of the period is now known. By the end of the century, too, the wax-work show had arrived in London, and has continued, probably with hardly a break, until today; about 1700, Ned Ward was much astonished at the liveliness of the figures at Bartholomew Fair, "art's nicest imitation of human nature", but the wax figures of course were even more perishable than the plaster busts.

Very important, as a disseminator of the fashionable face, was the popularisation of engraving. Portrait engravings were published towards the end of the sixteenth century, but they remained for long small in scale and woodenly inferior in quality to the painted portraits. With the beginnings of Wenceslaus Hollar, a Czech, in England, they took a livelier turn, and his small etchings from his own drawings from the life anticipate Loggan already in the sixteen-forties. But line-engraving, at the pitch of excellence to which it was brought by 1660 by William Faithorne (who had learned much from Nanteuil in France) and then mezzotint-engraving, sponsored in England by Prince Rupert and John Evelyn in the 'sixties, with its almost magical illusion of the sensuous depth and chiaroscuro of oils—these brought the portraits of those in high fashion out from the private palaces into the public print-shops of St. Paul's Churchyard.

The popular illustrated magazine is almost in sight, and it is to Pepys, of course, that one turns again for the first account of that enduring phenomenon, the pin-up girl. The first one was not an actress; Nell Gwyn is now firmly established, I suppose, as the archetype, as it were, of the average English-man's bawdy—"pretty, witty Nell" as Pepys described her, and she is recreated by each age in its own fashion; but she was not the first. The honour fell to Charles II's first mistress of con-sequence, Barbara Villiers, Lady Castlemaine, later Duchess of Cleveland. In 1662 Pepys saw at Lely's studio "the so much desired by me picture of my Lady Castlemaine, which is a most blessed picture; and one that I must have a copy of". This may well have been the whole-length of her, head on hand, melancholily arranged as a Repentant Magdalene in a wilder-ness (one version of this belonged to Pepys' master, Montagu,

and is still in the Montagu house at Hinchingbroke) but thereafter, although Pepys' exclamations of wonder at the original
lady are frequent, the portrait is lost sight of until suddenly, on
the 7th November 1668, he found Faithorne with the Castlemaine picture "done by him from Lilly's, in red chalk and
other colours, by which he hath cut it in copper to be printed
... the finest thing I ever saw in my life".

Faithorne, however, would not part with the drawing as he
had not finished the engraving; he promised that Pepys should
have it as soon as the engraving was done, but he seems to have
failed to keep it (it is probably the drawing now in the Victoria
and Albert Museum) and the last sight we have of the
portrait is of Pepys calling at Faithorne's again on 1st December, publication-day of the engraving, and buying three prints
of it. This was an entirely respectable engraving, superficially
at least; others that were to come, particularly of Nell Gwyn,
were less so, décolletée to the waist, or even nude, lightly disguised as cupid with a pair of wings. Charles II had a painting
by Lely, a whole-length nude; it was kept behind a sliding
panel on which one Danckerts had painted a landscape, a
device that was used again in Victorian days to camouflage
more than one of Etty's nudes. The head of what may well be
this very painting is here reproduced; it is one of the least
mannered and most charming of Lely's heads, and, if it really
be Nell Gwyn, explains her persistent charm better than any
other portrait (the remainder of the painting is mildly but fairly
ably pornographic).

Plate 57

It is now impossible to gauge the demand for all these
pictures of beautiful women, but it must have been considerable, apart from the engravings; Lely's stock, when sold in 1682
after his death, included no less than twelve paintings of Lady
Castlemaine. From the sixteen-seventies onwards, the output
of engraved portraits was relatively very large, and their scope
very wide. The Royal faces, as ever, were probably the most

popular, but most people who achieved some public fame or notoriety were now recorded by their visual journalism; not only the actresses and the politicians, but the major criminals from Titus Oates downwards (though these tended to be very crude woodcuts incorporated in broadsides, often showing only an unrecognisable body dangling from the gallows). Really resonant *causes célèbres* would produce a host of prints, mostly pirated; Sir Edmundbury Godfrey's face was everywhere on the prints after his murder on Primrose Hill, as were those of the Seven Bishops whom James II consigned to the Tower. And a little later, in Thoresby's Diary, we find ingenious men of learning exchanging engravings of themselves somewhat like visiting cards.

But there are hardly any serious portraits yet of the less than well-to-do. Servants, odd pages, even negro boys, occur in formal portraits occasionally, but as decoration, as trappings; there are a few isolated studies, like Riley's well-known painting of the scullion at Christ Church, Oxford, but they are exceptional. Only one odd glimpse would I preserve here, from Peter Angelis' record of a ceremonial occasion with 'Queen Anne and the Knights of the Garter' about 1713, in all the billowing baroque of their great blue and white robes and their powdered wigs; amongst them, solid and expressionless, a Beef-eater, already a century out of date in costume and in face yet almost precisely, except for the lack of a ruff, as you can see him at the Tower of London today. There are not even any crowd scenes; one or two Dutch or Flemish artists of genre painting, Heemskirk, Tilborg, were working over here at the close of the seventeenth century, but their crowd characters seem indistinguishable from the Dutch low-life they were accustomed to paint. Some writers already perceived a lively, swarming and lusty picturesque in English everyday life, like Ned Ward in the Royal Exchange distinguishing French from Spaniards ("lank-haired formalists . . . walking with as much

Plate 65

state and gravity as a snail o'er a leaf of a cabbage"), "the Lord's vagabonds, the Jews", and then

a kind of lean, carrionly creatures, with reddish hair and freckly faces, very much given to scratching and shrugging, as if they held lousiness no shame and the itch no scandal; stooping a little in the shoulders, as if their backs had been us'd to a pedlar's pack. . . . These, I found, were a compound of Scotch and Irish. . . .

The painters had yet to turn their eyes to this kind of subject-matter; when the *London Spy* began to appear, in November 1698, Hogarth was but one year old.

Chapter VII

HOGARTH–CHARACTER NOT CARICATURE

AT THE BEGINNING of the eighteenth century, a long-nourished resentment against the low standing generally allotted to painting among the other arts began to find public expression. Painting was in fact not widely admitted as a genteel occupation; the painters' concern, though not openly avowed, when formulating its claims as a liberal art, was as much with their own social position as with the honour of their art. It was generally acknowledged that painting in classical times had been a liberal art, for the unimpeachable evidence of great Greek and Latin authorities was a record to that effect, but it was held that in modern times the art had declined from grace into a mechanical trade.

Elyot, in the widely-read and influential book *The Governour,* 1531, had already as good as stated this; Stow in his *Annals* of 1580 said so specifically:

sure I am, it [the art of Painting] is now accounted base and mechanicall, and a meere mestier of an Artificer and handy Craftsman. Insomuch as fewe or no gentleman, or generous or liberal person, will adventure the practising this Art.

Hilliard's passionate apologia of the art of limning as a gentleman's art may well have been provoked by this passage, but Hilliard's manuscript remained unpublished until the twentieth century. There were of course distinguished amateurs, practitioners of the arts, as distinct from connoisseurs, men like Sir Nicholas Bacon and General Lambert, but they did not practise professionally. Sir Anthony Van Dyck was knighted by Charles I, and so was Lely, while Kneller was the first to achieve, in 1715, a baronetcy—but these were exceptions (besides being all foreigners) and the truth was that painters had not the social recognition that was readily accorded to men of letters.

Poets indeed were soon to have almost a fan-following, and in the late 'twenties, Voltaire observed that the "picture of the Prime Minister hangs over the chimney of his own closet, but I have seen that of Mr. Pope in twenty noblemen's houses". Addison, Congreve, Steele, Garth, Vanbrugh, all hang on a level with men of the noblest blood in the informal precincts of the Kit-Cat Club, but no painter is represented; Kneller's portrait belonged to Tonson, but not as part of the series, almost as it were on sufferance—and on almost a miniature scale. It was well over a century after Sidney wrote his *Apologie for Poetry,* about 1581, that Jonathan Richardson, painter, attempted an apology for painting in various publications dating from the first quarter of the eighteenth century.

Richardson maintained that a great painter had to be endowed with a learning equal to that of great scholars, plus an intimate knowledge of anatomy, osteology, geometry, perspective, architecture; he had also to be a poet, a man of imaginative genius. In addition to all this, he had also to be a

Curious Artificer, whereby he becomes Superior to one who equally possesses the other Talents, but wants That. A *Rafaëlle* therefore is not only Equal, but Superior to a *Virgil*, or a *Livy*, a *Thucydides* or a *Homer*.

The justification for such a contention would naturally be found in that branch of painting which gives the widest scope to all these qualities, and that was not portrait-painting, but "history-painting", the imaginative representation of scenes from history and mythology.

It has been said of Painting [wrote the English connoisseur John Elsum in 1703] that it is like Musick, best in Concert. History-Painting is that Concert, comprizing all the other Parts of Painting, and the principal end of it is to move the Passions.[50]

Richardson, connoisseur though he was, and man of letters, panegyrist of Milton, was also by profession a portrait-painter, and so had to stress the liberal side of that branch of the art as well as of history-painting.

His argument much resembles that of the Italian theorists of the Renaissance (particularly Lomazzo); against the charge that portraiture is a mechanical copy of nature, he stresses its imaginative and its interpretative aspects. Likeness is not enough.

Thus to raise the Character: To divest an Unbred Person of his Rusticity, and give him something at least of a Gentleman. To make one of a moderate Share of good Sense appear to have a Competency, a Wise Man to be more Wise, and a Brave Man to be more so, a Modest, Discreet Woman to have an Air something Angelical, and so of the rest; and then to add that Joy, or Peace of Mind at least, and in such a manner as is suitable to the several Characters, is absolutely necessary to a good Face-Painter. . . .[51]

It is still a good text for portrait-painters who would have a fashionable prosperity, though some would resume it more tersely: flatter.

Portraiture, indeed, cannot but fit awkwardly into any intellectual theory of painting as a liberal manifestation of the imagination; it is tied too closely to imitation. A greater intellect than Richardson, the third Earl of Shaftesbury, writing (1712) at much the same time with a similar pre-occupation, was more logically drastic: he deleted face-painting from the canon of true art altogether. "Tis an abuse of real art which should (aye and will) be reserved for better purpose." The only exception he makes is "for small portraiture of heads only (for bodies would be mere puppets and ridiculous as everyone presently sees) which convenience and use renders agreeable and friendship amicable". But any further claims for the face-painter he dismisses as ridiculous; it is not a liberal art nor to be so esteemed;

158

Earl of Winchelsea 1726
Jonathan Richardson

69 *Earl of Winchelsea c.1724*
J. M. Rysbrack

67 *Earl of Winchelsea c.1710 (?) Sir Godfrey Kneller*

70

72

71

70 Dr Mead 1739 A. Pond

71 Dr Mead 1739 Jonathan Richardson

72 Mrs Emma Harvey 1751 (?) Allan R

as requiring no liberal knowledge, genius, education, converse, man-
ners, moral-science, mathematics, optics, but merely practical and vulgar.
Therefore not deserving honour, gentility, knighthood conferred
(Glance at Sir Kneller).[52]

These notes, from Shaftesbury's uncompleted work on plastic
art, were not published, and he was in advance of his time.
But the unease they reflect was to spread widely until all
British painters yearned to be history-painters. It was not that
form of art, however, that was to prove the characteristic mould
for the great eighteenth-century school of British painting. It
was rather the despised art of portraiture, enlarged to the scale
of history-painting, to concert-pitch, by Reynolds. His reading
in Richardson's book is said to have played a large part in his
decision to become a painter.

But Reynolds is still a long way off; and before his establishment in the seventeen-fifties thousands of faces had to be
painted. The front on which he was to unleash his attack
meanwhile was in some sectors softening up; in another, that
of formal society portraiture, it set almost into a rigor. Richardson's own painting scarcely bore out his theories. In his larger,
formal portraits he was not a remarkable innovator, though
able enough, and it is his smaller, informal head-and-shoulder
portraits that now have most appeal, for in them he seems to
rely on an honest, fresh and literal transcription of his sitter's
head, in exact opposite to his theory. In his treatment of the
face he is notably more detailed and more particular than
Kneller. Richardson had a heavy, accurate, rather leathery
technique in painting the flesh which he passed on to his
pupil, Hudson, who became one of England's leading society
painters. In Hudson's work, and in that of his rivals, Hoare,
Ramsay (with some reservations), Pond, and others, from
the seventeen-thirties through the 'forties, and lingering on even
into the 'sixties, society portraiture at last found a solution that
seems logical to that dichotomy that oppresses all its practi-

tioners—the cleavage between the necessary representation of the brute facts about a given face and the claims of the picture as a work of art.

We have seen Van Dyck's age, and Lely's, and Kneller's; the seventeen-thirties and 'forties are neither Hudson's, nor Hoare's, nor Vanderbank's—in society painting they belong to Joseph van Aken. He came to England before 1720 and died in 1749, and towards the end of his life was painting much of Hudson's, Ramsay's, Highmore's and others' portraits. They did the face, the brute facts, and then the canvas was sent over to Van Aken who painted the body, fashionably attired and fashionably clothed. Hamlet Winstanley, a pupil of Kneller's with a large practice in the north, was perhaps his most extreme employer: he

travelled about and drew pictures from the life in oil colours—often on small pieces of cloth, only the face; pasted them when sent to London on larger clothes,

and sent them off to Van Aken in London, who did the rest with that

excellent, free, genteel and florid manner of pencilling, silks, satins, velvets, gold lace, etc.

which gave the finished product that essential, as it were Savile Row, cachet.

These compositions, gradually pitched higher and sharper in colour and light, are generally still within that tradition in which Kneller had worked; but the poses become more forced, and affected, and a certain sartorial precision is apparent, a crisp laundering of linen with a sometimes pleasantly Rococo life of its own; in the male portraits the swirling drapery is abandoned, although the fashion for Van Dyckian fancy-dress was in evidence during the middle of the eighteenth century. There was in general a shift of sympathy towards the French tradition

of portraiture as described not entirely unjustly by Addison
some time earlier (in 1711)—the faces

very remarkable for their smiles and a certain smirking Air . . . bestowed indifferently on every Age and Degree of either Sex. The
Toujours Gai appeared even in Judges, Bishops and Privy-Counsellors
. . . every part of the Dress was in a Flutter, and endeavoured to distinguish itself above the rest.

When J. B. van Loo arrived in London from Paris in 1737,
he had a rush to his studio of the most fashionable sitters; he
had a waxier *chic,* and a more minute technique in the rendering
of the features than any British painter then working. The
progression of this part of the art seemed to be indeed towards
the ideal of presenting a two-dimensional illusion of a wax
tailor's dummy.

At the end of the 'thirties, the Abbé le Blanc commented
that in London the portrait painters were more numerous and
more unskilful than ever they were before.

At a distance one would take a dozen of their portraits for twelve
copies of the same original. . . . Excepting the single countenance or
likeness they have all the same neck, the same arms, the same colouring
and the same attitude. In short these pretended portraits are as void of
life and action as of design in the painter.[53]

The faces, more detailed though they are, are still of the
Augustan expression; polite and unimpassionable masks—the
face of Lord Chesterfield, the urbane and cynical author of the
Letters to His Son: the face of the well-entrenched Whig, at
one (in expression, at least) with Sir Robert Walpole for
stability and prosperity at home, and peace abroad.

There may be in some faces, outside the Royal Household,
a certain thickening, a Hanoverian heaviness, but overall the
ideally fashionable features have not changed much. They are
still burdened with wigs, but always powdered from the

seventeen-twenties onwards, and beginning to freak in decadence. The wig generally used for polite occasions shrinks up from the full-bottom in the seventeen-twenties and 'thirties; by 1753 the only members of the House of Commons wearing a full-bottomed wig were the Speaker and the Attorney-General.[54] For their two offices the already obsolete fashion had fossilised, and the Speaker and Judges still wear full-bottomed wigs today. By that date, the variety of wigs was sporting in full profusion; there were the pigeon's wing, the comet, the cauliflower, the royal bird, the staircase, the wild boar's back, the she-dragon, the rose, the negligent, the cut bob, the long bob, the drop wig, the snail back, the spinage seed. . . . But even amongst this medley, Lady Mary Wortley Montagu's son caused a certain furore when he arrived back from Paris, in 1751, with an iron wig, spun out of the finest wire.[55]

Certain professions appropriated their own peculiar shape of wig: soldiers, the clergy (a very thick bob wig), coachmen and others. But a wig of some kind was essential for social occasions; virtuosi and even the nobility might be painted wigless, in a velvet turban-cap, but not for a more formal portrait.

A curious illustration of the effect of the wig on the appearance is offered by three portraits of Daniel, Earl of Nottingham and Winchilsea; a triple head by Kneller (reminiscent of Van Dyck's Charles I) in which he is seen bald from three angles; a formal portrait in peer's robes by Richardson, much bewigged; and a senatorial bust by Rysbrack, with his head sprouting a crisp crop of little curls. All three in their different ways are also examples of rejuvenation—the sitter is near or in his seventies.

Arthur Pond, in the late 'thirties, issued a rather scratchy etching of the celebrated Dr. Mead, a connoisseur and physician with a European reputation, without a wig on; the doctor

Plate 67

Plate 68
Plate 69

Plate 70

Sir Robert Walpole c.1726 J. M. Rysbrack

74
Jack Sheppard 1724
Sir James Thornhill

75
Sarah Malcolm 1733
William Hogarth

"passionately desired Mr. Pond to suppress it", probably because, as a contemporary wrote, it appeared "like an old mumper, as Rhimebrandt's heads usually do: such works give pleasure to virtuosi but not the publick eye . . . and debase the idea of a polite person".[56] (It was Lord Chesterfield who wrote, in 1751: "I love la belle Nature; Rembrandt paints caricatures.") Soon after, Richardson issued a wigged version of the doctor, conceivably as counter-blast.

Plate 71

The formal portraiture of the women continued on the same lines as that of the men. In the 'twenties and 'thirties, with painters as different as Jervas and Vanderbank, the vertical line of Kneller is drawn still further out; slender women, "who seem rather intended to hang up in the hall of an anatomist than for any other purpose" (as Fielding's Fanny was not); the necks stretch from the narrow, almost naked shoulders, scarcely expanding into the narrow but alert faces that sprout on top with hair. Spry, monotonous, plain faces; there were no doubt characters as visually expressive as the Kielmansegge, later Countess of Darlington, beloved of George I and described by Walpole as with

large fierce black eyes rolling beneath lofty arched eyebrows, two acres of cheeks spread with crimson, an ocean of neck that overflowed and was not distinguishable from the lower part of her body, and no portion of which was restrained by stays.[57]

But the Anglicised portrait-painters subdued them into a variant of the common mould. Sometimes they were enlivened by fancy dress; the pastoral conventions died hard, and society shepherdesses were not uncommon, while the Duchess of Queensberry anticipated Marie Antoinette as a milk-maid. In the 'twenties there was a sudden vogue for being painted in Persian dress, with a fancy turban, and in the 'thirties, 'forties and 'fifties, a prudent rather gauche version of Rubens costume, with large-feathered hat, occurs again and again, often no doubt supplied by the expert modiste, Van Aken, to the works of Hudson, Ramsay, Knapton, Bardwell and others.

The faces are so uniform that a suspicion that they were modulated to the fashionable ideal, not only by the artist's paint but by their own, seems legitimate; some paint was probably used by women of fashion throughout the reigns of the four Georges, and certainly towards the end of the eighteenth century, but the evidence, as always with cosmetics, is very uncertain. The toilet preparations best described by Pope in the *Rape of the Lock* were probably not over-exaggerated, and satirical comment is vociferous through the century. Madame du Bocage, in London in 1750, may have been guilty of a Gallic condescension when she described the women "who use no paint and are always laced (as was the custom formerly in *France*) . . . in their court-dresses they resemble the pictures of our great grandmothers";[58] other witnesses are emphatic to the contrary, as Horace Walpole, calling for Lady Caroline Petersham and friend, in the June after Madame du Bocage was in town, found them "having just finished their last layer of red, and looked as handsome as crimson could make them . . . gloriously jolly and handsome".[59] Yet they probably were, by Parisian standards, archaic almost in dress, and English female portraits of the time show little or nothing of the paint and powder, glazed to a porcelain finish, of the faces of their French contemporaries.

The conservative school of society-painters, their doyen Thomas Hudson, worked on into the seventeen-sixties; Hudson, who died in 1779, encompassed in his life-time the careers not only of the sculptor Roubiliac (died 1762) and of Hogarth (died 1764) but a great deal of his improbable pupil, Reynolds, who broke the Hudsonian tradition into fragments. But the sculptured faces that the first part of the eighteenth century has left us should first be considered; they are the first in time of the new movement. Sculptural portraiture remained, of course, firmly rooted in its funereal functions; the projects that brought in the big money for the sculptors were the great tombs of the great dead. Curiously, some of the liveliest, most animated, most baroque portraits of the late seventeenth century are to be found on tombs, where the effigies had long since risen from the old horizontal tradition into a fluid movement, sometimes approaching ecstatic aspiration. But in the third decade of the eighteenth century the three-dimensional likeness, in the shape of what were known as bustoes, began to win its place as a more domestic furnishing until, by about 1740, the bust-makers were so fashionable that they were said to be threatening the prosperity of the painters.

These busts tended to answer, not to the Baroque but to that precocious neo-classic taste, the Palladian, of which the third Earl of Burlington was the great protagonist. It was Burlington who imported the Italian sculptor, Guelfi, to England, and Burlington who employed Rysbrack to sculpture the statues of Inigo Jones and of Palladio that flank the stairs at Chiswick House. Rysbrack[60] made busts of those two pillars of the Burlington gospel, William Kent in the arts, Pope in literature; and he worked on busts for the Temple of Fame at Stowe and for Queen Caroline's Grotto. His busts of the living are generalised polished statements, tending often to the senatorial, with a hint of toga; they seem to have been good likenesses, and for some characters are admirable—for Sir *Plate 73* Robert Walpole, endowed with gloss, but a burly, genially cynical, well-fed, well-wined, most British Roman, the man who would say to young aspirants with their honest hearts yet untainted: *Well, are you to be an old Roman? a patriot? You'll soon come off of that and grow wiser.* It was said to be very like him.

It may be noted that in the classical bust, though a formal object, wigs were not considered essential for the conveying of the idea of a polite person; the same Dr. Mead, who objected to the bald etching made of him by Pond, was celebrated posthumously by a bust by Roubiliac, commissioned by Askew especially "from a laudable veneration for the memory and public character of so great a patron of learning etc." In most busts in the more classical manner, there were overtones of a similar celebration; it was by busts that the Ancients had immortalised their great men; it was by similar busts that the modern patrons of classical learning, and the artists who were rivalling the great classical artists, could be glorified. Non-funereal busts of women, and of purely society figures, are relatively rare; it was men like Pope and Handel, Bolingbroke and the Duke of Argyll and Walpole, who were suitable subjects and attuned patrons. A more informal note was introduced by Roubiliac in some of his best busts. Rysbrack was a Fleming, Roubiliac[61] a Frenchman, with that same deft feeling for the characteristic niceties, the quirks of an individual face, as had for example Van Loo, but with a far greater vitality, conveyed through an astonishing technique.

Roubiliac worked in England from the early seventeen-thirties until his death in 1764; he could compose in terms of a classic dignity, and so he created in 1745 even the diminutive Chesterfield with a naked deep-barrelled chest, eliciting from him the compliment that "Roubiliac only was a statuary, the rest stone-cutters"; so, too, he preserved Pope in 1741, a head of quick intellectual beauty, and also, according to George Vertue, the most like portrait of the poet, while to Hogarth *Plate 76* he gave a truculence more lucidly purposeful than Hogarth ever found in his own countenance, though this again was said to be very like.

The subjects which gave Roubiliac's remarkable realism its full scope were the old, particularly those whose features had been fired into extraordinary shapes by stubborn eccentricity— Martin Folkes, antiquary, of 1747, a bust acclaimed by Vertue as "equal to any of present or former ages; his features strong

William Hogarth c.1740 (?) *L. F. Roubiliac*

77 *Colley Cibber* c.1740/50 *L. F. Roubiliac*

and musculous with a natural and just air of likeness as much as any work of this kind ever seen"; or, perhaps most extra-ordinary of all, beside the marmoreal beauty of Pope, Pope's chief victim of the revised *Dunciad,* the aged actor Colley Cibber "coloured from the life and extremely like", as Horace Walpole said; clever as a wax-work—with the glass-eyes and the turban-cap that lifts off to reveal the blue-veined bald pate—it avoids by a hair's-breadth that dead life-likeness of wax, and survives, inexplicably and disturbingly, in our midst, an old man with genial eyes, dreaming backwards perhaps in time but not unhappily, the mouth smiling on its toothless gums.

Plate 77

In fluid paint, the Baroque tradition tended to smooth out the minute particularity of such realism, even though it was by now generally breaking from its large sweep into the surface splash and ripple of the Rococo. The interest was nevertheless there, from 1730 onwards, betraying itself even in those engaged also in the most formal kind of portraiture, like Highmore. Highmore could and did produce state-portraits, more shim-mering in texture, but as broadly grand as any of Kneller's and in Kneller's tradition. When dealing with his humbler clients, he produced portraits of an unassuming familiarity and relaxation that broke new ground, until, in the 'forties, he was capable of the astonishing 'Mr. Oldham and his Guests' in the Tate, a portrait of friends of the middle-class, including himself, having a drink together, and unsurpassed in its natural-ness, its directness, its affection, by any conversation-piece painted in England. It is perhaps the most relaxed portrait painted in the eighteenth century. Before then, of course, portrait-painting had begun to explore levels which, though considered by the contemporary fashion to be beneath that of the society state-painters, are now considered high above them.

Plate 81

The vogue for the sort of 'conversation-piece' that is now recognised by that name, small-scale groups of figures, caught on in England a little earlier than 1730. Part of their importance is that they set their subjects in a social context; we see them *engagés,* performing the actions of everyday life. This type of group-portrait, that merges into the genre painting of Vermeer and de Hooch, had had a considerable success in Holland in the previous century in the hands of masters like Terborch; there it had flourished in a bourgeois society, in which dignity was not to be conveyed by the regalia of nobility nor by the sartorial conceits of courtiers, but by the air of solid, decent prosperity with which the sitters occupy their compartments in time and space; the sitters are shown for what they are (though dressed, naturally, in their best) and with what they are, which includes, by a sort of empathy, even their furniture, the capital sunk in their plate, their harpsichords, their pictures and carpets. There are odd isolated examples in England before the eighteenth century; the Elizabethan group (though life-size, this) of card players at Knowsley; the Dutch painter H. G. Pot, visitor to England in 1632, was responsible for a conversation-piece of Charles I and Henrietta Maria, but he was before his time and had no following. About 1700, on three occasions, the admiral Edward Russell, Earl of Orford, had himself painted with different groups of friends; other Stuart conversation-pieces, though larger in scale than those of the eighteenth century, are known.

The first sustained vogue took a rather different but characteristically English form—horse pictures; from the hunting scenes that Jan Wyck painted in the sixteen-nineties grew the paddock-scenes, groom or owner and favourite horse, that his pupil Wootton, and Peter Tillemans, were painting from early in the seventeen-twenties onward, if not earlier. By 1735 several painters, including the Frenchman Mercier, Philips, G. Hamilton, and Hogarth, with whose name the conversation-piece is for ever linked, were busily employed painting people in their homes, engaged in their ordinary occupations—taking tea was a favourite subject—at some specific moment in time.

These pictures, like the Dutch ones, are not merely portraits of people, but include their furniture, their dogs and horses, houses, and familiar landscapes. The fashion was by no means confined to the middle-classes, as is sometimes suggested; it went as high as George II and his family, but it might show even almost the grandest busy with pursuits common to all classes with money enough to order a picture—not only could everyone drink tea, but everyone did.

Some of them have the air as of a number of single portraits rather awkwardly brought together, but in the best of them we have a kind of portraiture in which, at last, the effigy has vanished from the scene. The faces are animated, the thoughts set not on the eternal, not entirely on the duty of looking one's best for posterity, but also on the here-and-now. This immediacy is predominantly the characteristic of Hogarth's essays in the new manner, though not confined entirely to his work. And in such essays the intention is no longer the impossible one that all portrait-painters sigh after, to capture a man's whole character, to paint his spiritual and physical biography in the composed confine of a face, but to catch the character in action, reacting to a specific impulse, the features in movement before passion, like water in a wind.

Thus the art widens in scope from that of portraiture into dramatic painting. For Hogarth all the world was a stage— "my Picture was my Stage and men and women my actors who were by Means of certain Actions and expressions to Exhibit a dumb show". In the course of time, it has even become uncertain whether some of his pictures are portrait con-versation-pieces, or whether they are, more broadly, scenes from domestic life—such as Lord Northbrook's 'The Broken Fan' —and, which ever they are, they are all so closely based on the life that through paint and through the engraver's burin come at last, teeming, the faces of the English crowd. In the truly dramatic pictures the faces are, of course, to some extent generalised, but Hogarth himself insisted, notably in a well-known engraving, on the fundamental difference between his art, which he called that of character, and that of caricature, as practised by the Italians from Leonardo da Vinci to Ghezzi.

In the engraving, he refers the "reader" to the preface of Fielding's *Joseph Andrews* for further enlightenment; there Fielding had written that

He who should call the ingenious Hogarth a burlesque [or caricature] painter, would, in my opinion, do him very little honour; for sure it is much easier, much less the subject of admiration, to paint a man with a nose, or any other feature, of a preposterous size, or to expose him in some absurd or monstrous attitude, than *to express the affections of men on canvas*.

Hazlitt's claim that Hogarth took his faces to the verge of caricature, but never went beyond it, is exaggerated. (The Earl of Iveagh's 'Taste à la Mode' is surely caricature, and in many pictures individual heads overstrain the bounds of possibility.) But generally speaking his appraisal is luminously just: Hogarth's faces

carry all the conviction of reality with them, as if we had seen the actual faces for the first time, from the precision, consistency, and good sense with which the whole and every part is made out. They exhibit the most uncommon features, with the most uncommon expressions, but which yet are as familiar and intelligible as possible, because with all the bold-ness, they have all the truth of nature . . . *memorable* faces, in their memor-able moments.

As has been well said, "he supplied his public not only with the strip-picture and the caption, but also, and above all, with the close-up".[62]

It was part of Hogarth's genius to catch in paint the human face at that pitch of contortion in which it becomes as it were a caricature of itself; while still individual and essentially

'The Shrimp Girl' c.1750 (?) William Hogarth

Hogarth's Servants   c.1750/60 (?)   *William Hogarth*

Marriage à la Mode   c.1743   *William Hogarth*

81 *Joseph Highmore and a schoolmaster* c.1750 *Joseph Highmore*

human, the face becomes also a symbol of some quality. That these qualities are usually of a low if not vicious order is due, first, to Hogarth's satirical purpose; second, to the fact that a vast number of faces are, at their most memorable moments, almost exactly as he depicts them; third, to an inherent short‚ coming in nature. This Hogarth has described in the *Analysis of Beauty:*

it is strange that nature hath afforded us so many lines and shapes to indicate the deficiencies and blemishes of the mind, while there are none at all that point out the perfections of it beyond the appearance of com‚ mon sense and placidity.

It is the perpetual struggle of the formal portrait‚painter to prevent the unequal combat with the pictorial representation of common‚sense and placidity resolving itself in the tedious, plain, and insipid clichés of society portraiture. Later com‚ mentators have again and again observed how true to the English face Hogarth's interpretation remains. It can be most strikingly demonstrated to the Englishman himself when, abroad, he suddenly sees perhaps a bus‚load of compatriots unloaded in a remote French village, or spilled from a *vaporetto* on to the Piazza of San Marco.

How closely the characters in the series like the 'Progresses' were related to living contemporaries remains a matter for argument. Contemporary evidence on the engravings of 'Industry and Idleness' suggests that many were immediately and unmistakably recognisable (though Hogarth himself denied that it was meant to be so), just as were his topographical settings. He certainly exploited that universal human curiosity so well defined by Browning—"we're made so that we love First when we see them painted, things we have passed Perhaps a hundred times nor cared to see". Not only did the public turn to Hogarth with delight to discover themselves ("Bob ——, Beadle of St. —— Parish . . . see his Nose, his

Chin, and the damn'd sour Look so natural to poor Bob"),
but Fielding,[63] father of the English novel, refers back to him
for description of his own characters—for the immortal Mrs.
Bridget Allworthy, in *Tom Jones*: "I would attempt to draw
her picture, but that is done already by a more able master,
Mr. Hogarth himself"—the woman walking to church in
Hogarth's 'Morning'.

In some cases, his aim was more specifically journalistic;
faces, as the engravers in the late seventeenth century had
already found, might be news. Thus celebrated criminals were
portrayed in broadsides, but the quality, at least of the artistic
execution, was very low. In 1724 Hogarth's father-in-law, Sir
James Thornhill, whose rare portraits are the most truly Baroque
essays at portraiture by an English painter, turned his hand to
Plate 74 the portrayal, for a print, of the great highwayman, Jack
Sheppard, as he awaited execution in Paris. It is curious to
see Jack Sheppard, in spite of his cropped bullet-head, assume
exactly the *contraposto,* the desirable Baroque twist of body on
head, with which Thornhill endowed his intellectual portraits
of Newton and Bentley. Early in March 1733, Thornhill seems
to have accompanied Hogarth to Newgate, where the sensational murderess Sarah Malcolm was awaiting execution.
Plate 75 Hogarth's view of Sarah Malcolm (although he is said to have
claimed to see in her features "that she is capable of any
wickedness") is as remarkable for its lack of sensationalism as
for its direct honesty: she is painted on the same scale as the
conversation-pieces Hogarth was then producing. She is
distinguished from his sitters of higher class not only by her
clothes, but by her attitude, which is entirely unforced and
wonderfully observed, the muscular bare forearms resting on
the table as on a kitchen-table. The face is not prepossessing,
but calm. Later, in 1746, when he drew the Jacobite rebel,
Lord Lovat, he had a sensational subject with a sensational
appearance. He did not waste the opportunity, but the result

is said also to have been very like. The engraving had a huge success, and Hogarth for some weeks made the then fabulous sum of £12 a day out of it.

In his life-size, more formal portraits, Hogarth still conveys a liveliness, even here emphasising expression in the face of his sitter. This is much more marked than in the portraits of his contemporaries, such as Highmore and Mercier, who were tending towards a greater degree of informality, which was, of course, at variance with the composed expressions that charac-terised the portraits of the old school. His women sometimes almost beam with cheerfulness, and his men appear busy, or about to be busy; it is a business that can even smack of fussiness, or seem a little affected, as though, in some cases, the single portraits were details snatched out of a conversation-piece, and left conversing with no one. Here, the necessary formal isolation deprived him of occasion for his most characteristic talent, for drama. His portraits are nevertheless a most refreshing break in the tradition of portrait-painting, and most of them are indeed of members of an unpretentious middle-class, particularly of his friends, like the Hoadleys, or his relations; as a society-painter he never achieved a great success, and his output of life-size portraits was small, and, outside the years 1735-42, sporadic.

He himself blamed his failure to catch on to a deliberate and malicious campaign against him by his rivals, alleging that the "whole nest of Phizmongers" ran down his portraits of women as "harlots" and his men as "charicatures". His artistic theories, as based on the famous Line of Beauty and elaborated in that confused and confusing book, his *Analysis of Beauty,* need not concern us greatly in this context. The line of beauty, the serpentine line, which might apply also to the structural undulation of the Baroque, is in Hogarth's practice the broken serpentine of the Rococo, descriptive or ornamental, rather than structural. His faces, in comparison with the ideally pure

Knellerian oval, tend to accumulate more roundly in an inter-
play of plump convexities, cheek, and chin, and chin again,
and popping eye; his mouths are full and fleshy, yet vigorous
with a wiry flick of humour in the corners, and in a somewhat
schematised drawing of a mouth (from the manuscript of the
Analysis) one can see, for once, precisely how, in the shading

Fig. 1

of the upper lip, the S-line of beauty may apply; in the second
sketch of a mouth, immediately below, a typical Hogarthian
dramatic mouth in full expression, the theory of the S-line is
detonated into fragments in the toothful grin of a spherical face.

Fig. 1

His attitude to the interpretation of the human face, while
by no means entirely sceptical of a causal relationship of
character on feature—or rather, as always with him, on the
expression of the features—was sensibly empirical: "it is reason-
able to believe that aspect to be a true and legible representation
of the mind, which gives everyone the same idea at first sight;
and is afterwards confirmed in fact." A foolish or a wicked mind
may lie behind a handsome face; it is likely to betray itself in
expression when excited by passion, but even so the "character
of a hypocrite is entirely out of the power of the pencil" without
some non-facial circumstance to help the characterisation "as
smiling and stabbing at the same time". Yet how far Hogarth

Mary Monckton 1777/8 *Sir Joshua Reynolds*

83   Charles James Fox   c.1802   J. Nollekens

could go, in catching living comedy on the canvas in an
isolated character, is for ever shown in the phenomenal 'Shrimp
Girl' vibrating still with the silent echo of her cry; on the other
hand, some may find a more profound, more rounded, achievement in that wonderful canvas on which, in all sobriety and
humility, he set down one by one the faces of his servants; no
king could hope for such sympathy combined with such
veracity from his portrait-painter.

Plate 78

Plate 80

Hogarth had no true following. Highmore, in his 'Mr.
Oldham and his Guests', comes near to the breath-taking simplicity of Hogarth's servants, but in no other work yet known.
His illustrations to Richardson's *Pamela* are strictly illustrations,
genteel, charming and, compared with Hogarth's comedies,
inexpressive. For Richardson's more robust readers, Mercier
produced a painting, which was engraved, that is pure pin-up;
Pamela rising from bed, with a plump and lavish display of
breast and thigh. But after Hogarth we generally see the
lower classes either through patronising or hygienic eyes (as in
Wheatley's unusual 'Mr. Howard offering Relief to Prisoners',
1787), or in the picturesquely bucolic character given them by
Hayman (as in his Vauxhall decorations) and Gainsborough;
or reduced to caricature ridiculousness by Rowlandson. Only
Stubbs, and perhaps Ben Marshall—rather than Morland—
will survey them with a clear but sympathetic eye. But by 1764,
when Hogarth died, the greatest movement in British portraiture was in full flower; Reynolds was firmly established in
London, and Gainsborough in Bath; Romney had just arrived
in London from Westmoreland, Stubbs from Lincolnshire
and Zoffany from the Continent; miniatures, in the hands of
Meyer, Richard Crosse, Smart and Cosway, all already busy
in London, were achieving a new stature and shaking off their
temporary servility to the life-size portrait; and two years later,
in 1766, the author of *Tristram Shandy* sat to Nollekens in
Rome. The golden age of the British society portrait has begun.

Plate 81

187

Chapter VIII

THE GOLDEN AGE OF THE SOCIETY PORTRAIT

THE SHAPE of the feminine head in the eighteenth century moved from the tall Knellerian oval of about 1700, gradu-ally plumping out in the 'twenties, until, particularly when supplemented by the popular mob-cap, it blossomed into the Hogarthian sphere of about 1740. Then the hair was closer curled, softening the outline and echoed by the deckle edge of the mob-cap. But hardly had this fashion established itself than the head began to lengthen once more; in the 'fifties the hair again tends to be drawn tight and smooth, back from brow and cheek; in the 'sixties it begins to mount above the forehead, a rise accelerating to the fantastic peaks reached in the decade between 1770 and 1780, those top-heavy artifices of wire, grease, powder, with many artificial flowers and feathers, and some natural hair, an unrepeatable and eagerly-grasped opportunity for the furious delight of the caricaturists.

Soon after 1780 the tall cumuli began to shrink, and by 1785 had melted almost away into a broadening crowd of curls at the sides of the head again, although height was still often lent by fountains of feathers erupting from the crowns of vast-brimmed "picture"-hats; in the last five years of the century the face again narrows towards the oval, the curls, thinning in quantity, moving from the sides of the head forward to the brow, sometimes almost into a fringe, but brushed or twisted forward with much of the carefully calculated disorder of the *gamine* hair-line of 1955: Sir Thomas Lawrence's romanticised version of the austere Empire style.

From at least 1740 onwards the dependence of the fashion-able woman on artificial aids to smartness, if not beauty, seems to have been considerable. As early as 1737, approximately,

Mrs. Delany described Lady Baltimore at a royal birthday party as "like a *frightened owl*, her locks strutted out and most furiously greased, or rather *gummed* and powdered . . ."[64] (Mrs. Delany was probably prejudiced, as she was describing the wife of one of her own former suitors.) But the fortunes of the cosmeticians and coiffeurs must have reached their height simultaneously with that of the tall style of hair, in the 'seventies. In 1770 a Bill was at least tabled for the consideration of Parliament—

that all women of whatever rank, profession or degree, whether virgins, maids or widows, that shall from and after such Act, impose upon, seduce and betray into matrimony, any of his Majesty's subjects by the scents, paints, cosmetic washes; artificial teeth, false hair, Spanish wool [a form of rouge pad], iron stays, hoops, high-heeled shoes and bolstered hips, shall incur the penalty of the law now in force against witchcraft and like misdemeanours, and that the marriage upon conviction shall be null and void.

An appearance as artificial as that which prevailed in the 'seventies was obviously a matter of some concern for the painters of portraits. Gainsborough, as was his nature, recorded it tolerably faithfully; in 1771 he was engaged in a portrait of Lady Dartmouth, which had not been found satisfactory; it appears to have been dressed in some kind of compromise, against the painter's wishes, and he writes to ask permission to

dress it in the modern way . . . I am vastly out in my notion if the face does not immediately look like; but I must know if Lady Dartmouth powders [probably meaning her hair] or not in common.

As for the complexion, Gainsborough was criticised more than once for exaggerating; in 1772 it was for "too glowing" colours, coupled with an admonition to "borrow a little of the modest colouring of Sir Joshua Reynolds".

As always, the fashion of face-painting was most prevalent and most remarkable amongst the courtesans—though it was not only Kitty Fisher but also the Countess of Coventry who was said to have died from the abuse of cosmetics—and the portrait practice of Gainsborough was further extended in that direction than was that of Reynolds. "A favourite among the demi-reps" the *Morning Chronicle* called Gainsborough à propos of the Royal Academy Exhibition of 1778, where were hung three portraits of women of that kind:

> very fit subjects for Mr. Gainsborough's pencil, since he is rather apt to put that sort of complexion upon the countenance of his female portraits which is laughingly described in the School for Scandal as "coming in the morning and going away at night", than to blend what is, properly speaking, Nature's own red and white.

The colour scheme for the fashionable face seems indeed to have been a vivid red mouth, and cheeks sometimes almost amounting to purple, on powder-white; the hair heavily powdered. Reynolds' testimony is often more modest indeed than Gainsborough's, in the 'seventies and 'eighties, but its value is difficult to assess as his flesh colours have faded, some-times to an almost monochrome pinkish sallowness. In portraits, of course, the sitters are generally fully-dressed as for formal social occasions, and undoubtedly display more furs and more paint and powder than they would normally in their homes.

For the men, the same period saw the very gradual emancipa-tion of the face from the wig. In 1700, the full-bottomed wig was in its perfect bloom, and worn by all men of society for formal dress; by 1725 it could still be found frequently in undiminished luxuriance, though now grey-blonde with powder; by 1740 it was already obsolescent, and by 1753, as we have seen, the full-bottomed wig was already dead, sur-viving only in fossilised condition as an attribute of certain offices and professions.

Medicine was one profession that retained it beyond its natural term; in 1747 Dr. Mead was shown in a wig in his

Margaret Gainsborough c.1772 *Thomas Gainsborough*

85 *Georgiana, Duchess of Devonshire*   1787   *John Downman*

state-portrait painted for the Foundling Hospital, but by 1778 Boswell diagnosed, gloomily, "a general levity in the age. We have physicians now in bag-wigs". The real shrink and freaking of the wig took place between 1720 and 1740, when it dropped almost flat on top of the head, and reduced its length till it was often clear of the shoulders: the sides might be a frizz of hair, or a simple or elaborate arrangement of curls; at the back the long tail might be plaited into one or more pigtails, but an enduringly popular mode was the bag-wig. As the powder grew thicker on the wig, the thicker it shed upon the shoulders and back, so that it was found convenient to shave or crop one's own hair in order to wear a wig; to powder the wig heavily, and then to encase its back extremities in a bag so that the powder did not snow upon the clothes; and then, often (to prevent the disturbing flip-flap of the bag upon the back), to harness the bag about the throat by a black ribbon, tied at the front in a bow; this was called the *solitaire*, and has been claimed as the direct ancestor of the modern "black tie".

A hair-dresser, writing in 1782, looked back with some regret to the mid-century when you could tell a man by his wig:

the tradesman by the snug bob, or natty scratch: the country gentleman by the natural fly and hunting peruke. All conditions of men were distinguished by the cut of the wig, and none more so than the coach-man, who wore his, as some do to this day, in imitation of the curled hair of the water-dog.[65]

The varieties, the refinements, were endless; the expense very great. The variety was not, however, a sign of health, and certainly by 1760 many men were wearing their own hair, although they acknowledged, by the use of grease and tongs and powder, the supremacy of the wig, disguising their own hair to look like one.

By 1765 the wig seemed to be no longer dynamic, for in

that year the master peruke-makers, in a petition to George III, set forth their distress "from the almost universal decline of the trade, occasioned by the present mode of men in all stations wearing their own hair". A company of Body-Carpenters was thereupon promptly invented, exhorting his majesty to wear a wooden leg, and to enjoin all his subjects to appear in the royal presence with the same badge of honour.[66] In fact, the wig was far from done for, and within five years had sprouted again into its most extraordinary form yet: the wigs of the Macaroni.

These rivalled the simultaneous elevation of woman's hair; at first the hair was brushed stiffly up from the forehead, and suddenly it soared, out of control, while the *queue* behind was bound into a greased club: powder, pomade and even plaster-of-paris were the ingredients, besides hair, but especially powder, greyish, pink, blue, violet, laced with scent. It is extremely difficult to get an exact idea of the heights to which these toupets grew: the evidence of the caricaturists, particularly Darley, is profuse but obviously exaggerated, and even the Macaroni seem to have hesitated to perpetuate themselves at the full height of fashion in formal commissioned portraits. There is a disparity literally of feet between the head-dressings shown even in the most modish portraits of Reynolds and Gainsborough in the 'seventies, and those shown by the cartoonists.

To judge by the more formal portraits, a fairly modest form of wig, or dressing of the hair in imitation of the wig, seems to have consolidated itself, rather than given way to the natural hair, between 1770 and about 1789. The French Revolution probably had something to do with the death of the wig, sweeping it in France from such heads as it spared; there was Rousseau's taunt at the rich depriving the poor of bread by using all the flour for their own heads; but a movement towards a greater relaxation in dress generally, headed by *Plate 85* characters of the eminence of the Duchess of Devonshire and

Charles James Fox, seems to have been under way in England   *Plate 83*
through the 'eighties. Soon young men at the Universities
were cropping their hair, wearing it unashamed in its natural
colour, unwaxed, braving the fury of the proctors and the
nickname of "Apollos". The abandonment of the wig and of
powder was however still gradual; about 1799 a bishop
(Dr. Randolph of Oxford) ventured to lay his aside, but he
was severely rebuked. Powder was taxed by Pitt, after a bad
wheat harvest; in 1795 a group of eminent Whigs, in order to
deprive him of some revenue, ceremonially washed their hair
at Woburn Abbey, and forbore to powder. The practice
continued unabated in the army, with such devotion that, when
during a flour-famine in July 1800, the consumption of flour
for pastry was forbidden in the Royal Household (rice being
used instead), the 250,000 members of the armed forces were
still reckoned to be using a pound of flour per head per week.[67]

From 1740 onwards, in spite of its vagaries, the general
tendency of the wig is to recede from the face, leaving it more
visible. Yet the face of the period is almost impossible to define;
one can see the fashion-plate ideal perhaps behind the work
of some of the more mannered, minor portrait-takers, especially
in such as Downman, and to an extent even in Romney. The
women approximate to a sharper-featured, less rounded type;
one of the most celebrated of them all, Georgiana, Duchess of   *Plate 85*
Devonshire, could indicate her own shortcomings thus: "a
moderate drawing might surely comprize A snub nose, a wide
mouth and a pair of grey eyes"—and be described (by a writer
in the *St. James Chronicle* in 1783) as

in our opinion by no means an elegant woman. There is a hoydening
affability about her, sanctified by her rank and fortune, which has
rendered her popular. Mr. Gainsborough has given her as she might
have been if retouched and educated by the Graces.

Downman gives her almost as if sophisticated by nature.

The men too are less plump, often fleshy but no longer swagged with fat, and the young men tend towards a clean-cut face, that sometimes conveys an almost hygienic impression, like an advertisement for after-shaving lotion, and has an assured, sharply defined jaw-line. From Romney's portraits one could at last take faces, again and again, that might be submitted with confidence for star-leads in modern films. But anyone who knows the latter part of the eighteenth century well will not be deceived by such generalisations, for our deeper knowledge of its people is conditioned visually neither by Downman nor by Romney, but by Gainsborough, and above all, by Sir Joshua Reynolds.[68]

Joshua Reynolds returned from his journey to Italy in 1752, aged 29; early in 1753 he set up in London, and there, for forty years until his death in 1792, he remained the dominant figure in British art. His triumph was one of application rather than of formal exploration and discovery; he applied the discoveries of the Old Masters to the British portrait. He is said to have been fixed in his determination to be a painter by the reading, when he was a boy, of Richardson's theoretical works, and in theory, like Richardson, he suffered from intellectual pretentions. He wished to be a history-painter, to paint subjects of a more general, spiritual and intellectual order than portraits: a realm of the pure imagination.

Fortunately—for he was not at his best there—the British public was not ready for such art, and so not prepared to support it in terms of hard cash; Reynolds therefore was doomed to remain primarily a painter of portraits. But to his portraits he brought his wide learning, of technique and of theory, of the Old Masters, and he treated his sitters honourably as material not merely for portrait-effigies but for imaginative compositions. A portrait must also be a picture, composed in terms of colour, of light and shade, of a pictorial architecture;

Dr Johnson c.1769 *Sir Joshua Reynolds (? studio)*

87   *Admiral Rodney   1789   Sir Joshua Reynolds*

and to the requirements of a picture the sitter must in a sense yield; at least he must admit some compromise.

Behind almost all society portraiture before Reynolds there is a basic, and dead, symmetry; on the surface of the picture is disposed the sitter, dead-centre; behind him, like a drop-set, or series of drop-sets receding in depth, is the background. By no means is it always as simple as this, but such a description applies to almost all the portrait-maker's work immediately preceding Reynolds, that of Hudson and Hoare, and even, in the 'forties, of Ramsay and of Hogarth. Symmetry again is observed in the painting of the face; every sitter (except when seen in profile) has two eyes, two eye-brows, two nostrils and two modulated segments of the bow of the mouth; every face, though each departs in its individuality from the norm of the oval, acknowledges nevertheless that it is an oval. Very often, in a portrait by Reynolds, we find that his sitter is not in the middle of the canvas; his body being perhaps chopped off at a most unorthodox place and angle by the picture's edge. Often, too, the play of light and shade, deployed in much stronger contrast than by any previous British painter, seems to be active even between the spectator and the person in the picture; the sitter is involved in a shifting weather.

Further, the sitter's face, no longer composed into the sym-metrical oval mask, may be involved with, or even corroded by, the shifting weather of life. Hogarth of course had shown faces similarly involved in action, but faces shattered from a basic symmetry occur only in his comic history pieces, not in his portraits, and the shattering is achieved by a faithful recording of the features when violently distorted by passion. Naturally, Reynolds' sitters, including the politest of polite society, did not distort their faces violently with passion when confronted by his urbane, if calculating, stare; their involvement with life is more subtle, less definable, but no less positive; they may be obviously doing nothing except pose for their picture, but Reynolds' recording transmits his own agreeable and sometimes faintly ironic acknowledgement of the fact (this applies particularly to his portraits of women).

In his best portraits there is much more than that. When asked to produce a written character of Johnson, Reynolds wrote that he doubted if he had the ability—

the habits of my profession unluckily extend to the consideration of so much only of character as is on the surface, as is expressed in the lineaments of the countenance.

He goes on nevertheless to attempt his best, asking that his presumption to "investigate the peculiar colouring of [Johnson's] mind as distinguished from all other minds" be excused.[69] He has, in fact, in his portraits, abandoned the classic attempt to present a summary but rounded definition, for eternity, of a character; he deals with "so much only of character as is on the surface", but he deals with it in action, involved with the moment. Titian and Vandyck, said Northcote, painted hours; Sir Joshua moments. For him each portrait presented a fresh problem, not merely that of recording an individual facial likeness, but of *producing*—with all the theatrical implications of that word—a convincing, coherent character in action. Whereas Hogarth's conversation-pieces sometimes show a group in action, Reynolds at his best stages men and women in soliloquy; he may have abandoned the attempt to paint the mind (his panegyrists, of course, claimed that he did, as had been claimed for every portrait-painter from Holbein onwards), but few painters can rival him in the almost palpable rendering of the cast of thought.

Technically, he had grave shortcomings. He could not draw (as is perhaps too often stressed, for he could paint) and he was sometimes glaringly slip-shod; he experimented—with an irresponsibility to posterity curious in his character—dangerously, almost haphazardly, with tricks of technique. Even before his death, many of his portraits, painted with perishable media, had faded badly. Sometimes, as in some of his grandiose semi-allegorical portraits painted for exhibition at the Royal Academy in the 'seventies, he lost his sense of judgement to the point of painting actually ridiculous pictures; many times—inevitably, considering his huge output—he fell back on stock solutions. Yet, in his overall range and general variety, he stands unsurpassed amongst all great portrait-painters, and the inexhaustible marvel of his genius was recognised by his rival, Gainsborough, in his famous ejaculation of envy—"Damn him, how various he is!" To the faces of his sitters he brought every time a fresh eye and that extraordinary sensitivity to the atmospherics of character-producing.

With all his formal preoccupations and his borrowings from the Old Masters, he produced nevertheless a new naturalism. Commissioned though he was to take a likeness, his eye leant impartially upon each face and he painted it as he saw it, not as a concept. Thus in his portrait of the aged Admiral Rodney *Plate 87* the light falls on each accident of the face, on the sunken eye, the craggy nose, the shrunk grim mouth that disdains false teeth; on the shadowy side of the face, he records, not—as Lely or Hudson would have done—the symmetrical anatomy of eye and cheek, but their submergence and dissolution into shadow. No longer is there a set formula of outline and of colour for each feature; Reynolds, painting a face, with an extraordinary, though by no means infallible, feeling for tonal modulation, paints the surface of an object as it is revealed in colour and shadow, and in depth, by light. There is no standard "Reynolds mouth" as there is a standard "Kneller mouth". The portrait of Rodney is a very late work (exhibited at the Academy in 1789), but Reynolds indicated his range in works painted in his first years in London, in paintings such as those of Lord and Lady Cathcart (1753/5), and the first portrait of Admiral Keppel (1753/4), in the National Maritime Museum.

The latter is a key-piece, for it has not only the broad treat-ment of the face, lit by the stormy sea-light, a face painted—not drawn in terms of line—massively and freely, the far side sunk in shadow with but the glint of an eye, but it is based in pose on the 'Apollo Belvedere', probably in direct emulation of Ramsay's similarly posed 'Chief of Macleod', painted five years before. Ramsay had done much to soften up the conventions of society portraiture in the 'forties; yet his Macleod is a lay figure, symmetrically disposed on the surface of the picture, whereas Reynolds' Keppel walks and breathes in the broken light of the cloudy sea-shore. It was with works such as these, right at the beginning of his career, that Reynolds transformed the whole conception of British portraiture; and it was within the new freedom that he gave it that not only he but the other masters of the late eighteenth century were to deploy their forces.

It may come as a surprise to those who are not specialists in English painting to know that Reynolds was notoriously unreliable in his ability to satisfy clients with a likeness; Hoppner once said that he was surprised that Reynolds dared send home some of his portraits, so little did they resemble the originals. Part of the reason for this doubtless lay in the fact that he painted moments, not hours; that he could produce almost snap-shot effects, sometimes perhaps fixing his sitters in expressions unusual to them. If you take a series of instan-taneous photographs of anybody, a proportion of them will inevitably be judged, not only by the sitter, to be "not like", or not "characteristic". However that may be, and though the accusation should not be forgotten, it is nevertheless now almost entirely academic, for it is precisely by the coherence and conviction of his characterisations that Reynolds now im-presses most people—and by their range.

Largely aloof from politics, yet urbane and sociable, widely-read, a man-of-letters, a man of substance, Reynolds was sought out by an astonishing proportion of the cream of his time; he painted the aristocracy of blood and of intellect, of sensibility and even of professional sex. He painted the soldiers and the great admirals; he painted Rockingham, Bute, Burke, Charles James Fox (but the Pitts eluded him), he painted royalty and dukes, he painted bishops and Beckford, he painted high fashion, Georgiana, Duchess of Devonshire, or Kitty Fisher; he painted lawyers, virtuosi, actors (or *the* actor, Garrick), surgeons and country gentlemen; he painted Horace Walpole and he painted Dr. Johnson.

It is perhaps in his portraits of the Johnson circle, of which he was himself an intimate, that his finest achievement, at least in male portraiture, lies. Laurence Sterne, practical joker, was not a member of the circle, and is earlier (1760) than most of the literary portraits, but is the most disturbing and hypnotic face; of the circle proper Reynolds has left us Goldsmith, Dr. Burney, Boswell and others, but above all Dr. Johnson *Plate 86* himself. Reynolds' views of Johnson, from the first sprawling three-quarter-length of 1756 in the National Portrait Gallery to the last fantastic imaginary reconstruction of Johnson as a naked infant (1783) will add another dimension even to Boswell's account, and, in conjunction with it, bring anyone as close to that magic hulk as they will ever get. Reynolds' images of him, together, admit the validity of all the astonished reactions of Johnson's contemporaries.

Dr. Campbell on first meeting him, was revolted—

"the aspect of an idiot, without the faintest ray of sense gleaming from any one feature; with the most awkward garb and unpowdered grey wig on one side of his head, he is forever dancing the Devil's jig, and sometimes he makes the most driveling effort to whistle some thought in his absent paroxisms." "His person was large, robust, I may say approaching to the gigantic, and grown unwieldy from corpulency," wrote Boswell lucidly but affectionately: "His countenance was naturally of the cast of an ancient statue, but somewhat disfigured by the scars of that *evil* which it was formerly imagined the *royal touch* could cure."

The "ancient statue" is, of course, special pleading; there can be no more doubt that Johnson was physically appalling than that his fascination was all but irresistible. Here is Mrs. Piozzi:

... his Sight was near, and otherwise imperfect, yet his Eyes though of a light blue Colour were so wild, so piercing, and at Times so fierce; that Fear was I believe the first Emotion in the hearts of all his Beholders.

Later in the same description, though in a figurative passage, she almost succeeds in conveying the physical impact of his presence: "Suffice it at once that he was great on all Occasions, and like a Cube in Architecture you beheld him on each Side, as his Size still appeared undiminished."[70]

But words lap vainly at the contours of his physique as at some invincible continent; it is only Reynolds who was able to map the compatibility of that vast intellect with that vast mis-shape, and in the portrait reproduced here we have Johnson wrenching, half physically, thought into words.

Plate 86

With women, Reynolds was liable to be less successful than with men. He was profoundly a bachelor ("Married!" exclaimed Sir Joshua to an aspiring young painter: "then you are ruined as an artist");[71] as he grew older he tended to become distressingly avuncular in his attitude to the opposite sex, and to children; he often painted, not women, but the Ladies, who are only too prone to express themselves with a coyly roguish smirk; most of his children (and with them I would include even pieces such as the famous Master Crewe as Henry VIII) may fill the heart of a modern parent with a sickened rage of frustrated iconoclasm. But against his lapses there is always to be set a superb range of successes, from the grave, intimate candour of his portraits of the 'fifties and early 'sixties, when his approach to women was still direct and unaffected, to the justly famous Duchess of Devonshire and daughter, of the 'eighties, and the extraordinarily revealing head and shoulders of the Duchess's rival and successor, Lady Betty Foster.

Plate 82

Reynolds painted the moment, but he defined it with a massive finality. It was the special genius of his rival and contemporary, Thomas Gainsborough,[72] to catch the moment in transience; Reynolds gives us the "still", Gainsborough seems to catch the face actually in motion. His career ran, in time, almost parallel with Reynolds'; in his first period, in Suffolk and in London, he was painting those direct little masterpieces, of which the greatest is the famous 'Mr. and Mrs. Andrews' in a cornfield. His sitters are involved in no psychological drama; instead we have a direct and vivid record of country gentry at their ease in their countryside, their faces open and ingenuous and unconstrained by fashion. But in 1759 Gainsborough moved from Suffolk to Bath, and in that fashionable resort he had to come to terms with fashion; gradually he did so, without ever entirely losing that informality that at first seems to have shocked, not entirely disagreeably, the mannered visitors to Bath; thus Mrs. Delany reacted in October 1760 to his whole-length of 'Miss Ford with a Guitar'—"a most extraordinary figure, handsome and bold; but I should be very sorry to have anyone I loved set forth in such a manner". "Splendid impositions", she called his portraits. Thence he learned to ally his informality with a necessary social dignity, and all the time his style was opening out into that feathery flickering touch that renders his later paintings, after his establishment in London in 1774, almost airborne.

Plates 84, 88

It was during his Bath period, however, that he produced perhaps his most sensitive appreciations of individual faces, modelled with a minute delicacy of touch that is only equalled by Van Dyck, on whom he was at the time deliberately remodelling himself. Such is the 'Mrs. Portman' in the Tate Gallery. Later, in his looser manner, he seems still to have retained his power of catching a likeness, for which, unlike Reynolds, he was famous. Personally, in contrast again to Reynolds, he conducted his business of painting almost as a tradesman, without intellectual or social overtones ("many a real genius is lost in the fictitious character of a gentleman"). His avowed intention was to satisfy the client by the delivery of a likeness, which he described as "the principal beauty and intention of a portrait".[73] To achieve this, he liked to begin his portrait in a reduced light, even by candlelight; by this method, according to his colleague Ozias Humphrey,

with incessant study and exertion, he acquired the power of giving the masses and general forms of his models with the utmost exactness. Having thus settled the groundwork of his portraits he let in (of necessity) more light for the finishing of them . . .

Of the finished product, no more acute or revealing account has ever been given than that included by Reynolds in his Fourteenth Discourse, after Gainsborough's death in 1788; it is a passage that every painter of portraits should know.

The likeness of a portrait . . . consists more in preserving the general effect of the countenance, than in the most minute finishing of the features, or any of the particular parts. Now Gainsborough's portraits were often little more, in regard to finishing, or determining the form of the features, than what generally attends a dead colour; but as he was always attentive to the general effect, or whole together, I have often imagined that the unfinished manner contributed even to that striking resemblance for which his portraits are so remarkable. Though this opinion may be considered as fanciful, yet I think a plausible reason may be given why such a mode of painting should have such an effect. It is presupposed, that in this undetermined manner there is the general effect; enough to remind the spectator of the original; the imagination supplies the rest, and perhaps more satisfactorily to himself, if not more exactly, than the artist, with all his care, could have done. At the same time it must be acknowledged there is one evil attending this mode; that if the portrait were seen, previous to any knowledge of the original, different persons would form different ideas, and be disappointed at not finding the original correspond with their own conceptions; under the greater latitude which indistinctness gives to the imagination what character or form it pleases.

88 *Sir Henry Bate-Dudley* c.1780 *Thomas Gainsborough*

89

90 *Mrs Siddons* c.1797 *Sir Thomas Lawrence*   91 *Mrs Siddons* 1785 *Thomas Gainsbor*

89   *Mrs Siddons   1784   after Reynolds*

Reynolds' own characterisations can be remarkable for the intensity of their definition; in Gainsborough's later portraits he uses in his characterisation (but not in his colour) a kind of impressionism; the light but incomparably deft brush indi-cates, but does not define, a contour, or suggests, with three or four slight strokes, the upper eyelid and the tremulous mobility of the eyelashes. He gives the onlooker scope to move and to imagine, to adjust the sitter's expression according to his own fancy; the key-points of the features, those that control the expression, especially the eyes and the corners of the mouth, remain ambivalent, hovering amongst possibilities.

Plate 84

He was, however, concerned, as indicated by a letter already quoted, to paint his sitters as they were, even to paint, powder and all the ephemeral vagaries of fashion. Reynolds, in practice and in theory, in his Seventh Discourse, was strongly against such practice suggesting as compromise that the painter dresses

his figure something with the general air of the antique for the sake of dignity and preserves something of the modern for the sake of likeness.

The result, as Reynolds had to admit in Gainsborough's case, was to contemporaries usually a striking likeness, yet the strange thing is that, now that the originals have gone down into dust, and that the question of "like or not like" is academic, it is Reynolds' portraits, unlike though they may have been, that carry in most cases the more vivid and positive impressions of living individuals.

Gainsborough's people, in his later portraits, are so loosely defined that they tend to merge one into the other, the stuff that dreams are made of, under the veil of his brilliant most personal paint; and it is in sheer paint that Gainsborough's enduring magic resides. One can catch a glance of the spell being woven through Northcote's eyes, when he describes Gainsborough and his nephew Dupont sitting up all night by candlelight working on the whole-length of Queen Charlotte

—"'Tis actual motion, and done with such a light airy facility. Oh! it delighted me . . .":[74] a rhythmic modulation of line and colour that, like music, can catch into incredulous sharp pleasure the hearts of those who are in love with it.

Reynolds was a dramatic painter; it is Gainsborough who endowed our history with lyric faces. His clientele was much narrower than Reynolds', and largely confined to Suffolk and Bath of course for the first twenty-five years of his painting career. Portraits of an intellectual weight, such as were Reynolds' forte, were not for him, and his finest portraits tend to be those of his family and his intimates, who were not members of the Johnson circle, but included musicians, eccentrics and demi-reps. When Reynolds painted Mrs. Siddons, he turned to Michelangelo for inspiration, and painted her, on stage, in draperies—as 'The Tragic Muse'; when Gainsborough painted her, he painted her as she sat in his studio, a smart woman of fashion, with a sharp, spry and eloquent nose, and a great deal of powder, ready for the Mall.

Plate 89

Plate 91

Reynolds and Gainsborough are the two supreme portrait-painters in the later eighteenth century, and, in the forty years between 1750 and 1790, they covered a great deal of ground, producing well over 2,000 portraits between them, no in-considerable proportion of the top strata of society from which almost all their sitters came.

They held of course no monopoly. The later careers of some of the best of the conventional painters of the preceding era overlapped even the early maturity of Reynolds and Gains-borough. Ramsay, who, in his constant search for fresh designs, had prepared the way in the 'forties for Reynolds, lived on until 1784, but painted very little after 1770. Although contemporaries had noted in his earlier portraits a novel com-plexion (achieved by an underpainting of the flesh in bright red) and a "licked" brushwork that was reminiscent of French painting, the expression and character of most of the portraits of the period is little different from those of Hoare and Hudson (who died respectively only in 1792 and 1779), the pillars of the old school. In Ramsay's later work there is a certain debt to the new freedom bestowed upon portraiture by Reynolds, but also a subtlety and reticence, particularly in his portraits of women, that was outside Reynolds' own range; he could be a painter of perfect tact and courtesy, without blandishment.

Plate 72

Hudson and Hoare both soldiered on with few concessions to the new freedom of manner; in this they seem curiously like provincial adherents of the conventional portraiture of the Continent, from which Reynolds, with all his debts to the great Mediterranean masters, stood clearly apart. In 1778, Northcote wrote from Rome that artists there delighted in running Sir Joshua down. In Rome, the twin deities in portraiture were the German-born Mengs, and Batoni, both—but especially the latter —much patronised by Englishmen in Italy on the grand tour.

Batoni's whole-lengths of young, gravely holiday English-men, shown steeped in the antique, in a world of statuary, drawings, urns and elegant ruins and excellent clothes, still hang in many English houses. It was perhaps from Batoni that George Romney, on his Italian journey in 1773-5, learned that air of amiable but nobly aloof nonchalance that distinguishes perhaps too many of his portraits. For many of his con-temporaries Romney's star was as bright as those of Reynolds and Gainsborough; though it is dimmer now, he was at one time seriously encroaching on Reynolds' clientele. He is, *par excellence*, a painter of handsome men and women, and the interpreter of a certain high-bred, aquiline sensibility of re-pression.

By the quick or tardy movement of the fibres around the lips, he was accustomed to estimate the degrees of sensibility in his sitters; and of himself, in this particular, it might have been said with truth,

His own example strengthens all his laws:
He is himself, THE SENSITIVE he draws.

So wrote his panegyrist, Hayley; in fact he was at his best, not with women and men, whom he over-clarified often into a banal fashion-tailored line of brow and nose and chin, but with adolescents. He can be seen at his best in the Provost's Lodge at Eton, for which he painted several of the fine series of "leaving portraits". In these, awkwardness hesitates into elegance, shy yet splendidly-mannered, and Romney's clarity is here vernally delicate, avoiding slickness by a hair's breadth. And elsewhere, at his very best, he could pull effects out of the bag that no one else had in their power—as in the pastel head

Plate 92

of that archetypal poet of sensibility, William Cowper. Romney himself considered this the "nearest approach that he had ever made to a perfect representation of life and character", an attempt to catch "the poet's eye in a fine frenzy rolling". Cowper himself rose to the occasion in a sonnet to Romney, praising the painter, once again, for tracing "The mind's impression too on every face".[75]

William Cowper 1792 *George Romney*

93

John Wilkinson
Money token 1787
Artist Unknown

94

95 *John Wilkinson* c.1790 (?) *L. F. Abbot*

Chapter IX

MINIATURES — PROFILES — SILHOUETTES

THE TAKING of portraits, the presentation of likenesses, was practised in the late eighteenth century as never before in all media. One extreme was the literal naturalism of the London dentist Van Burtchell, who in 1775 kept his embalmed wife in a glass-case in the drawing-room ("and though she has been dead three months she looks as well as when alive");[76] another novelty was the art of the "shade" or silhouette, which, in its basic form, is not a portrait at all, but one's shadow fixed on paper.

In particular, the art of miniature-painting, lost for a century in the servile imitation in small of the type of image purveyed by the oil-painters, found itself again; where the miniaturists were influenced by the life-size painters—as Humphrey gener-ally was by Reynolds, and Meyer sometimes apparently by Cotes and by Gainsborough—the effect was not disastrous, as the life-size painters themselves were now so concerned with the transcription of the particularities of their sitters' faces. The most naturalistic of the miniature-painters was John Smart, who aimed above all at exactness of likeness, had no truck with the frills and graces, yet achieved a sparkling prettiness. In sculpture, fashion rejected scornfully the rococo animation of Roubiliac, and settled severely into antique taste. In their portraiture men like Wilton, Bacon, Nollekens and then Flaxman, only too often carved into boring practice the theory laid down by Reynolds, but happily only rarely acknowledged by him in the painting of his faces: that

the whole beauty and grandeur of art consists, in my opinion, in being able to get above all singular forms, local customs, particularities, and details of every kind.

A sentimental taste for the antique lay behind the success of profile portraits in the second half of the eighteenth century. Life-size representations of the head in profile are difficult to manage, the centre of the picture being a plateau or tundra of cheek, and the pose, turned decisively away from the onlooker, cold and unfriendly. But reduced to miniature size, the profile can assume a fragile exquisiteness and a flattering classic simplicity. Such portraits were made in wax by Isaac Gosset, for example; in ivory; and, by the prolific Tassies, in a hard paste in imitation of antique gems; and above all they were made by the silhouettists, from 1780 onwards.

As I have already indicated, the silhouette is not really a portrait at all: in its basic form it is made by tracing the shadow —it is not merely a portrait of one's shadow, it is virtually the actual shadow, stilled and fixed on paper. However, even if it be not a true portrait—and the relationship of the person to his shadow is doubtless open to philosophical argument—it is absurd not to admit that at the time it was (barring masks taken from the face) the most exact method of recording the outline of anybody's profile. It was for that reason that Lavater, the Swiss apostle of the science of physiognomy, largely used silhouettes to illustrate his treatises. They had an extraordinarily wide vogue throughout Europe, not merely with cranks but with men of the calibre of Goethe downwards, from 1780 until well into the nineteenth century.

The prestige given by Lavater to the silhouette must in turn have augmented considerably its appeal. Burke, in line with his friend Reynolds, had written that "a portrait is the ideal of an individual, not of men in general", but Lavater's comment on this definition was that

a perfect portrait is neither more nor less than the circular form of a man reduced to a flat surface, and which shall have the exact appearance of the person for whom it was painted, seen in a camera obscura.[77]

Failing that, the best experimental material for one who hoped to demonstrate precisely the character of the man from his features was, apart from the man himself, the facsimile of his profile offered by the silhouette.

For ornamental purposes, however, a life-size silhouette is unwieldy and even incoherent; reduced to miniature scale, they

Fig. 2—Miss Tydell by Hamlet of Bath

can be decorative trifles. They are, moreover, both extremely quick and cheap to make, whether cut out of paper, or drawn or painted; hence, partly, their popularity—they have been called "the poor man's miniature". Artistically, the best are those that were taken freehand without the help of any mechanical appliance; such was the early work of John Miers, in Leeds and London, in the seventeen-eighties—head-and-shoulder profiles, painted in jet-black on a white plaster ground, with a very sensitive outline that softens with feathery delicacy

217

in the hair. Few however were of this order, and the cutting of silhouettes was also a tremendous parlour-game for amateurs.

The professionals who, to begin with, often made a virtue out of the severe limitations of their art, soon, in a hunt for novelty, went whoring after other dimensions. They hatched their black with gold or bronze, touching their black faces with pink nigger-minstrel lips, and even setting black, flat faces in portraits that were otherwise normal miniatures in full colour. A large display of silhouettes is as repulsive as smallpox, but taken singly the best examples of this very minor art do support contemplation, and distil, from their remote and final simplicity, a disturbing poignancy; it is as though, instead of Peter Schlemihl losing his shadow, the shadow had lost Peter.

Technically, the silhouette is of considerable interest as it heralds and in some ways anticipates the portrait-photograph. Many professionals used mechanical contrivances to ensure the accuracy of their likenesses; such were the Ediograph, the Prosopographus and the Physionotrace; such was Charles Schmalkalder's Delineator, Copier and Proportionometer, registered at the Patent Office in 1806, which, at one end, passed a steel rod delicately over the sitter's features, while, at the other end, it simultaneously drew, or cut out, a miniature silhouette of them.

Other devices worked very like a camera—such was a box with an opening towards the sitter. Inside the box was a mirror so angled that it threw the image of the sitter on to a piece of frosted glass let in at the top of the box. Like the photographer, the silhouettist could offer his subject a sitting of only a minute or two; he could also repeat his portraits if wanted. John Miers charged, to start with, half-a-crown (including frame), and always kept a copy himself, as a photographer keeps his negative, so that he could provide further "prints" (two shillings each) if wanted. Those who cut out

'Experiment with the Air-Pump'   c.1768   Joseph Wright

97   *Peter Dollond and Assistant   1772   Johann Zof*

98   *Richard Cosway   1740-1821   Self Portrait*

their silhouettes, could make a "negative" without trouble by cutting the original out of a folded sheet of paper.[78]

The list of media in which portraits were taken towards the end of the eighteenth century is far from exhausted; the interest in them was reaching its peak, and so, inevitably, freaking a good deal. Thus the Society of Artists in the 'seventies, a serious body, admitted portraits such as that of a 'Nobleman Worked With a Needle in His Own Hair', submitted by one or other of the Misses Lane, who specialised in that line. A mock advertisement in a paper on behalf of a "Mynheer — , just come over from Germany", who had invented a method of taking a likeness by the sitter looking into a mirror and having the glass heated so as to bake the impression, is said to have produced a queue of would-be clients next day at an innocent perfumer's shop in Bond Street.[79]

Portraiture, both of the present and the past, seems to have fascinated people. It was the age of Granger, one of the first serious students of historical portraiture, whose *Biographical History of England* (1769) sparked off the fashion to which he gave his name—Grangerising, the extra-illustration by engravings of standard historical works such as Clarendon and Burnet, and Granger's own History. Meanwhile, in the hands of the contemporary practitioners, British engraving had reached its highest pitch of quality, as a method of reproduction. Earlier in the century, portrait-painters had been well served for publicity by excellent mezzotint engravers like John Smith and Simon, and later by John Faber the younger; when there were no public galleries, and pictures were only to be seen in the houses of the well-to-do or at auctions, the mezzotinters and line-engravers were invaluable. They were broadcast by the print-shops, the windows of which fulfilled to some extent the functions of the illustrated dailies and weeklies of today. We have already seen Thornhill and Hogarth practising this sort of visual journalism; in 1761 Goldsmith, disguised as a

Chinaman, approached a print-shop somewhat optimistically:

Here, thought I, the painter only reflects the public voice. . . . But, guess my surprise when I came to examine this depository of noted faces! All distinctions were levelled here, as in the grave, and I could not but regard it as a catacomb of real merit. The brickdust man took up as much room as the truncheoned hero, and the judge was elbowed by the thief-taker; quacks, pimps and buffoons increased the group, and noted stallions only made room for more noted strumpets.[80]

The subjects were not all "straight" portraits of course. Indeed, the chief revenue of the print-shops was probably derived from the sale of satirical, grotesque and caricature prints—but with those I shall deal briefly in the next chapter. Respectable, pretty genre pieces, featuring pretty girls in domestic occupations, were engraved by McArdell after Mercier in the 'fifties— 'Girl with Cat', 'Girl taking Tea'; similar works by Gravelot and Arthur Pond were popularised, and later those by Henry Morland and others. In the 'seventies a more saccharine sweetness of sentimental attitude was dispensed, notably by the engravings of J. R. Smith after the works of the Reverend Peters—'Hebe', 'Love in Her Eye Sits Playing'—in a distressing style based on Reynolds, isolating his latent arch roguery and spreading it with an unction for which the word has only recently been invented: cheesecake.

But Smith, in his subject-matter, was fairly comprehensive; he engraved, for more delicate sensibilities, topical matters such as the 'Lady coming from the Circulating Library', after Singleton, of 1781, to the very genteel anglicised *Sturm und Drang* of the 'First Interview of Werther and Charlotte', of 1782. There is, in such works, no more profound study of the face than a mannered rendering of the fashionable expression, which was —in the case of Peters—refined vulgarity. But the masters of serious portraiture had no cause to complain of their engravers; after a falling away in quality in the 'forties and early 'fifties (apart from Hogarth, who was served by himself), engraving revived, particularly in the hands of the mezzotinters. James McArdell, who died before he was forty, in 1765, led in the great school of British mezzotint engraving. Reynolds once expressed the opinion (not foreseeing the public gallery and the photograph) that it was through McArdell's reproductions of his paintings that he, Reynolds, would be immortalised, and when McArdell died he was succeeded by engravers of almost equal ability like Valentine Green; and their works dispensed the new aesthetic throughout the country.

The vast majority of the clients of the masters came of course as always from the top levels of society, although the clients were now far more variously rendered than they had been before. More and more people were being painted, but the tendency of the portrait was still to level them desirably up, fashionably and socially. Population had increased enormously; the industrial revolution was changing the face of the countryside and the life of the people; Rousseau was busy in men's imaginations like yeast in the dough; France was about to explode in political and social revolution.

There is little sign of any reflection of such portents in the faces of the time as they survive for us. Romney returning from "the Sussex Peasants, with faces round with health, and expressions of contentment everywhere" might remark on the approach to London of the "sharpness of countenance" of the Londoners, "with passions so strongly marked . . . deep design, disappointed ambition, envy, hatred, melancholy, disease and poverty"[81]—but Romney did not paint these faces. Hogarth (aided, admittedly, by a natural squint in his sitter's eye and some malice in his own) had shown how to draw a radical agitator in the face of Wilkes; Romney did draw Tom Paine, but he drew him as a gentleman and little more. The Russian visitor, Karamzin, coming from France ("where beauty is so rare a phenomenon") found England "the land of female

223

beauty," but ranged the male physiognomies in three classes:

surly, good-natured or brutish. I can safely swear that in no other country have I seen so many brutish faces as here, and I am now convinced that William Hogarth drew from nature.[82]

Hogarth, however, had no true successors of any ability. Though Wright of Derby painted Sir Brook Boothby (National Gallery) prone in a landscape with a volume of Rousseau in his hand, nature is still a park and Sir Brook's face emotionless, painted firmly and composedly in a style that reminds one that Wright was Hudson's pupil. There are no industrial faces, as such, but occasionally one does get a glimpse of a face that is bluntly tough, with an atmosphere that has not been caught

Plate 95

before. Such perhaps is Wilkinson's face, by Abbott in the National Portrait Gallery, and Arkwright's, by Wright of Derby; faces that sit well and aptly on an iron-master (who ultimately had himself buried in an iron coffin) and on the inventor of the spinning-jenny. Opie, in his still brilliant youth, could strike with a vivid and almost unsentimental naturalism the faces of village children at a school, and once,

Plate 99

in his painting of a Cornish mine-owner and his manager, 1786, he achieved a most unusual and contemporary characterisation, coarse, powerful and vital.

The practitioners of the conversation-pieces are, for faces, disappointing; here, in the painting of faces involved with and uninhibited by action, Hogarth again had little following. Devis's charm rests in his colour and in his doll's-house naïveté; if you isolate the faces of his men and women they are almost always as blank as dolls, painfully stupid; Zoffany, more sophisticated, may be but little more illuminating, painting group-portraits more often than conversation-pieces—but he produced some remarkable exceptions to that generalisation: for example, in his extraordinary tour-de-force of the 'Royal Academy Life Class', you see artists as they are, void of

99 Ralph Daniell and
Captain Morcom
1786 John Opie

100 A Jockey c.1770
George Stubbs

101   *Duke of Wellington   1814   Sir Thomas Lawrence*

2 *Duke of Wellington* *1812* *Francisco Goya*

103 Byron 1817 B. Thorwaldsen

104 Byron c.1809 George Sandars

glamour, sharp with their intent precise vision, in all the idiosyncrasies of their flesh: a close-up not unworthy of Hogarth. And in his painting of the optician Dollond and his assistant in his workshop, there is a fascinating literal reflection of the artisan craftsman; but this was not a picture that appealed to the arbiters of taste and the patrons. "Extremely natural", Horace Walpole commented on it at the Academy in 1772, "but the characters too common nature and the chiaroscuro destroyed by his servility in imitating the reflexions of the glasses". Zoffany did not repeat the experiment: academic art could not yet stomach "characters too common nature", but they are to be found outside the Academy. The young Gainsborough, before he sought the patronage of society, had painted country gentlemen to their ordinary life, and Stubbs, despised as an "animal painter", painted grooms and coachmen, country gentry and even soldiers, with the same veracious dispassionate sympathy as he painted horses; his jockey, with that fine nose thrusting to the post, ages not. These are truly rural faces, as distinct from the picturesque rustic or bucolic faces that even Morland generally paints. The unusual atmosphere in Wright of Derby's candle-lit pieces, though striking and sympathetic, is achieved by a by no means new technical trick of illumination rather than by a new approach to character.

Plate 97

Plate 100

Plate 96

Chapter X

LAWRENCE–GILLRAY AND THE NEW WORLD OF INDUSTRY

THE LEADERS of late Georgian society expressed, by their patronage, their confidence in Thomas Lawrence's flair and ability to paint them at their best. Lawrence[83] first showed his full powers in the paintings that he sent to the Royal Academy in 1790, when he was twenty-one years old. They included two female whole-lengths that still rank among his masterpieces: the portrait of the actress, Elizabeth Farren, and that of Queen Charlotte now in the National Gallery. His early style was based on the late style of Reynolds, and Reynolds, at the private view in the Academy of 1790, is said to have indicated that it was on Lawrence that his mantle should fall: "In you, Sir, the world will expect to see accom-plished what I have failed to achieve." The world's expectation was to be deceived, if Reynolds thought that Lawrence would prove at last to be the world's awaited history-painter.

Lawrence in practice confined his interest to portraiture—despite his theatrical ventures, like the 'Satan' and the 'Cato'—far more exclusively and far more happily than did Reynolds. Even there he was a more limited artist than Reynolds himself. In the 'nineties he heightened portraiture with a more flowing elegance, a greater clarity and splash of colour, and a more brilliant expression. His faces are pointed and heightened by often exaggerated lights, that sit palpably as tears in the eyes or as salve on the lips; the great end of painting, he had written when but eighteen, is "the expressing with truth the human heart in the traits of the countenance", a sentiment which Reynolds would surely never have expressed: the human mind or the human soul perhaps, but not the heart.

230

Lawrence's characterisations tend in fact to have a double aim: to portray the public, superficial creature of fashion and society in poise and dress, and, primarily in the face, to indicate the more private sensibilities of the heart, in the parted lips, the dilated brilliant eyes, the sable curls in profusion on the forehead high and pale. In tonality indeed he often anticipates a Byronic beauty; his sitters mostly wear their own hair, and it seems generally to be dark against a pale skin—but they lack the physical vigour and conviction of a Corsair or a Don Juan. They may be at once stagey and curiously asexual.

Lawrence never painted Byron himself, but late in his career he set down a verbal portrait that shows a close sympathy:

Lavater's system never asserted its truth more forcibly than in Byron's countenance, in which you see all the character: its keen and rapid genius, its pale intelligence, its profligacy, and its bitterness; its original symmetry distorted by the passions, his laugh of mingled merriment and scorn; the forehead clear and open, the brow boldly prominent, the eyes bright and dissimilar, the nose finely cut, and the nostril acutely formed; the mouth wellmade, but wide and contemptuous even in its smile, falling singularly at the corners, and its vindictive and disdainful expression heightened by the massive firmness of the chin, which springs at once from the centre of the full underlip; the hair dark and curling, but irregular in its growth. . . .[84]

Sandars' portrait of the poet, though not approved ("It does not *flatter* me, I think, but the subject is a bad one . . ."), offers at least a windswept cloudiness, in strong contrast to the neoclassic clarity of Thorwaldsen's bust of him. Looking back, in 1858, Trelawney described Byron's appearance as the realisation of that ideal standard with which imagination adorns genius. Although hints of it are visible already in the characters of some of the Gothick novels, notably those of Ann Radcliffe, it may be that Byron not merely realised but formulated that standard.

Many of Lawrence's male portraits point towards it, keen

Plate 104

Plate 103

and rapid, with brilliant eyes, dark and irregular hair, flaring nostril and curling upper lip. Bitterness and vindictiveness however escape Lawrence, and disdain, though ineradicable from certain mouths, is always softened by the expression of the eyes. If Lawrence had drawn Byron, he would probably have caught more of the "succinctness and gentlemanliness" of his appearance, as noted by Leigh Hunt, than of that inimitable cohabitation of sharp irony and romantic imagination; it is, of course, Delacroix who should have painted the poet.

Lawrence was after all a society-painter, and his work as a whole is a retraction from the wider horizons established by Reynolds to those of the drawing-room. If he escapes the drawing-room, it is most often for the parade-ground or the stage, and his characters are bathed in a soft limelight. North-cote called him "a sort of man-milliner painter—a meteor of fashion"; Northcote was biased and extremely jealous, but his criticism is not entirely unjust. Magnificently successful as are, within their convention, Lawrence's series of whole-length masterpieces of the victorious allied statesmen and generals in the Waterloo Chamber at Windsor, the convention is that of the stage, theatrical rather than essentially dramatic, of martial glamour rather than of true martial grandeur as demonstrated, for example, by Reynolds in his 'Lord Heath-field'.

Plate 101   Lawrence's face of Wellington, well-drawn as it is, well-fitting as a glove, is perhaps too conscious of the work of the barber, too defined in the eyes, those perfect steady irises, lit each by one perfectly-placed and formulated highlight.
Plate 102   Compare the tough, almost hostile sensitivity of Goya's handling of the same face, in Madrid in 1812; it is that of an explorer, rather than of a tailor. Lawrence paints the lion of Waterloo in his social context as an English aristocrat, fresh from a bath after exercise on the playing fields, perhaps, of Eton; Goya, who knew nothing of the playing fields of Eton,

Wordsworth   1842   B. R. Haydon

106 John Keats   1816   B. R. Haydon (life-mask)

saw a conqueror, a bleak, high-blooded man with the strained and fanatic stare of war.

But for a surface recording of Regency society, Lawrence's brilliance and *chic* were exactly right, as right as Lely's for the Restoration Court, except that Lawrence omits the visible evidence of profligacy that was certainly there. He is one of the most valuable witnesses for the Crown against the overwhelming condemnation of history. In 1815 he exhibited a portrait of the Prince Regent aged fifty-two; it was noticed by Hazlitt:

Sir Thomas Lawrence has with the magic of his pencil recreated the Prince Regent as a well-fleshed Adonis of thirty-three . . . we could not, as we stood before this very admirable picture, but derive a high degree of good-natured pleasure from imagining to ourselves the transports with which His Royal Highness must have welcomed this improved version of himself. It goes far beyond all that wigs, powders and pomatums have been able to effect for the last twenty years.

Lawrence generally painted his sitters within a tight social context; one can scarcely blame him for failing with the irreducible egg-head of Sir Walter Scott—it baffled all the many artists who attempted it. Even the portrait by Raeburn (here, one might have thought, on his home-ground) was dismissed by the *Repository of Arts* in 1810:

This last of the minstrels shows how lamentably the race is degenerate, for never was a more unpoetical physiognomy delineated on canvas; we might take him for an auctioneer, a travelling dealer or chapman; in short for any character but a bard.

Scott's face appears to have been incompatible with the authorship of *Marmion* and the Waverley novels.

But Lawrence badly misplaces other characters, especially upstarts on the wave of industrial and scientific progress. Humphrey Davy is an exception, for that poor Cornish boy was born not only a brilliant chemist but meat for Lawrence, outwardly a natural aristocrat. But in the case of James Watt, father of steam-power, Lawrence has reduced a face of Scots granite to glossy alabaster. It was Lawrence's later style, gradually tightening towards both a greater solidity and a more uniform polish in the painting of the flesh, that beat the retreat to the drawing-room. And in the drawing-room it could be entirely adequate and successful, as is his 'Countess of Blessing-ton' of 1822, which would be perfect illustration to a perhaps more metropolitan version of *Sense and Sensibility*.

Plate 110

The society portraiture of the years between 1790 and 1840 was almost entirely conditioned by the achievements of Rey-nolds and Lawrence. Most of the painters worked somewhere between their two styles, although in the 'thirties some painters, influenced by their Italian visits, like John Partridge and Hayter, were moving back towards the continental academic tradition, in a more precise and tight style. Hoppner, notorious for his swing from one to the other, died in 1810, four years after Opie; and in the last twenty years of his life, between 1810 and 1830, Lawrence had no near rival. There were numerous other painters of ability, but none with that personal genius that stamps the face of an epoch with its own imprint: Owen, Beechey, Northcote and Jackson, then the rising stars of Martin Archer Shee and Thomas Phillips, and the close followers of Lawrence like the short-lived George Harlow, Evans and Lane.

In Scotland, however, a more individual course was taken by Raeburn, painting steadily away in Edinburgh from after his return from his Italian visit in 1787 until his death in 1823. By using forced lighting Raeburn revealed the faces before him, often almost brutally; he is the master of a new realism, painting his sitter "in his habit as he lived", from the Edinburgh urban blacks and greys to the Tartan picturesque clamour of the plaid and the kilt. His use of chiaroscuro had of course distinguished antecedents; as R. L. Stevenson remarked, his Mr. Wardrop (now in Melbourne) might be palmed off on a layman as a Rembrandt, but Raeburn had in fact a far less subtle attack than either Rembrandt or Reynolds, and the concentration of light tends too often to lead not to greater penetration, but to a Hollywood production of the obvious. Already in 1801, Farington wrote of Raeburn's work that "that which strikes the eye is a kind of Camera Obscura effect", the effect, in fact, of an over-illuminated photograph. His portraits tell wonderfully when reproduced in size in the half-tone block or the photogravure. Confronted in the paint, they are often very vulgar—particularly his portraits of children and of young men and women of fashion. In older faces it was Raeburn's forte, with that direct, forthright certainty, the famous "square touch" of the brush, to discover an enduring structure of character and experience. He is the first truly Scottish portrait-painter of more than minor stature; Jamieson, in the early 17th century, is like a lesser Cornelius Johnson; later the Scougalls have a recognisable but dull style; Medina was a contemporary of Kneller and his work is often confused with that of Kneller; Aikman, and later Allan Ramsay, that impressive painter, both moved to set up practice in London. Raeburn, though he made unsuccessful forays to London to see if it would support him, practised and throve in his home town, the northern capital rather than a city of the provinces, with a vigorous, enlightened and very independent society.

From Raeburn depends a whole native Scottish School of portrait-painters, from Watson-Gordon to Fiddes Watt, but more interesting was the work of Dyce in Scotland in the 'thirties, earning scanty bread by portraiture which included some fascinating excursions into the manner of Titian, and that of the émigré Scotsman, David Wilkie in London. After his continental travels, and particularly after Lawrence's death in

237

1830, Wilkie largely abandoned the small-scale genre-painting that had brought him fame and prosperity, and began working in a much broader manner that some alleged to be Spanish, but which was, as Haydon observed, "something like Lawrence and Raeburn, and not like himself; and yet fine, but not original". They have indeed (those that have not been eaten away by bitumen) still something of the glamour and bravura of Lawrence.

There were also some odd little pockets of achievement, never followed up, by painters who were later to turn away from portraiture. Such was a remarkable group of paintings by William Etty in his early twenties, of members of his family, recorded unconventionally with a deeply felt intimacy and an entire lack of conventional inhibition. Such, too, were the portraits by Constable, painted with a searching, almost heavy, veracity, between 1810 and 1820. And later there was Haydon, forced into loathed common portraiture by poverty. His real pot-boilers are drearily bad, while of the ninety-seven portraits included in his large painting of the 'Reform Banquet', Lord Jeffrey found he was unable to recognise a single one. Yet, in those few heroic portraits that he took on deliberately (pursuing the Duke of Wellington with letter upon letter until he sat), there is more than a hint that here, given only a greater technical ability, might have been a worthy successor to Reynolds.

Plate 105 Haydon, in his Wordsworth brooding on Helvellyn, achieves a characterisation of a mind in action that is no mean performance. It is far more truly a heroic portrait than any of Lawrence's, despite its clumsy and sluggish paint. (When Wordsworth sat, the delighted Haydon "found him, to my wonder, eight heads high, or 5 feet 9⅞ inches, and of very fine heroic proportions".[85])

In all other media the spate of portraiture continued. Between about 1780 and 1805 Cosway was painting his finest miniatures, often as large as 3 inches high, in thin colour

Nelson   c.1805 (?)   Catherine Andras

108   *Lady Hamilton   c.1790   George Romney*

109 'Dido in Despair' (Lady Hamilton) 1801 James Gillray

110 *Lady Blessington 1822*
     Sir Thomas Lawrence

111 *Maria Siddons (?) 1797 after Lau*

brilliant over the white ivory. Himself a sartorial fop of prowess, a notable eccentric, claiming to have had several *Plate 98* sittings from the Virgin Mary for her picture, and a personal friend of George, Prince of Wales, he was even better fitted than Lawrence to present sympathetically the *bel idéal* in Regency faces. His characters are winsome with enormous melting eyes, a little hectic in the cheek and with a calculated negligence in the hair; sometimes their heads are almost as wide as their shoulders; but they are presented with such three-dimensional skill that they convince. A curious, brief but intense freak of the miniature-art that now came into fashion was the eye-miniature, which aimed to capture the most intimate glance of "the windows of the soul"; more often, it captured a repulsively detailed, almost anatomical, account of the mere surface of the eye and the contiguous flesh, and the human eye, hardly more than that of a fish, is not an object that profits from detachment from its context. They are not common now, but may sometimes be found jostled together in a cardboard box in an auction-room, viz.:

Lot 18. An Eye Miniature inset in the bezel of a ring which is inscribed 'Genl. Arabins Right Eye 1798'; another in paste frame and mounted as a brooch; another inset in the lid of a Vinaigrette, $1\frac{1}{4}$ in., contained in leather case; and five other Eye Miniatures all mounted as brooches.

From the bottom of the cardboard box, the General's eye stares up, the veins of the white a little blood-shot as is only proper in a General, the iris a steady military grey; on one of the other eyes—its original owner long lost and unidentified— there glistens, almost wet, a *trompe-l'œil* tear.

Like miniatures, the small-scale portrait drawing also throve. Cosway practised them; Edridge and Thomas Heaphy, amongst others, had a thriving practice in them. They are able enough. Forerunners of the cabinet photograph, they seem destined to stand upon a piano, but they offer no novel facial characterisation, and are, when confronted by one of the many drawings in the same format that Ingres made of British visitors to Rome after the peace of 1815, suddenly naïve and gauche. On a life-size scale, and smaller, the pastellists also flourished. The Swiss artist Liotard, active in England in the seventeen-fifties, had set a standard of almost libellous verisimilitude; as Professor Waterhouse has pointed out, it is from Liotard's portraits that we can tell which of the children of Frederick, Prince of Wales, had adenoids. From this standard the pastellists gradually withdrew; Francis Cotes, in his pastels, achieved a liveliness rare in his oils, but his successor was John Russell, a Methodist of stern principles but with a saccharine sweetness and affectation in his portraits. Broader, indeed sloshy, effects were needed by an emulator of Reynolds, Daniel Gardner, and to achieve them he mixed his pastels in a heady concoction that included brandy.

The bust-makers continued in fashion, by no means always for funereal purposes. Nollekens, whose exhibiting career at the Academy lasted from 1771 to 1814, had an enormous practice, dependent upon his ability to convey a lively likeness within a limited senatorial formula. Although he rarely achieved the vividness of his early busts, such as that of Sterne, the best works of his later period, from his Dr. Johnson to his *Plate 83* second bust of Fox (1802) and as late as his Wellington (1813), are strong characterisations—in the case of Fox, formidably Roman. In the work of Nollekens' successor as the most fashionable sculptor, Sir Francis Chantrey, the vigour is visibly abating in the cold zone of the ever-spreading neo-classic taste as formulated by Winckelmann in the seventeen-sixties. A major tenet was that "expression detracts from beauty", a theory upheld by Reynolds in his Fifth Discourse of 1772 though often forgotten in his portraits, but put into interminable practice by the most famous sculptor in Europe, Canova. Chantrey, in his best work, like the bust of Southey, escapes its limitations, but the large bulk of his work abides inexpressively within them, whereas the busts of some sculptors such as Westmacott are no longer portraits but variations on a classic head.

Some of the less mannered portraits in the round may now be found more interesting: the wax mask of Nelson's face *Plate 107* from his effigy in Westminster Abbey, modelled by Catherine Andras and said to be very like, or the vivid life-mask of Keats, taken by B. R. Haydon in December 1816. *Plate 106*

The popularity of busts was remarkable, and it was felt natural to enshrine the great popular figures, the party leaders, in marble as household tutelaries; Nollekens is said to have sold 100 busts of Fox, and 150 of Pitt. The ensuing prosperity of the sculptors may be judged by the fortunes they made. Nollekens, though admittedly of a notorious miserliness and very long-lived, accumulated well over £200,000; Chantrey, who died aged only sixty-one in 1842, is said to have been worth £150,000.

In sharp contrast to the extremes of neo-classicism represented in their differing ways by Westmacott and the tenderly severe Flaxman, but parallel with a boom in popularity of the Dutch seventeenth-century masters of low-life painting, came the British School of painters of contemporary low-life. It was headed, of course, by David Wilkie,[86] who arrived in London from Edinburgh in 1805, aged twenty, and who, by the time he was twenty-five, had scored a resonant success that was not only popular, but was supported by the approval and active patronage of the great connoisseurs headed by Sir George Beaumont.

Wilkie's was not, like Hogarth's, satirical or moral painting; no incubus of responsibility was placed upon the spectator.

He was endowed with a shrewd, accurate and, above all, an enjoying eye, and he painted in many of his best pictures a society, that of the Scottish village, that was in its relaxation sprightlier and less inhibited than its English counterpart. He had a remarkable memory for facial expressions and quirks of character and his work teems with portraits, from that of his father (who, as a strict minister, was furious when he found out) in his early 'Pitlessie Fair' of 1804, to the veterans in the 'Chelsea Pensioners reading the Gazette of the Battle of Waterloo', suggested to Wilkie by the Duke of Wellington in 1816.

After 1830, generally speaking, he fell victim to a blight of artistic theory. His patrons and his public found him to be the British Teniers, though he rarely shows Teniers' interest in the grotesque; compared with Hogarth he shows as very much a *petit maître*, choreographer of a pretty, vivid and small world as if seen through the wrong end of a telescope. But part of his success undoubtedly came from the fact that he appealed to a growing public taste for the laughable and the quaint, and for sentimental anecdote, although he himself painted almost always without condescension and without sentimentality. The same is true of his much-neglected English contemporary, William Mulready,[87] a painter with a sometimes most admirable grasp of sheer pictorial values, but beloved by the public for his subject-matter, especially for his small boys, generally fighting. In the generation following Wilkie and Mulready, the sentimental approach of the public to the contemporary scene would swiftly corrupt the painters.

Other facets of society, already seen, continued to be portrayed. Ben Marshall, with an entirely different technique, preserved something of Stubbs' sturdy transcriptions of jockeys and grooms, and painted some remarkable portraits of prize-fighters. John Ferneley specialised in the painting of the English sportsman astride, austerely but intimately involved in a wintry inexpressive bliss amongst the hounds; and Francis Grant, in his early sporting pictures of the 'thirties, caught for ever the essence of the dandaisical ennui of the sporting gentleman, best perhaps in the cold dawn limbo of his famous 'Melton Breakfast'.

The propagation of portraits by the engravers also continued prosperously, in the hands of engravers as skilful as Charles Turner, who in his long life-time (1774-1857) reduplicated over 600 portraits; the demand for public heroes, the Nelsons and Wellingtons, was insatiable, and we find also "personalities", in the modern sense, commissioning Turner to engrave their portraits and publishing themselves in aid of their own publicity campaigns; thus the prize-fighter Belcher published his own portrait in 1810, as had the famous fat man, Daniel Lambert, in 1806. But print-sellers, besides disseminating in reproduction many "straight" portraits, were also sponsors of one of the most remarkable efflorescences in British art: the satiric caricature.[88] A host of artists, working in this medium, sprang up between 1770 and 1830, representing all facets of middle-class opinions suddenly and brutally involved in politics.

The genius of the personal caricature was Gillray; Rowlandson, though capable, as in his portrait of George Morland, of vivid even naturalistic likenesses, was in his satire more generally social than political or individual. Caricatures are sometimes— and to me, it seems, wrongly—disallowed as portraits. They were presented along a range between the manner of Hogarth, the comic history-painter, and that of Ghezzi, of the traditional Italian caricature. But however far they go in distortion—and Gillray in extremes developed a fantastic romantic expressionism—the best of them remain of, and well rooted in, the person on whom they are based. By emphasising the physical eccentricities of their subject, they focus a shocked astonishment in ridicule upon them.

These faces are often much more than ridiculous, they may particularise some specific energy. Often Gillray seems to be illustrating the man-in-the-street's distrust and incomprehension of—and helplessness before, those forces now often referred to as "They": arbitrary forces that move mysteriously and out of sight, dispensing, unaccountable and unappeasable as the weather, now war, now peace; now famine, now plenty; but all the time a rain of laws, ordinances, decrees, regulations. In the political cartoons, these forces become incarnate in faces recognisable as those of the Royal Family, of Napoleon, of Pitt and of Fox: faces still just human but also the figurehead, now of a self-indulgent gluttony of a court or party indifferent to the misery of country, now of invading war toppling not only the established kingdoms of Europe but the established over-seas markets of England, and so on. It is heroic portraiture turned inside out; whereas the society-portrait ennobles the particular towards an agreed ideal of beauty, without losing sight of its subject, satirists like Gillray distort the particular as far as possible away from the same agreed ideal of beauty, to the extent that this is consonant with retaining the human identity of his sitter. Just as the portrait-painter enhances his subject with attributes (as Reynolds' 'Lord Heathfield' with his wonderful key), with official robes, or even turns them into gods or goddesses, so Gillray in reverse.

Gillray ridicules excess in terms of excess, but his ridicule is fired by a profound distrust, and by fear that sometimes seems to try to control a hostile, superhuman force by giving it a known human face. His hero, often John Bull in one form or another, is usually being imposed upon: a sucker. At other times, his caricatures seem to be statements of pure revulsion against the mendacious uplift of fashionable high art. Romney had glamorised Lady Hamilton endlessly in terms of a flaw-less, almost synthetic, beauty; to Gillray, Lady Hamilton was stouter than she ought to be and also a strumpet, and so he

Plate 108
Plate 109

drew her as 'Dido in Despair', in 1801, but elephantine—cat-
aracting from her bed (in a gesture borrowed from the most
heroic of all Reynolds' paintings, his 'Death of Dido'), while
outside the window the top-sails of her sailor lover vanish
beyond the horizon, towards the triumph of the Nile. But
Gillray's range was remarkably large; he did not always need
to exaggerate, and one may reasonably suspect that his 'Vol-
uptuary under the Horrors of Indigestion' comes nearer to the
life than any other portrait of the Prince of Wales, later George
IV, now left to us.

The raw material that served all these diverse takers of
portraits was conditioned, as ever, by shifting sartorial fashion
and by the fashionable facial expressions of the moment. With
women, the neo-classic—or now, more strictly what was conceived to be neo-Hellenic—taste, had pushed the waist high,
and with it, inevitably, the breasts. The hair was worn, if not
necessarily cut short, with a short appearance, gathered in a
bun high at the back, with a rich profusion of curls at brow
and temples.

In about 1797 we find Lawrence compounding this fashion
with his own vision of ideal feminine beauty, which he seems
to have found personified in the women of the Kemble family,
especially Mrs. Siddons and her two daughters Sally and Maria,
with all three of whom he was more or less, from time to time,
in love. A profile drawing of Sally, about 1800, has the classic
Greek outline, the nose continuing the forehead in almost a
straight line, the chin large and firmly shaped; in paint, as in
his 'Mrs. Siddons' of 1797, the classic regularity is softened by   *Plate 90*
the clustering curl and a dark, liquid melancholy in the eyes.
(Byron records that his own "first dash into poetry"—at the age
of twelve, in 1800—was an ebullition of passion for his cousin
Margaret Parker: "Her dark eyes! her long eye-lashes! her
completely Greek cast of face and figure!"). And classicism,

for Lawrence, was diluted, if not contradicted, by the influence of the curious view of it expounded in England by the German-Swiss Fuseli, whom Lawrence acknowledged gratefully as "the noblest poetically inventive genius that perhaps our modern ages have produced".

It was to Fuseli that a new Mannerism was primarily indebted, for its attenuation of form and that "tip-toe" effect in whole-lengths derided by Haydon. (Lawrence's debt is most obvious, of course, in his 'Satan', but it is also there in the transfigurations of the Waterloo Chamber.) It was also Fuseli who, with his dark and violent atmospherics, illustrated best that sensibility for the "horrid" that found its expression else-where in the *Sturm und Drang* of the young Goethe, in the Gothick novels, at Fonthill, and also still in Coleridge's *Christabel* and in one part of Byron.

Lawrence reflects these atmospherics perhaps sometimes in the eyes and in the forced twist of the neck on the head, but most palpably in the lowering backgrounds against which the spot-lit figures of his more heroic portraits are set. For the face, in a society-portrait, they were obviously unsuitable, and it is only very rarely that one finds a characterisation entirely in their terms; such a one is perhaps Lawrence's unfinished *Plate 111* portrait of Maria Siddons. The daemonic appearance of this, so far removed from the clarity of Lawrence's drawing of her, has led to the suggestion that he painted it after her death—in hatred and fear, almost in an attempt at exorcism. Lawrence, it will be remembered, had first been in love with her sister Sally, had transferred his affections, in a temporary infatuation, to Maria; when that was over, he had reverted to Sally. Maria's vengeance was the promise that she, on her deathbed, extracted from Sally, that Sally should never marry Lawrence.[89]

Almost all Lawrence's female portraits concentrate rather on the brilliant reflection of youth, of prettiness if not beauty, and of elegance. The curls gradually vanish from the brow, and in his 'Countess of Blessington' of 1822, and still more in *Plate 110* his drawing of his last Kemble love, Fanny, about 1828, the smooth hair, symmetrically parted in the middle and drawn back, anticipates the propriety of the prevailing mode of the early Victorians. The brooding, that has the faintest threat of violence in Mrs. Siddons, has become purely wistful. Such of the heart as is visible in the face would not seem to register other than domestic longings.

For men, the period saw a complete revolution in dress. By 1800, not only had the wig vanished, but so had colour from clothes, and gradually the male splendour subsided into the drab which is only now, in America, being relieved; the sartorial glamour of the Regency was built, not on colour, but on cut and outline. Byron, the outlaw from society, may have worn (though he certainly did not usually do so) the open collar the better to display the noble column of his throat, but the significant figure for the future appearance of nineteenth-century man was neither he nor the over-lavish, flamboyant Prince Regent himself, but Beau Brummell. The codification of manners and dress begins with Beau Nash at Bath; Mrs. Thrale observed that Johnson had been forestalled, by some twenty years, in the famous phrase he applied to Addison— "an Arbiter Elegantiarum, a judge of propriety, was yet wanting"—by the author of the epitaph on Nash's memorial at Bath. Nash, however, had to cope with such elementary crudities as squires who wished to attend functions at the Pump Room in hunting boots; he but prepared the ground for Brummell.

Byron described Brummell as having nothing remarkable in his dress, only "a certain exquisite propriety". Any undue emphasis or flamboyance would be profoundly distasteful to him, including that of the wig, of powder, of scent. No man of fashion should use perfumes, he said, but should instead send his linen to be washed and dried on Hampstead Heath.

According to legend, he employed three hair-dressers who worked in unison upon his hair, but the desired result was no more and no less than the concealed but self-sufficient perfection of art. One of the worst things that could happen to a gentle-man was to attract attention to his outward appearance. Brummell relied on cleanliness, disciplined elegance and the best tailors. The face, it may be, was for him a mortification. There it was, necessarily exposed, and there was little that could be done about it, beyond keeping it trim and clean—and his own face, indeed, almost escapes us. All that is known (apart from a betrayal beyond his control, when his mother—presumably—had Reynolds paint him still in the fluffy skirts of a four-year-old) is an engraving from a lost miniature; it seems distressingly pert.

The metaphysics of Brummell, and of Dandyism, did not concern Englishmen very much until Oscar Wilde. (Partly distilled from Brummell's legend, and partly invented, in a sort of satanism, by writers like Barbey d'Aurevilly and Baudelaire, it had earlier a great *succès d'estime* in France.) But the practice of Brummell, the insistence on cut, on sobriety, and above all upon not standing out from one's fellow men, which became, in the hands of ordinary mortals, mere con-formity—these were to develop, persist and fossilise, not in Dandyism, but in the dark urban uniform we still acknowledge today. By about 1810, trousers were established instead of breeches, the white cravat was about to yield to the black, and the head, stripped of the wig, accepted the burden of the top-hat. The face itself, after more than a century of clean-shaving, was threatened by the first out-flanking movement of hair, advancing in side-board whiskers down the cheeks.

For the vanguard of fashion, Brummell's discipline was too severe an imposition. Chateaubriand, writing in the 'forties, remembered the English so-called dandy of the 'twenties as presenting, by duty, an unhappy and ailing figure; he was expected to have something neglected about his person: long nails; beard worn neither full nor shaved, but seeming to have sprouted at a given moment by surprise, through forgetfulness, amid the pre-occupations of despair; a waving lock of hair; a profound, sublime, wandering and fatal glance; lips contracted in scorn of the human race; a heart bored, Byronian, drowned in the disgust and mystery of existence.[90]

(Romantic beauty was often ailing; Lawrence found it in the consumptive Misses Siddons; it is sharp and eager in the face of Keats, and in Byron it was enhanced by a club-foot.) This, one suspects, may have been a fashion mainly cultivated in *avant-garde* literary circles, rather than in high society.

In the 'thirties, d'Orsay, radiant with health and scent, led a more bluff and colourful assault on uniformity in dress, with a neat close-curled beard now fully encircling his face; he had known Byron, and he mingled a dash of the Byronic with the precision of Brummell, restraining but not stifling a true French loudness. He had no wide influence; the presentation of body and face was henceforward to be, perhaps not controlled by, but anchored in, the urban middle-classes.

It was of the middle-classes that Fielding had written already in 1751:

Nothing has wrought such an alteration in this order of people, as the introduction of trade. This hath indeed given a new face to the whole nation, hath in great measure subverted the former state of affairs, and hath almost totally changed the manners, customs, and habits of the people, more especially of the lower sort. The narrowness of their future is changed into wealth; their frugality into luxury, their humility into pride, and their subjection into equality.[91]

The ranks of the traders were soon to be swollen by the industrial pioneers and magnates. But in the uniform now worn by society for the ordinary formal business in life, it is trade— and specifically the trade in magic money—that still prevails now: the uniform of the City. Even the Brigade of Guards climbs quickly out of its gorgeous uniform, as soon as off-parade, into that of the City gent.; its badge should be reversible, and one side would show crossed umbrellas over a bowler hat.

In the latter part of the eighteenth century and in the first half of the nineteenth century, men of talent, determination and accomplishment could rise with little embarrassment, as James Watt did from the family of a bankrupt small merchant, as Stephenson did from far humbler origins, and as did countless others. The portrait-painters to whom they sat in due course, as one of the normal consequences of their success, incorporated them without effort into the top-ranks of society, of those who had had their portraits painted. Some painters, like Wright of Derby, had a natural plainness of vision that might preserve something of the unaffected in sitters like Arkwright, and the unknown painter of Macadam seems to have caught the tough, hard-wearing surface of the roads in their maker. But normally the painter tidied up the sitter into the polite format, disguising them, as it were, in Academy dress.

Very occasionally the industrialists themselves sponsored curious novelties. Such were the money tokens issued by Plates 93, 94 Wilkinson, the iron-master, to his workmen in the shape of coins: on one of them, where normally would be the royal head, and Britannia or another emblem, the symbols of the power behind the money, he has set his own head and his massive tilt-forge; the whole thing as potent an emblem of *auctoritas* as ever was. But of that other nation that was beginning to form up, at first in the 'seventies in hysterical mobs of machine-workers, and then gradually coalescing over the next seventy-five years into Unions, the working-classes, the *proletariat,* their faces are scarcely glimpsed at all. The genre painting of the period, from Gainsborough, Wheatley and Morland through Wilkie and Mulready to the beginnings of the true Victorian anecdotal painters like Webster and Frith, is confined to rural (if not bucolic) and metropolitan subjects. By the time Victoria ascended the throne, revolution had threat-ened, as in the "Massacre of Peterloo" in Manchester in 1819, more than once, and the division of society, between masters and men, was acknowledged. Men, from the masters' point of view, were not a picturesque subject, and radical journalists like Cobbett did not yet tour England with an artist to record what they saw.[92]

But also, by the time of Victoria's accession in 1837, the heroic period of portraiture in England was over. With the exception of Lawrence, the opinion of the best artists had been hardening steadily against the slavery of the portrait. Fuseli, of course, and Barry, abominated it; even Opie told the students at the Academy that his very soul was sick with hearing crowd after crowd revolving round the exhibitions with only two questions: *Who is that?* and *Is it like?* Fuseli and Opie and then Haydon still believed that the alternative was the *ignis fatuus* of history-painting, but, as Opie spoke, the three real geniuses active in English painting were already forging their own realms of imagination: Blake (to whom the name of Reynolds was anathema) in the visionary; Turner and Constable in land-scape. There was no comparable genius in portraiture, and the society-portrait between 1790 and 1840 shows a steady regres-sion, all in all, from the dramatic, involved painting of Reynolds to the depiction of effigies once more.

Chapter XI

PRE-RAPHAELITE YEARNING

IN 1837 Queen Victoria succeeded to the throne of England; also in 1837, in France, Louis Daguerre became the first man to fix permanently the image of the camera obscura, and established the first practicable process of photography.[93] In 1841 Richard Beard opened in London the first public photographic portrait studio in Britain; by the end of the next year London had two more; by 1851 about a dozen; by 1861 over 200, of which 35 were in Regent Street. In those twenty years, photography arrived.

The reaction amongst artists was varied; Paul Delaroche, on first seeing a daguerreotype, was appalled and announced that painting was dead, while even Turner was moved to see in it the end of Art: "Thank God I have had my day."[94] Their fears of course were exaggerated, but there were casualties—not only the crude forerunner of the photographic shadow-picture, the silhouette—but miniature-painting itself as a living craft. On his death-bed the last of the important miniaturists, Sir William Ross, lamented that "it was all up with future miniature-painting"; that was about 1860, and his announcement was correct, but belated.

For the first ten years of portrait-photography, two methods in the main were used. The first was that patented and baptised by Daguerre, and when Beard patented in England the refine-ment of tinted daguerreotypes, photography offered a completely satisfactory substitute for the miniature-painting, plus various advantages—that of novelty, to begin with; of speed—a single exposure sometimes of much less than a minute (depending on the weather), compared with several sittings each perhaps of an hour or more; and, of course, of veracity. Veracity, however, was a double-edged quality in portraiture, and it was precisely on this that the painter Chalon's confidence rested when he made his famous rejoinder to the Queen's doubts that the camera would ruin the miniature: "Ah non, Madame, photo-graphie can't flattère." Photographers soon found that the photograph was open to titivation, and any query could be turned by the truism that the camera cannot lie.

But seen backwards in historical perspective, the miniature looks as though it had been straining upon self-immolation in the photograph since about 1800. In 1801 Andrew Robertson arrived in London from Edinburgh, where he had been much encouraged by Raeburn; Robertson's aim was to give to the miniature the substantiality of oil-painting, and he claimed to have been amongst the first "to explode the pink cheek and lips, and blue beards of the old style, and to introduce truth, warmth and harmony". He acknowledged that what had recommended him to the public was his "careful drawing and correct form".

In place of the artifact, the heightened conceits of Cosway, miniaturists began to attempt to supply their clients with a facsimile in miniature. Their paintings grew steadily larger, until one of the most popular formulas was a three-quarter-length seated, with one hand resting on a table by the chair, set in a mount with a slightly arched top: it was a life-size formula in small, but even more was it the precise formula that *Plate 112* was to make the fortunes of Beard and of Claudet, when applied to the daguerreotype; several miniaturists moved from the practice of painting their sitters to that of photographing them with little effort of adjustment. Henry Collen was one of them, and his miniature of Lord Langdale might almost *Plate 113* be a coloured photograph—but it was painted in 1829.

One of the qualities that endeared the daguerreotype to the early Victorian public was its brilliant rendering of minute detail, and it was the daguerreotype that monopolised the atten-tion of the professional studio photographers all through the 'forties. The rival method, the first to use the now standard

257

negative/positive process, known as the calotype, is associated with the name of that brilliant but unattractively jealous pioneer, Fox Talbot. It produced a broader effect that found less favour with the contemporary public, but it did help those two great Scottish photographers, David Octavius Hill and Robert Adamson, to make masterpieces which in artistic quality have still to be surpassed.

In 1851, another technical advance—the wet collodion process, invented by Frederick Scott Archer—combined the advantages of the daguerreotype—its fine detail—with those of the calotype: a larger size and the negative/positive system by which it could be reduplicated (daguerreotypes were generally less than four inches high, and each was unique); twenty years later, dry-plate photography began to be developed, and thence it was only a short matter of time before the hand-camera came in. The first Kodak was marketed in Britain in 1888, and man was finally exposed indefensibly before the myriad ruthless recording eyes of the snap-shooters and the press photographers.

The impact of photography upon life-scale portraiture—in paint or in sculpture—was initially probably very slight. It may well have endangered the livelihood of many second-rank painters, particularly in the provinces, but it could offer nothing that seriously disturbed the prestige of the life-scale portrait as an object of pomp and circumstance. As far as quality goes, the situation with the painters was not good; of the Academy Exhibition in 1838, the *Athenaeum* observed that the place of Sir Thomas Lawrence was as far from being filled as ever. While acknowledging the power of some of Wilkie's portraits, it disparaged the affectation and false colouring in others; and then—

Willing as we are to give all honour due to Phillips, and Pickersgill, and Shee, and Briggs, and Wood, and Say, and Eddis, and Laurence, each of whom exhibits works rather above than below his recognised standard of excellence, we are still compelled to confess that none of them rose above mediocrity.

Mrs. Beeton   c.1860   anon.

Lord Langdale 1829 H. Collen

114

115

114 Jane Morris 1865 anon.

115 'Beata Beatrix' (Elizabeth Sidd[c]
1863 D. G. Rossetti

116 'The Front Row at the Opera'
c.1870 (?) W. Holyoake

117 Mrs Madox Brown
c.1852 F. Madox Brown

117

118 *Charlotte Brontë 1835*
Branwell Brontë

119 *Charlotte Brontë 1850*
George Richmond

Posterity has endorsed the verdict of the *Athenaeum*, and forgotten all the names of these painters, save that of Wilkie, and he is remembered not for his portraits but for his genre painting.

Nor was the situation, in the ranks of the orthodox Academy painters, to improve for a long time. The standard of technical ability remained very high, but of artistic exploration and discovery there was almost nothing. Now those painters named, and others like Margaret Carpenter, were followed by men such as Sir Francis Grant, J. P. Knight, J. C. Horsley in the 'forties, 'fifties and 'sixties; by Millais and then Holl in the 'seventies and 'eighties. Through these long years, as the figures stand out more and more sharply against the backgrounds, more and more entries in the catalogues of the Academy exhibitions are followed by the note—Presentation Portrait.

Simultaneously, that mute invasion of the squares and parks of British cities (and of the cities of the Empire) by whole-length statues gathers way; piety becomes public, and sites its monuments no longer only in the churches, but in the highway, and in the board-rooms and the council-chambers of public and semi-public institutions, that now become in part also shrines: town halls, water boards, charity commissions, schools, universities. In 1856 this mood created its focus in the National Portrait Gallery, the first of its kind in the world, and the kind apparently peculiar to the British taste, for it has hardly been adopted outside these islands; it may also not be irrelevant to remark that at the time of the founding of the Portrait Gallery, professional British portrait-painting was at one of the lowest ebbs in its history.

The Gallery's purpose was to be not artistic, but historic; decently sentimental, and not merely educational, but inspiring. "There cannot", said Palmerston when moving the Vote for its financial support, there cannot be a greater incentive to mental exertion, to noble actions, to good conduct on the part of the living, than for them to see before them the features of those who have done things which are worthy of our admiration and whose example we are more induced to imitate when they are brought before us in the visible and tangible shape of portraits.

The official school of portraiture was in full sympathy with such sentiments; the difficulty was to paint them in the features of their sitters. In their portraits of public men they could no longer indicate them by a heroic orchestration of rich colour; colour had gone out of dress, and power resided more in the frock-coated House of Commons than in the Lords, who any-way were becoming increasingly self-conscious about ermine. The formulas became more and more static, more and more those of the effigy. It may seem incongruous at first thought, but the artistic forebear to whom the painters perhaps most referred was no longer Lawrence, nor Reynolds, nor Van Dyck, but Velazquez. Francis Grant acknowledged that he "owed much of his success to Velazquez";[95] Millais was much interested in him and was only deterred from studying him in the Prado by the well-known discomforts of travelling in Spain; Frank Holl was actually dubbed "the English Velaz-quez". None of them—not even Holl—recognised in Velazquez what we now recognise as his genius, the way he used paint in the building of pictures (as of course their near-contemporary Manet did in France); they were interested by the icon that he produced, a resolution in matchless dignity of the problem of painting a state-portrait of a man dressed in sombre, boring and difficult blacks and greys.

With women, the problem was different; colour abounded, but the shape of clothes somewhat offset it. By about 1840 the hooped skirt was on its way in, and soon the crinoline was in full flower; the society-portrait painters hesitated before it, and seem to have preferred if possible to minimise its extravagance by showing its wearer seated. It was left to the painters especially patronised by the court, to catch it in its wide prime; and amongst them, above all, to the famous international court⁄painter, Winterhalter. He—and to a lesser degree the English painters affected by continental academism, like Hayter and Partridge (they all stood apart from the English Academy)—worked in what was in effect at once a more smoothly polished and more naturalistic style than did the painters in the English tradition.

But it seems odd that Winterhalter should have been rebuked by English critics for too earthy an approach, now that he is remembered as the most quaint and "period" of Victorian portrait⁄painters: "The Queen and Prince [Consort]", said the *Athenaeum,* of the sentimentally delightful portrait⁄group by Winterhalter of the Queen and her family in 1847,

"though likenesses, are yet sensual and fleshy versions of those distin⁄guished persons." The Queen's arms and hands, it was found, were "expressed in contours that speak more of hard work in the kitchen than of the occupations of a palace," and there was such "a coarseness in the details—such an odour, we may say, of paint, and such a want of taste—as make us frankly rejoice that it is not from the hands of an Englishman".

The English painters, indeed, specialised in a more sweetly spiritual key, particularly when dealing with young women; here the paragon among artists was George Richmond, who admitted that a portrait should represent the truth—"Ah! but the truth lovingly told".[96] He was the most accomplished of a considerable number of portraitists who challenged the photo⁄graphers with chalk drawings of heads—sometimes life⁄size. The head is tilted on the long neck, meek yet resilient as a narcissus bud that fills to flower; the expression may be over⁄sweet, but it is wrong to dismiss it as a simper; smooth though he was, and though one may doubt the claim that his portrait of Ruskin was "more exact than any photograph", he was famous for his power of catching a likeness, and some truth surely remains behind the highlights of love.

Plate 119

As an extreme example, one may take his portrait of Charlotte Brontë: some may reject out of hand this suave account of a successful society authoress, with the melting eyes, and turn rather to the primitive version of the authoress of

Plate 118

Jane Eyre, the only begetter of Mr. Rochester, by her brother Branwell. Yet the truth probably ranges all the way between the two portraits. Richmond left a curious record of his conversation with her when she sat; she arrived on the 13th June 1850, aged 34, wearing a hat, and nervous: she took off her hat, showing a small square of merino resting on top of her head.

George Richmond: "Miss Brontë, you have a little pad of brown merino on top of your head—I wonder if I might ask you to remove it."

Miss Brontë: (bursts into tears).[97]

The Pre-Raphaelites, in their brief and vivid spring, in the 'fifties, scrutinised faces with eyes more piercing and (except in the case of Rossetti) more minutely loyal to accident. Portraiture, as art, did not interest them much, but with their insistence on faithfulness to nature, they filled their compositions with real faces drawn from the life, the faces of themselves, and of their friends and relations. So Elizabeth Siddal lay immersed in a large bath for Millais' 'Ophelia', and one of the results (according to W. M. Rossetti) was probably the best likeness ever taken of her; both the Rossettis, W. B. Scott, F. G. Stephens and Millais' father and his sister-in-law are said to appear in 'Lorenzo and Isabella'; for the two depressed

Plate 117

emigrants in the 'Last of England', Ford Madox Brown used himself and his wife, and

to insure the peculiar look of *light all round* which objects have on a dull day at sea, it was painted for the most part in the open air on dull days, and, when the flesh was being painted, on cold days.[98]

But the creation of a new type of face was the achievement of Rossetti; a face that is often wrongly called the typical Pre/Raphaelite[99] face, and (perhaps also partly wrongly) the face of Elizabeth Siddal, Rossetti's wife and lost dead love. It is a face hazed with a mystically sensuous contemplation, the mouth clearly defined for love, the eyes cast down, the golden hair about the shoulders.

Plate 115

> Look in my face; my name is Might/have/been;
> I am also called No/more, Too/late, Farewell.

And yet also:

> Above the long lithe throat
> The mouth's mould testifies of voice and kiss,
> The shadowed eyes remember and foresee.
> Her face is made her shrine . . .

It is the shrine of an ideal love rather than of the image of Elizabeth Siddal, known as Guggums. That so characteristic line of jaw is in some of the drawings almost masculine, and well it might be, for it is Dante's; in modern English women Rossetti found it more in Jane Borden, later Mrs. Morris, than in his wife. His 'Beata Beatrix', painted in 1863, the year after Lizzie Siddal died, is his haunted memory of his wife, but the face is already nearer to Jane Morris—the face that glows palely until the end of the century. That it is a typical mid/Victorian face is hardly true; it burns on, a personification of a certain state of exaltation that finally faints in the truly never/never mediae/valism of Burne/Jones. But the rich new patrons from the North who were amongst Rossetti's best clients would have been dismayed to find their wives as intense within such monastic draperies as are Rossetti's women; only in the mid/'seventies, with the beginning of the "aesthetic" movement in dress, did the figures from the Rossetti and then the Burne/Jones pictures move out from the canvases into the drawing/rooms and streets of London, into 'The Front Row at the Opera'.

Plate 114

Plate 116

For a deliberate attempt to sum up the Victorian face for posterity, one has to turn to George Frederick Watts.[100]

Watts spans the Victorian age; he exhibited first at the Academy in the year of the Queen's accession to the throne; he survived her by three years. As painting, some of his early work, done partly in Italy, is the most satisfying; under the impact of the South and of the warm colour of the Venetians, the withdrawn and ascetic young man from London became almost resplendent. Upon his return to England, his capture by the Pattle sisters, and his settling into the establishment at Little Holland House in an atmosphere of high thinking and discreetly high living, he settled to his vocation which was moral. Art was the means to an end, "to affect the mind seriously by nobility of line and colour". In his main attack, he failed, or so it seems at present. It was to present visually a new mythology, to illustrate the unwritten bible of agnosticism.

Fundamentally a religious painter, he had no religion—no basic plot, no coherent tradition of imagery with all its accumulation of associations, upon which to draw. He was not, unlike Blake, passionate enough in his vision to invent a new symbolism; he borrowed, and the result is pastiche; he tried to invent, and was restrained by good taste and propriety into flaccidity. It is not then his mythological and allegorical pictures that are now of most interest, under-rated though many of them are, but his portraits. W. M. Rossetti indicated accurately the reason for this as early as 1862:

In portraiture Watts is still as ideal as the form of art allows him to be so; but this controls the tendency, and prevents it from passing into vagueness. Ideal tendency in ideal subject is always in danger of losing itself "as Water does in Water".[101]

Watts' imagination, impulsive but weak in architectural skill, needed a recalcitrant material, a stubborn irreducible fact, to work against, in order to bring out his best; the immutable skeleton of his sitter's head provided just that.

Already by about 1860 he had hit on the idea of a series of portraits of the worthies of his time, a sort of Victorian pan⁄theon, which he would (and did) bequeath to the National Portrait Gallery. He painted most of them to a standard size, about 25 by 20 inches, which just allows a life⁄sized head and some indication of the shoulders; the focus is on the face. The mood is monumental, and his portraits are variations on the theme: Let us now praise famous men. When Tennyson sat to him in 1859 (for the portrait now belonging to Lord Somers) the poet asked him what he wished to achieve in painting a portrait, and Watts' answer is said to be incorporated in the lines in *Lancelot and Elaine:*

> a painter poring on a face,
> Divinely thro' all hindrance finds the man
> Behind it, and so paints him that his face,
> The shape and colour of a mind and life,
> Lives for his children, ever at its best
> And fullest.

There is nothing new in such purpose, nor was it foreign to some of Watts' contemporaries—Holl spoke of his aim as "to drag upon canvas the identity of the man himself". What was new was the intensity and concentration with which Watts dwelt on the face as the arena in which the character is shown; allegorical allusion and rhetoric of pose and body play little part in his portraits, he is intent upon soul and mind and their achievement scored on the face. That he should fail was inevitable; the greater part of his portraits are probably dead for most people, and he has paid, as have most successful portrait⁄painters, the penalty of painting too many portraits. Nevertheless, his best paintings will be found, I think—given a fair scrutiny—both evocative and commensurable with such mental grandeur as their subjects have bequeathed to posterity. These faces, many of them, can support their owners' genius, and to make them able to do so, Watts arrived, about 1860, at a technique that can almost foreshadow that of expressionism.

It is far removed from the hard naturalism of Millais' later style, or from that of any of Watts' British contemporaries. It is becoming visible, already in 1859, in his portrait of Gladstone, in his Lord Lawrence of 1862, and he never carried it *Plate 122* further than in his Tennyson of 1863. Here is the poet, the bard, of *In Memoriam*; sombre, searching, and yet somehow rather sumptuous in doubt. Watts was not often to achieve portraits of this order again, but almost right up to his death in 1904 he did from time to time rival them, in, for example, the *Plate 123* Swinburne, the Manning, the Walter Crane (1891); and it is these and others that place him fairly in the ranks of the great English portrait-painters, and as a heroic painter.

With women, he is generally less happy; although some of his whole-lengths, such as the Mrs. Huth in Dublin, are gracious and noble ventures in the grand English manner, and his portraits of his brief, unsuitable wife Ellen Terry are enchanting and beautifully painted sentiments, as also is that of *Plate 120* Miss Treherne, he tends generally to over-sweeten his young women with Venetian memories, and to worry the life out of old women. He was almost certainly frightened of the sex, not only of George Eliot, which is comprehensible enough (he longed for her, but knew "that the features belonged to a type he would have found most difficult; and afraid of not doing the great mind justice, he did not venture to make the attempt"), but of any strange women, other than those who dominated him, those to whom he was used, and those who had built a chaste affection about him like a studio.

His approach to the great men of his time was not made in pure adulation; he chose them from the men whom he thought would hereafter be deemed to have made or marred their o   *Georgina Treherne*   1858   *G. F. Watts*

121   *Tennyson*   c.1867   *Julia Margaret Cameron*

2 *Tennyson* *1863/4*   *G. F. Watts*

123   *Cardinal Manning*   *1882*   *G. F. Watts*

country, and he confessed to Cecil Rhodes, during a sitting: "I'm not sure myself which you are doing." There was also some bias in his selection; Gladstone, of course, but it is difficult to imagine him even considering the possibility of painting Disraeli. Nor did all his sitters approve of their images; Carlyle, to whom I shall return, was furious, Rossetti uncertain, and Morris's friends thought the portrait almost libellous; Watts was tough in his integrity to his conception, and it was a heroic conception. Sir Henry Taylor wished to be immortalised as a "jovial modern"; Watts insisted on a "modern Jove".

The achievement of Watts links the evaporating glory of Lawrence's school in the 'forties with the kindling blaze of Sargent in the 'seventies. By 1870 the photograph had already taken a heavy toll in the ranks of the portrait-painters; a comparison of figures at the Academy Exhibition is significant. A hundred years earlier, at the second exhibition of the newly founded Academy, some 265 objects were shown; over a third were portraits, including six sculptured portraits. Sixty years later, in 1830, in the by now enormously swollen show, just over half the exhibits were portraits, about 643 out of 1,278, of which about 300 were miniatures or small water-colours, and some 87 in sculpture. In the next forty years photography became a thriving business, and the figures at the 1870 Academy speak for themselves. Portraits account for a bare fifth of the exhibition, 247 out of 1,229. The miniatures have been decimated, 32 instead of 300, but three-dimensional portraits have actually increased to 117. They fulfilled a monumental function that photography could not, and a function in which the Victorians took a keen pleasure. (In the 'eighties and 'nineties there was even a revival, for the great Blougram-like prelates, of the false pride of the whole-length recumbent effigy.) The life-scale painted portraits in the Academy echo the monumental theme: gentlemen upright in dark and heavy respectability, an uprightness emphasised by the narrower, more vertical shape that Millais used for his three-quarter-lengths; the ladies as lavishly material and as congested with dress as their drawing-rooms, and often as vulgar. Millais and Sant had the true Midas-touch when they laid their brush on women. They are almost all parade portraits; either the continuation of the line, equal in size and state to those of the ancestors in the ancestral home, or they represent the founding of a new line, or they are household gods for institutions. The portrait that one gave away for love or friendship—that would now, or soon, be in the form of a photograph.

In the 'sixties the photograph album became a craze; they housed the kind of photograph known as the carte-de-visite, and were virtually portable portrait galleries. At the beginning of the book came the royal family, in full, followed by con-temporary celebrities, followed by the family and friends of the owners. About the same time various volumes of biographical notices of celebrities, together with their photographs, began to appear, and sold very well; the attitude of the sitters is not without interest. Between 1856 and 1860 a publication, the *National Gallery of Photographic Portraits,* was under way, and the preparatory correspondence has survived. A considerable proportion of the personalities involved were in no way averse, and fully content to be publicised, though there were excep-tions. Matthew Arnold considered himself insufficiently cele-brated; J. S. Mill wrote that he had no desire to figure in a collection and did not think that his personal appearance could be a matter of any interest to the general public; women of course were still in a minority, and their reactions varied sharply: Harriet Beecher Stowe was willing, Mrs. Gaskell was splendidly Victorian: "Other women may not object to having their portraits taken for the public, and sold indiscriminately, but I feel a strong insurmountable objection to it." But the root of feminine reluctance to be photographed was indicated by Helena Faucit Martin: "All the photographs of me have so signally failed that I have come to the conclusion never to undergo the ordeal again." The difficulty of obtaining raw, or untouched-up, studio photographs of feminine celebrities for record purposes still exists today.[102]

Pictorially, the professional photographers had still little to contribute. For their whole-lengths, they relied for the most part on the formulae sanctified by painters from Van Dyck to Lawrence, dropping a painted landscape backcloth behind their sitters, and furnishing them with the conventional poses and the conventional pillars and urns. The most remarkable work was being done by amateurs like Lewis Carroll, and most notably, by Julia Margaret Cameron.[103] The wife of a coffee-planter, she turned to photography as therapy for a fit of domestic depression in 1863. She was one of that energetic family, the Pattles, and one of her sisters was the dominant Mrs. Prinsep who housed and ordered Watts at Little Holland House, and it was there that Mrs. Cameron snared many of her most distinguished sitters. Watts himself she knew well, and he often advised her on questions of art.

Like Watts, she specialised in intellectual subjects, and concentrated on the seat of intellect, the head, often wrapping the shoulders in a loose dark drapery; her pietistic attitude to the great whom she photographed was again like that of Watts, though far less critical; when they were before her camera, she wrote, her

whole soul has endeavoured to do its duty towards them in recording faithfully the greatness of the inner as well as the features of the outer man. The photograph thus taken has been almost the embodiment of prayer.

The success of her portraits rested on the excellence of her eye, her insistence on a beautiful effect, and the deliberate "imper-fection" of her technique. She profited by accidents almost as much as some painters of the abstract expressionist school.

When focusing and coming to something which to my eye was very beautiful, I stopped there, instead of screwing on the lens to the more definite focus which all other photographers insist on.

Her portraits are visually in fact out-of-focus, and to the qualities of definition that were amongst the greatest virtues of photography for the ordinary exponent she was indifferent. She used very large plates, and also an abnormally long exposure, from three to seven minutes, for which length of time it is almost physically impossible for average sitters to remain still. They moved, giving Mrs. Cameron's portraits a still softer and broader modulation of form.

To compare the results achieved by Watts and Mrs. Cameron, *Plate 122* I reproduce the painter's Tennyson of about 1863 and the *Plate 121* photographer's version three or four years later. The comparison is not quite fair on Mrs. Cameron, as two of her other photographs of Tennyson are superior to this one, but it does indicate exactly what the two methods could achieve; Watts' simplification into general terms, his exaggeration of the length of the already long narrow face, his monumental quality. Mrs. Cameron's portrait tells more of the incidentals, the quirks, of Tennyson's face, especially of how his beard grew, but in spite of the deliberate softening of detail, an entirely coherent general statement on the poet's face is not achieved. On occasions, she was better than this; the famous photograph of *Plate 133* Sir John Herschel is an astonishing example, where all hazards have joined propitiously.

But the immediate future of the portrait-photograph did not lie in a development of Mrs. Cameron's methods; they were too rarefied and they were not what the public wanted. The public wanted the crisp definition of the professional studio photographer, and it got it. Of greater interest is the development of a more journalistic tendency, and here the photograph could offer something that the portrait-painter hardly ever attempted: the man on the job. J. C. Horsley was an able painter, decorously of his time—known to Whistler as Clothes-Horsley, from his objection to drawing from the nude. His portrait of the engineer Isambard Kingdom Brunel, painted in 1857, is an able and polished performance on traditional lines, the portrait of a successful engineering architect, sweetly dressed with his white plans in his office (very much so had Kneller painted Wren a hundred and fifty years earlier). But the extraordinary photograph of Brunel standing in front of the chains of his most ambitious creation, the biggest ship in the world, the *Great Eastern,* is an incomparably more vivid document—the engineer on the site, in his wrinkled working clothes, a cheroot thrust in the corner of his mouth.

Plate 134

Plate 135

Such unflattering, though trenchant, faithfulness was not the ideal of the thousands who now wished, and were able to, perpetuate their own likenesses. In 1861 *The Photographic News* exclaimed that

photographic portraiture is the best feature of the fine arts for the million that the ingenuity of man has yet devised. It has in the sense swept away many of the illiberal distinctions of rank and wealth, so that the poor man who possesses but a few shillings can command as perfect a life-like portrait of his wife or child as Sir Thomas Lawrence painted for the most distinguished sovereigns of Europe.

The standard of comparison is still that of the glamorous Lawrence; no one would have dreamed of comparison with the standards of the realist painters already vigorous in France, like Courbet, who proclaimed himself as a painter

not only socialist, but also democrat and republican, in short partisan of the whole revolution and further entirely a realist, sincere friend of the true truth.

In France indeed, in the 'sixties and 'seventies, art was in the melting-pot, and that technical exploration that was in the end

279

to undermine the central European tradition of painting as an imitation of nature, and particularly the art of portraiture, was already under way. In 1863, anti-academism received a semi-official, back-handed accolade in the establishment of the *Salon des Refusés*; in 1870 Monet and Renoir were in London (discovering, amongst other things, Turner). Although it was to be a long time before a similar spirit of investigation found its full scope amongst British artists, the *avant-garde* was busy in London from 1860 onwards, in the person of the American James McNeill Whistler.

Chapter XII

CARLYLE–THE FACE
OF HISTORY

IT IS CURIOUS to inspect the same object as seen from the very different points of artistic view that were taken up in the mid-nineteenth century; the most convenient object (in this context) is the face of Thomas Carlyle. He was, and is, in spite of his failings, a creative historian of considerable eminence; he was a public figure and a mind or at least a character of great influence, and he had a heroic view, which may be called fascist but which nevertheless had grandeur; he is now, more-over, very unfashionable; but he is very much of his time. Also he was undeniably picturesque, in a thorny and unorthodox way. His own position in relation to the arts is still held by a large number of people. "Ah well", he said to W. B. Scott,

I can make nothing of artists, nor of their work either. . . . Empty as other folk's kettles are, artists' kettles are emptier, and good for nothing but tying on the tails of mad dogs.[104]

In a picture, the only thing that interested him was the subject matter; although, when outraged by the subject, he might explode with a Munnings-like scorn (Holman Hunt's 'The Light of the World'—"a poor mis-shaped presentation . . . a mere papistical fantasy"), on the whole he was indifferent, with one exception: "Painting is worthless, except portrait-painting."[105] As a biographer, as a historian, portraits were for him serious, they were documents. Hence, with the added incentive of considerable vanity, his repeated long-suffering as a sitter for the artists.

He was born in 1795, but we know little of his appearance until he was in his late thirties, when he was chosen by Daniel Maclise for his series of what would now be called "Profiles" of

Plate 129

literary men in *Fraser's Magazine*. The drawing is a late development of the brief fashion, born in the seventeennineties, of small scale, cabinet, wholelength drawings, that had flourished in the hands of Cosway, Buck and especially Edridge; Maclise's drawings often border delicately upon caricature. Here is an unexpected Carlyle, neither the struggling, indignant and irritable writer and brilliant conversationalist of the early years in Scotland, nor the hardhitting, opinionated, courageous and irritable grand old man and *vieux terrible* of London in his last years; Maclise shows him oddly dandaisical.

Plate 125   Carlyle thought Woolner's portrait medallion of 1851 "a rather clever thing" (it is surely a little rejuvenated: he is 56 years old); it is also interesting as the view of the only sculptor who was amongst the original PreRaphaelite Brethren. Though Woolner was doubtless, if only for a brief spell, in full accord with the moral and artistic tenets of the Brethren, it is as difficult to lay one's finger on the visible evidence of those tenets in his work as it is in the very disparate painting of the young Millais, of Hunt and of Rossetti. It has, however, at this stage a clarity and a vigour that make most other Victorian sculpture of this period appear soft and sentimental in contrast. Later his style was less secure, often relapsing into a trite naturalism. Many of his busts only differed from others of the later Victorian period in his affectation of "growing" them out of a plain rectangle of marble rather than shaping them to the traditional socle (a device used by the extreme neoclassicist, Thorwaldsen). In 1865 he produced a bust of Carlyle, with some difficulty, commenting that his sitter's likeness was as difficult to catch as a flash of lightning; to assist him, Carlyle underwent "such a sitting to photographers as never was heard of", and the use of photographs may have been a factor in the deterioration of Woolner's style.[106]

Before this, in 1859, Carlyle had been sitting, also via a photographer, for Ford Madox Brown, who was already in

4   '*Arrangement in Grey and Black*' *(Carlyle)*   1873   *J. McNeill Whistler*

5   *Carlyle*   1851   *T. Woolner*

6   *Carlyle*   1868   *G. F. Watts*

7   *Carlyle*   1877   *Sir J. E. Millais*

8   *Carlyle*   1877   *Sir J. E. Boehm*

125

126

129

130

128

his prolonged travail with the satirical and propaganda picture called 'Work'. Rossetti said that it illustrated "all kinds of Carlylianisms", and it is in part a demonstration of the dignity and the unjust material poverty of work in the shape of a group of road-menders, contrasted with the butterfly condition of certain rich passers-by; in it figure Carlyle and the Christian Socialist parson, F. D. Maurice; in support of the physical labourers, they represent the brain-workers, who—in Brown's own words—

Plate 132

seeming to be idle, work, and are the cause of well-ordained work and happiness in others—sages, such as in ancient Greece published their opinions in the market square.

But the likeness of Carlyle is expressed in terms far from a neo-Grecian ideal beauty; it was widely criticised as a caricature—by Holman Hunt amongst others. It seems, however (from independent evidence), to have been a faithful recording of a characteristic grimace of Carlyle; Brown's own expressed intention was "to delineate types and not individuals", but he was not to be shifted from his view of Carlyle, for so the face had appeared to him in a moment of animation, and to typify did not involve a departure from the truth of an actual moment.[107]

Eight years later, in June 1867, Carlyle sat to a painter with ideas of truth far removed from the Pre-Raphaelite insistence on sheer physical actuality—to Watts. To Carlyle, Brown's Prophet of Work was opposed the Prophet of High Art; the battle appears to have been brisk but inconclusive. Carlyle would away with the whole of the Elgin Marbles, away with them all into space, on the grounds that there was not a clever man amongst the Grecian riders; their jaws were not prominent enough: "Neither God nor man can get on without a jaw." The long upper lip was a sign of intellect; Watts countered with the examples of Napoleon, Byron and Goethe. In the end, Carlyle found Watts "a very wearisome, washed-out

Plate 126

dilettante man". Watts found Carlyle very difficult, and made three fresh starts, maddening his sitter by refusing to let him see till the portrait was finished. When Carlyle at last saw himself, he restrained himself to an unusual degree: "Man, I would have you know I am in the habit of wearing clean linen." Later, in other company, he expressed his disgust at being turned into a

mad labourer . . . insufferable . . . a delirious looking mountebank full of violence, awkwardness, atrocity and stupidity, without recognisable likeness.

Yet Meredith found in the same portrait the look of Lear encountering the storm on the Kentish coast; and Chesterton caught in it

the strange combination of a score of sane and healthy visions and views, with something that was not sane, which bloodshot and embittered them all, the great tragedy of the vision of a strong countryside mind and body with a disease of the vitals and something like a disease of the spirit. In fact, Watts painted Carlyle "like a mad labourer" because Carlyle was a mad labourer.[108]

Plate 130

In sharp contrast to the opinions of Watts on Carlyle, and Meredith's and Chesterton's opinions, is another portrait taken at about the same time: a photograph by Mrs. Cameron. Carlyle was not enthusiastic about it, but he was not impolite, and he was perhaps worried by it:

It is as if suddenly the picture began to speak, terrifically ugly and woebegone, but has something of a likeness—my candid opinion.

As a picture it touched Roger Fry to the quick, and he wrote of it:

Neither Whistler nor Watts come near to this in the breadth of the conception, in the logic of the plastic evocations, and neither approach the poignancy of this revelation of character.

288

The first two of these contentions seem to me indisputable (though the crisper side-whiskers, nearer the lens and so presumably in a sharper focus, may be judged out of logic), but the third implies an over-simple conception of portraiture. This is certainly a most moving and a most beautiful portrait, but that it conveys more of Carlyle than Watts' image of him is very open to argument; it is possible that the very breadth and logic praised by Fry have suppressed the extraordinary paradoxes of the man, those indicated by Chesterton—and that bristly crankiness that gleams in the Madox Brown, the stamina that could seem at times almost of Scots granite, and the harsh vigour of the Boehm.[109]

Boehm's statue (a bronze of it presides over the gardens by Cheyne Walk) was made eight years later, in 1875, and is perhaps the sculptor's masterpiece. Boehm (an Austro-Hungarian from Vienna) settled in London in 1862 and immediately and permanently became immensely successful, everywhere from the court downwards, until his death in 1890. A sculptor of remarkable natural talent, with the help of a large studio team he produced far too much, capitalising on his skill in producing a sort of three-dimensional photograph, unpretentious, swift and completely indifferent to the plastic evocations that Fry was to reveal in art to a later generation. His work epitomises the movement of later Victorian sculptors away from the neo-classicism of sculptors like Baily, and especially of those like Macdonald and Gibson who worked in Rome, to a brisker but generally skin-deep naturalism.

Plate 128

Boehm seems to have got on very well with Carlyle (taking in good heart the writer's dishearteningly bluff opening gambit: "I'll give you twenty-two minutes to make what you can of me"). There is a thrust and drive, almost a rhythm, in spite of the limp and vapid coat collar, that is rare in his work. This is most marked in the bust taken by a "squeeze" from the original plaster done from the life (so much of late Victorian sculpture moves straight from the unpublished model from life to the monument in marble of certain death). The statue roused Ruskin to praise in his *Academy Notes* which ended with a just epitaph on much mid-Victorian sculpture:

> It is generally a note of weakness in an Englishman when he thinks he can conceive like a Greek; so that the plurality of modern Hellenic Academy sculpture consists merely of imperfect anatomical models peeped at through bath-towels. . . . Let us go back to less dignified work.

But a collar and tie are difficult subjects for sculptors, and the naked chests and throats often persist, the fine classical torsos sprouting a late Victorian head, often as uncomfortable as an English garden in a tropical exile.[110]

Plate 127
In 1877 Carlyle sat to the by now chosen painter of prosperity, Millais, fully weaned from Pre-Raphaelitism. Before it was finished, Millais had a brush with a sharp lady from Glasgow, Mrs. Anstruther, who describes it as

> in Millais' usual style, hard clever forcible painting. The outline, the features, all correctly given and with great power of brush. But merely the mask, no soul, no spirit behind. I said it looked modern, and in fact I did not like it. . . .

Millais never finished it, though the face is complete; it rejuvenates the 82-year-old considerably; it endows him with good health, a frank manly gaze (compare the Boehm and the Watts) and a certain slick and venerable romance in the hair. It is admirable evidence as to why Millais succeeded as a fashionable society-painter.[111]

Plate 124
To enumerate all the portraits of Carlyle would be wearisome; there are many more, but I will limit myself to the Whistler. The encounter seems improbable; it was arranged by Mme. Venturi, a friend of both parties, in 1873. Both

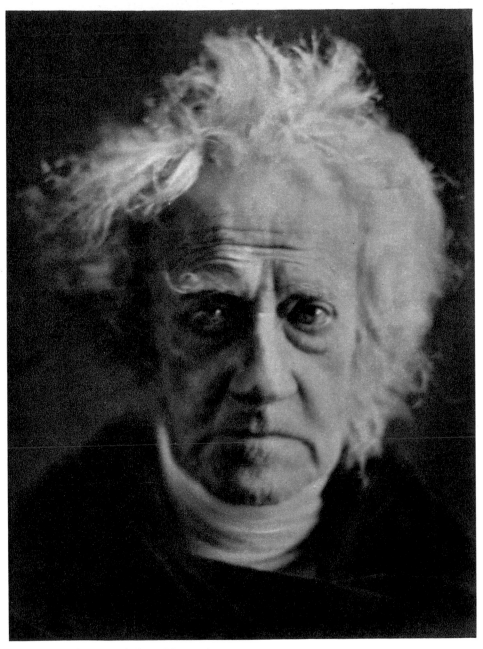

133   *Sir John Herschel   1867   Julia Margaret Cameron*

135 *Isambard Kingdom Brunel* c.1858 *anon.*

134 *Isambard Kingdom Brunel* 1857
J. C. Horsley

parties were baffled. Carlyle sat: "Now fire away, man." Seeing Whistler astounded, he added that if you were fighting battles or painting pictures, the only thing to do was to fire away. The sittings were innumerable; Carlyle complained that if he moved, Whistler would scream at him, but that at the same time the painter was far more concerned with the painting of the coat than of the face. When it was all over, he said: "Well, man, you have given me a clean collar and that's more than Mr. Watts has done."[112]

From Carlyle's constant sitting for portraits, and equally constant disappointment with the results, one may suspect that the apostle of the heroic creed hoped that one day he would find himself on canvas or in marble, perhaps warted, but also in heroic proportions, a blend of Cromwell and Frederick the Great, broadened with a dash of Goethe. Yet the portrait that in the end he said he liked the best was one by his friend, Mrs. Allingham, an amateur water-colour painter; it is perhaps that by her now in the Scottish National Portrait Gallery. It shows Carlyle, reclining whole-length in a chair, reading in his slippers and dressing-gown, a curiously comfortable portrait of a dear if slightly musty old man.[113]

Plate 131

The Carlylean anecdote has perhaps been liberally used in the preceding pages. It has been exercised not only for its own sake, but to illustrate the sort of resistance that a portrait-painter has to contend with. The result of the sittings to Whistler was one of the most enchanting British portraits to come out of the nineteenth century, even if not so successful a painting as a few others by Whistler. But Whistler was not a true portraitist, and the picture is significant of the direction in which the dominant interests in the best European painting were shifting. Carlyle's comment about Whistler's interest in his coat is not irrelevant, and Whistler called the picture, not 'Portrait of Carlyle', but 'Arrangement in Grey and Black'. As he had said of an earlier picture with the same title—

now that is what it is. To me it is interesting as a picture of my mother, but what can or ought the public to care about the identity of the portrait ?

Contrast Watts' creed as he himself formulated it:

A portrait should have in it something of the monumental; it is a summary of the life of a person, not the record of accidental position or arrangement of light and shadows.

A true portrait-painter must be not only interested in his sitter, but must yield to him. Soon painters will be organising in space; what they organise will be of slight importance; the movement is basically opposed to portraiture.

Chapter XIII

SARGENT –
THE WORLD AND ITS CENTRE

IN BRITAIN the infiltration of those values most conveniently labelled impressionist was relatively slow. The demand for portraiture in full fig was, and is, inextinguishable. The Academicians soldiered on in high prosperity, fulfilling an undeniable demand with a very high and very highly paid professional dexterity. On the extreme ideal right wing was Watts, for whom the grammar and syntax of painting had been hammered out to a final adequacy by Pheidias, Michelangelo and the Venetians, centuries before; on a more material plane, equally far to the right, were Millais, H. T. Wells, Sant and others, to be followed by Herkomer, Cope and Ouless (the "pocket Millais"); right of centre was the extremely gifted and serious Holl. On the left was Whistler, with his sitters, or standers, dissolving more and more indivisibly into a luminous haze of paint and light and dark as his career advanced.

But in the 'eighties, the centre revealed itself in a blaze of colour, a daring of elegance and high-light not seen since Lawrence, and a neo-Baroque movement of paint not seen since Lely; a grand talent, with his eye opened, at least, to the surprising colours of the rainbow by his friend, Monet; his eye made aware of the tonal transitions, that Velazquez had demonstrated, through the teaching if not the practice of his master, Carolus Duran, whose order of the day was: "Velazquez, Velazquez, Velazquez, étudiez sans relâche Velazquez!" —an exhortation which, as we have seen, Grant, Millais and Holl would have cordially seconded, but which was really put into action only by Manet. This talent was, like Whistler, an American; John Singer Sargent.[114]

Sargent's most profoundly influential mentor was, however, neither Velazquez, Duran nor any of his French contem/ poraries, but Frans Hals; he referred back again and again to Hals, generally in a technical sense, but more important than pure technique, for our subject, is Hals' approach to his sitters, particularly in his habit of catching those expressions which, while surely characteristic, are not those brave and arranged faces of a normal parade/portrait. Sargent's first appearances indeed were met with storms of disapproval; the famous 'Madame Gautreau' was considered a caricature at the Salon in 1884; of the 'Misses Vickers', at the Academy in 1886, the *Pall Mall Gazette Academy Extra* observed that Mr. Sargent was more eccentric than ever, and the paper's readers, in a referen/ dum, voted it the bottom picture of the year. (In the nineteenth century the word "eccentric" usually preludes an exciting departure; it was used, for example, of the Pre/Raphaelites.)

At this time Sargent himself was very conscious of the novelty of his art and of the opposition. But inside eight years he had become respectable, an A.R.A. paying his duty calls on his colleagues—"those whose names I had hated for years and years" he found, in 1894, often "men of the world and altogether delightful—Sant, for instance, whom one considered the Anti/ Christ". In but a few more years George Moore will be dubbing Sargent as but

the apotheosis of modern fashionable painting, doing what Messrs. J. J. Shannon, Hacker and Solomon would like to do but what they cannot do.

By then the centre had, as is perhaps normal, swung almost to the extreme right.

Sargent himself was very much a man of the world, and the world—that part of it that one is a man of—was altogether delightful. His vision was confined to the facets of a certain society; beyond that, for portraits, his eye was not interested and

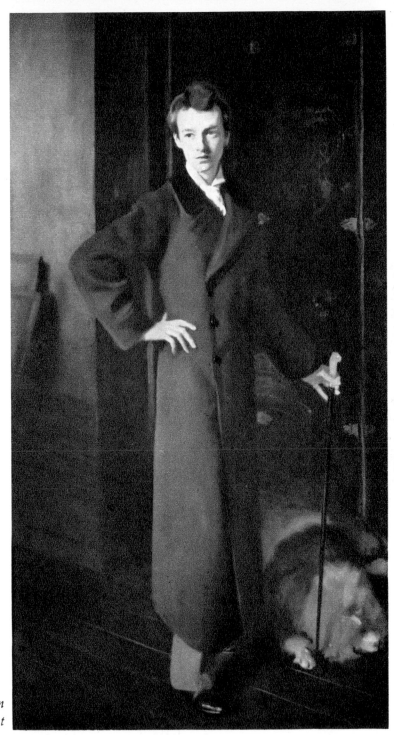

6 *Graham Robertson*
   1895 J. S. Sargent

137 'Vernon Lee' 1881 J. S. Sargent

George Moore   c.1891   W. R. Sickert

139 Colonel Burnaby 1870 J. G. Tissot

his imagination undisturbed. Only in 1918 does he seem to have grasped that there was a war on; and to the consequences of that war, including even the minor one that the Edwardian way of life was over, he remained blind. Yet he had very much, as Vernon Lee noted, an eye for the exotic, and it was his great virtue, in his best portraits, to discover the bizarre and the exotic in the heavily rich and smartly-whorled cream of society that he painted. Entranced with surface effects, he painted a great deal to which the criticism of "man-millinering", once applied to Lawrence, is only too apt. But on not a few occasions, his discernment in the choice of the surface-effect— a discernment which is in its way that of genius—was allied to a pictorial working-out of the picture which was at least adequate. At best, he was perhaps a sketcher, rather than any other kind, of genius; a superb example is the head of 'Vernon Lee', toothsome and bright, jewelled with spectacles; the portrait of a most sensitive intelligence, in which keenness and whimsy joined in style. Whimsy is now found almost obscene (like things that crawl out from under stones), and the style, the *belle-lettrisme*, in which it flourished, apart from the work of Henry James, thought as wearisome, washed-out, and as dilettante a thing as Carlyle thought Watts; that it produced remarkable achievements within its terms of reference is forgotten.

Plate 137

So, too, is Sargent's achievement; Roger Fry's obituary comment still blankets it—Fry was sure that

Sargent was no less distinguished and genuine a man than he was striking and undistinguished as an illustrator and non-existent as an artist.

Fry's view was almost puritanical in its specialisation; his comment is an over-statement though partly true; it was so formulated partly no doubt to *épater le bourgeois,* specifically those—and they were legion and included Sargent himself— who liked Sargent for the wrong reasons. But the criticism is really off-beam, almost as if a logician were criticising a novel, or Mme. Joachim Gasquet objecting that Cézanne's painting of her husband was not like him. Sargent was a taker and maker of characters.

He could also achieve a more purely pictorial splendour; although his broadness is too often vapid, he had a true feeling for the grand manner. He once indicated to a pupil:

Don't concentrate so much on the features, they are only like spots on an apple. Paint the head. Never leave empty spaces, every stroke of the brush should have significance. . . . That's not a head, that's a collection of features.

In comparison with his portraits, it is indeed only too clear that the other high Victorian artists collected features, that they all never left enough out and filled in too much.

With Sargent's more summary treatment he managed to retain the individuality of the sitters and, in his successes, to indicate in them types. The cultured, polished, and sometimes almost sinister, almost comic Jewish aristocracy, the Wertheimers (the powerful assurance of the elder generation, the affluent deprecation of the younger), the Sassoons; the last of the English aristocracy, high-faced as when Van Dyck saw them, splendid in their final extravagances, Lord Ribblesdale as M.F.H., Sir George Sitwell and family; the intellectuals, a little wispy, like Patmore and Gosse; the slender, under-slept, *Plate 136* aesthetic figure of the " 'Nineties" in Graham Robertson. All of these have something of the bizarre; with the chocolate-box beauty he was not generally successful, often getting no further than the chocolate-box, and in his whole-lengths of grand women of the *grands salons,* would force eccentricity by some fling of pose that puts such works fairly into what Sickert called the Wriggle-and-Chiffon school of Boldini. Yet even in some of these there is the shock of a more genuine bizarre, from the contrast of the turbulent froth of clothes with the bony unbeautiful intransigence of the individual face of the woman amongst it all.

In 1886, the year that Sargent was found so eccentric at the Academy, eccentricity much influenced by France found a focus, when the New English Art Club was founded. Earlier than this, in Scotland, about 1880, French values had been rooted in the Glasgow School. Academic portraiture in Scotland had followed much the same course as in England, the broad manner of Raeburn hardening into the higher polish and detail of Watson-Gordon, and still further into that of the Scottish counterparts of Millais, like George Reid. The Glasgow School set up in deliberate opposition their scale of values learned in Paris; amongst the portrait-painters were the young Guthrie and the young Lavery. In the New English, early exhibitors included Sargent himself, Maurice Grieffenhagen, Hacker, J. J. Shannon and also Lavery—all of them later to become popular academicians; Walter Sickert, later to become a somewhat unruly member of the fold, and others like Tonks and Steer who never came to terms with the Academy.

Steer, probably the finest painter amongst them, was very far from a professional portrait painter. Although he painted pictures of people from time to time—like the 'Mrs. Cyprian Williams and her Children' of 1890, at the Tate—the people yield to a greater interest in pictorial values. So also do the people in Sickert's portraits, though to a lesser extent. His George Moore of 1891, a straightforward head and shoulders composition, nevertheless struck horror; at the Academy banquet it was described as the portrait of an intoxicated mummy. Moore's face was famously provocative anyway; many people spent much time thinking up epithets about it, and it was attempted in paint by Manet, Degas, Forain, Tonks, Orpen and many others (though perhaps most successfully by Beerbohm, and, in wax, by Dulac). But Sickert's real interest is not in the recording of Moore's face as such, but in the problem of

Plate 138

303

organising the series of planes that Moore set before him; shape recedes architecturally from the luminous nose in a most exact interlocking of arches.

Thence the two trends continued and still continue, not in parallel course, but blending and breaking. The hard Academy polish was leavened by Sargent, and then loosened by his weakest works until the public eye became a pre-conditioned victim to the slash and slosh of de Laszlo, and the excesses of Lavery and Orpen in their later years. Yet all the time, into the 'twenties, Ouless was painting away, and the painters of polished effigies, with their brilliant sleight-of-hand, still bewitch those who require portraits of public men and of women whose beauty is public news. Yet the grand manner persists and did not die with Sargent; in the late 'nineties a painter, with comparable panache combined with a far more sardonic eye for the bizarre, was emerging: Augustus John. The British have a greater difficulty than the French in throwing portraiture overboard; Pasmore may abandon representational art for the abstract, but Sutherland returns, in excursions, from the world of thorns to portraiture, braving the anger of those who will have their bishops and prime ministers jolly.

In sculpture, naturally, the triumph of the Victorian effigy was even more marked than in painting. Headed by Gibson, who worked almost all his life in Rome, the British version of the style approved by Winckelmann and practised by Canova and Thorwaldsen wore on. Huskisson wore a top-hat upon the occasion, in 1830, when he became the first man to be run over by a railway locomotive; in his memorial statue, by Gibson, he wears a toga. By the 'fifties, trousers were becoming generally admissible in statuary; Gibson would have none of them, and would have refused to undertake the Sir Robert Peel in Westminster Abbey if modern dress had been insisted upon:

o   Oscar Wilde at the Royal Academy 1881   1881/2   W. P. Frith

142 Gladstone 1879 Sir J. E. Millais

141 Sir Sydney Waterlow 1900
F. A. Taubman

143 Sir George Grove 1896 Sir Alfred Gilb

The human figure concealed under a frock-coat and trousers is not a fit object for sculpture, and I would rather avoid contemplating such objects.

Gibson's stress in portraiture was upon the character of intellectual greatness:

It should give us an idea of [the subject's] soul, and this may be done by taste and judgement, without trespassing too much upon the individuality of the person.[115]

In practice, the trespass amounted almost to the obliteration of all individuality.

Although the neo-classic fascination held some sculptors in its grip throughout the century, by the time Gibson died (1865) a brisker movement had been abroad for some years, in the hands of sculptors like Baron Marochetti, an Italian artist of vigour, acumen and some cynicism ("For those who worship Gibson anything is good enough").[116] He celebrated George Stephenson in Euston Square in bronze trousers and frock-coat, with a suggestion of statesmanship added by the scroll in the right hand; to Brunel, he allowed a pair of compasses. In statuary, naturalism proliferated modern costume through the city squares and places of recreation of the British Isles, reaching peaks of one kind in Taubman's portrait of the merchant knight, Sir Sidney Waterlow, erected within his lifetime in 1900, in Waterlow Park, Highgate (in one hand he holds the bronze key to the park; in the other his bronze hat and bronze umbrella); and in the curious marble figure by Gleichen, of Queen Alexandra, wearing gown and marble mortar-board of a Master of Music, in the Royal College of Music.

Plate 141

But royalty, statesmen, and, above all perhaps, generals and field-marshals, were the most popular subjects, not only out of doors, but, usually bust-size, also in the churches, clubs and halls. In 1835, Madame Tussaud's peripatetic show of waxworks had come to rest at the first permanent establishment in

Baker Street, and through the years offered a more varied selection of up-to-the-minute effigies to the curious. They ranged
from the really celebrated criminals, from the Mannings,
Palmer the Poisoner and Charles Peace to sportsmen like Fred
Archer, to the Queen. The Madame Tussaud of marble,
though choosing his subjects within more select limits, was
Boehm, but he had many competitors in his business of catching a deft likeness in stone. More important than any of them
was one of his own assistants, who proved to be perhaps the
finest British portraitist in sculpture of the nineteenth century:
Plate 143 Alfred Gilbert. Gilbert demonstrated again, after a long lapse,
that a portrait-bust could convey a lively impression of an
individual without sacrificing a uniting, artistic rhythm.
Although—in a sense, like Watts—his full capability was
sapped by too great a dependence on the artistic heritage of the
past, so that he was unable to achieve a creation so coherent and
so compulsive as that of his elder contemporary, Rodin, Gilbert's was a brilliant talent with a sculptural feeling, particularly
for bronze, that is lacking in all his British contemporaries and
predecessors except Alfred Stevens.

In a few of Gilbert's busts of the 'eighties and 'nineties, there
is a movement and expressiveness that recalls Hogarth perhaps
rather than Roubiliac; it might be hoped that an expressiveness
of the same order would be found in the paintings of contemporary life and also the caricature in which the Victorian
period was so rich. On the whole, this is far from so. The
documentation of the aspect of the times is profuse; in the
'fifties the Pre-Raphaelites and their sympathisers opened up the
contemporary scene in paintings like Brown's 'Work', in the
early work of Millais and of W. B. Scott; in 1851 Frith too
turned his attention from the depiction of literary and "costume"
incidents to contemporary life. There remained however an
atmosphere of charade in his work; he did not disdain the use
of photographs as preliminary studies for his paintings, yet the

finished works remain contrivances, skilled as they are. On the sands at Margate the voluminous middle-classes disport themselves; on Derby Day the race-course crowds picturesquely behave themselves; at the Railway Station a celebrated criminal is arrested by two celebrated detectives with the rhetorical gestures of the stage. Only perhaps in 'The Private View at the Royal Academy, 1881', does a note, if not of passion, at least of indignation appear, in the looks cast upon Oscar Wilde by those at a safe distance from him.

Plate 140

With Hogarth, comic emotion was as passionate as the tragic; for the Victorians, in paint the comic became the laughable, or the quaint, as in Webster's 'Village Choir', and the tragic became the pathetic. Often the pathetic degenerated into the lachrymose or the pietistic (as Frith's series, 'The Road to Ruin'). But it could maintain a moving dignity of sentiment as in Egg's series of the faithless wife, and, later in the century, some of Fildes' and Holl's genre pieces. Of faces moved by passion, there is little trace; the unspeakable things must also be invisible; all is decency, and repentance is usually enough to indicate that there has been sin.

The world shown by the popular genre painters is one where poverty is neat and respectful, a world in which everyone knows his place. The scene abounds with courtesy, of the lover to the beloved, of the rich to the poor, of the painter to his subject; charity is graciously given and gratefully accepted. Such was the way of life, and few painters probed more deeply; Madox Brown, in his 'Work', was one, but none of them convey an underlying tension hinted at by some visitors, like the American, Nathaniel Hawthorne, at Liverpool in 1855. Hawthorne saw the poor in all manner of dirt and rags, waiting for soup tickets—

and waiting very patiently too, without outcry or disturbance or even sour looks—only patience and meekness in their faces . . . there does seem to be an insolence of riches and prosperity, which one day or another will have a downfall.[117]

Five years later Dostoevsky was in the Haymarket in London —"the district where in certain streets at night prostitutes gather in their thousands"—and the Haymarket teems in the gaslit dusk with his characters, like the consumptive prostitute, with a secret melancholy and a kind of thoughtful anxiousness: "certainly superior to that crowd of miserable women, or what meaning has the human face? but she was drinking gin . . ."[118] The misery and tragedy of urban and industrial England was not for the painters: why should it be? Dickens excelled in the portrayal of desolation and was the champion of the down-trodden; he was also a champion of Frith and the man who discovered in the freshness of Millais' 'Carpenter's Shop', which showed the Holy Family as a humble working family, "the lowest depths of what is mean, odious, repulsive, and revolt-ing". Even in the popular prints, satire died, after a dwindling rearguard action by Cruickshank and by C. J. Grant in the 'thirties.

The art-criticism of Thackeray indicates the rôle that art must play—elevating, doing good, making decent people more decent and warm and happy; an art from the heart to the heart. It was an art too that spoke continually of comfort, of the comfort of the conventional unshakeably fortressed against the unconventional, of a middle-class consolidated in wealth, until the working-class appears to be composed of a number of stock characters with stock "funny sayings" repeated endlessly in *Punch,* even below the drawings of the most brilliant and objective English draughtsman of the century, Charles Keene.

The socially-conscious group of illustrators who worked for the *Graphic* paper in the 'seventies were moved by a genuine interest and sympathy, but the school did not survive long, and the best-known of them—Holl, Herkomer and Fildes—all rapidly became leading society-portrait painters. John Thom-son, the first photographer with an interest in social documen-tation, followed exactly the same course. After his remarkable

14   *General Napier · c.1850 (?)   Smart*

145   *Edward Harrison*   c.1715   *Chinqua (?)*

Street Life in London, published in 1877, with its studies even of down-and-outs, he became a society-portrait photographer in Mayfair in the 'eighties. None of them, though Holl went to the lengths of borrowing real East End rags with which to drape his models, had the clear uncompromising eye for the starkly melodramatic horror of London that the foreigner Doré brought to it.

It was not Doré, however, that Ruskin recommended to the public; in that famous letter (1877) in *Fors Clavigera* in which he accused Whistler of flinging a pot of paint in the public's face, he suggests also that Tissot[119]—if only he would obey "his graver thoughts", instead of painting "mere coloured photographs of vulgar society"—would better occupy the attention of the public than Doré. Yet Tissot was far more than a mere photographer—an artist of extraordinary manual dexterity and deftness in composition. His people relax in an endless, admirable leisure, while time and sunlight circulate amongst them like money easily and well spent, and their eyebrows lift out of ennui at the gleam of pleasure. Frederick Gustavus *Plate 139* Burnaby was one of the many and varied personifications of that impulsive, exploratory and often eccentric Victorian energy that took shape also in people like Florence Nightingale, Livingstone, the Napiers and Jameson; an energy for which the confines of this island were generally too small, an energy which perhaps only the portrait-painters were able to tame. Yet Tissot's painting of Burnaby catches perhaps something of the man's character, more than the mere military dandy with the cigarette and the waxed moustache; six foot four in height, he could carry a small pony under one arm and was a master-balloonist, yet was obliged to travel for his health, and did so in the obscurer parts of Africa and the Middle East. He was painted by Tissot in 1870; fifteen years later he died with a dervish's spear through his throat.

None of this is of course explicit in the portrait, but the

painter had a power of evoking mystery out of the precision of everyday objects that is reminiscent of the best seventeenth-century masters in Holland: a mystery more demonstrable of course in his harbour scenes, with their promises of voyages and discovery, but the promise is also there behind the enigmatic faces of his women. Tissot returned to France in 1882; and though a somewhat similar rendering of high-life was pursued by Orchardson among others in the 'eighties and 'nineties, with more anecdotery, Orchardson's was a talent of great ability, but without magic. (Tissot's "vulgarity", *pace* Ruskin, was a true and honest vulgarity of pleasure in opulence, not to be confused with a taste for "low-life" subjects.)

One of the most typical forms of late Victorian genre painting was the recording on large canvases of social scenes; Frith's
Plate 140 'Private View at the Royal Academy, 1881', was one, and Jamyn Brooks and H. Barraud specialised in them. In spite of the academic sophistication of the technique, they tend to have a curiously "primitive" look, stuffed with people, for everybody or almost everybody has to be visible and recognisable. Private Views, Race Meetings, Royal Garden Parties, the Royal Yacht Club at Cowes, Jubilee Processions, they were all painted— and then engraved with the prospect of a reasonably certain subscription from at least the less celebrated participants in the scene. Simultaneously, the photographic portrait-groups, smaller in compass but even more diverse in range, begin to accumulate—the teams: the whiskered rugby players in three rows with tasselled caps, the cricketers and the Scottish shooting parties; the family groups, the fertile great-grandparents amidst their multiplication; the loyal employees, even the banded strikers with banners.

And what of the Victorian face amongst this medley? At the beginning of the reign, women's faces were meek, and respectable. In the 'forties, the hair was divided precisely and centrally by a parting; each cheek was veiled by a curtain of those long spaniel ringlets, forever associated with Mrs. Browning, and then still further blinkered by the huge wings of the poke bonnet. In the 'fifties the curls vanished and the hair sat close and smooth as a cap hiding the ears. Romanticism, like the art of cosmetics, was out; Thackeray demanded

a fresh, dewy, healthy rose out of Somersetshire; not one of those superb, tawdry, unwholesome exotics, which are only good to make poems about. Lord Byron wrote more cant of this sort than any poet I know of. . . .

In the portraits, the freshness and dew are glazed into a porcelain finish, and the rose is almost always a bud, hardly ever full-blown—such are the maidens; when they flower, they do so without riot and in full control, lifting their heads calmly to their matronly status ("locks not wide-dispersed, Madonna-wise on either side her head"), that of Tennyson's Isabel:

> The stately flower of female fortitude,
> Of perfect wifehood and pure lowlihead.

The exotics of course still existed, women like the formidable Caroline Norton, with a face "most dangerous, terrible, beautiful", hair "violet black . . . eyes very large with dark lashes, and black as death . . ."; or the great Florence Nightingale—but the dangerous and the terrible escaped the portrait-makers.

In the 'sixties the hair, still smooth, grows out of the back into a chignon (necessitating often false hair), and the bonnet gives way to the hat, though the hat by some was considered immoral. The entire packaging of the body, achieved by the combination in day-dress of bonnet and crinoline (with the face only naked, as at the window of the convent, peeping but not looking), is alleviated; in the 'seventies the crinoline is pushed behind, becomes the bustle; the counterpoise bosom and head thrust forward like a ship's figurehead; stateliness is upon woman. The chignon remains, enlarged by still more false hair, but the hair also begins to go up on top of the head, and to fringe the forehead, and ears emerge boldly; in the shoulders an apparently anatomical metamorphosis takes place. Surtees' heroines were shouldered like hock-bottles ("a fine girl—fine drooping shoulders"), but with the new thrust forward of the upper part of the body the shoulders quite suddenly, about 1880, become square, until in the great leg-of-mutton sleeves of the 'nineties they rise almost to the ear.

The Rossetti jaw emerges from the obscurity of an aesthetic coterie into high fashion, displacing the modest rounded early Victorian chin; the chignon draws up to a bun, the hair swells at the sides and the top; a masculine collar and a vast hat burdened with fruit, feather and flower sail forward into the Edwardian era. The faces are bolder, the heads straighten from their pensive droop. A Frenchman in England in the late 'seventies noted the lack of affectation compared with that of French women, and their candour and openness, valuing health above gracefulness: a hearty eater and a woman who, though she may not make love to her husband, will not make it to any other man either;[120] the tennis girls, the bicycling girls, and amongst them already, the militant suffragettes. Yet the parade-portraits, as by Millais and even Sargent, often produce an effect of glitter that is almost of brass in the jewelled ballroom women; the day of Sir Francis Grant, whose success, according to a contemporary, lay in the fact that his gentlemen were always gentlemen and his ladies ladies, was over by 1870.

In the male face, the dominant characteristic, of course, was hair. The wig had put its emphasis on the seat of reason, while faces were shaved clean; the Victorians often turned this habit upside down, arching the glistening bald dome from a luxuriant wilderness of beard. The beard, after an abeyance of almost two hundred years, was threatening in the 'forties; the last restraint was broken by the Crimean War in 1854. In November of the following year the address by the gallant Duke of Cambridge at a meeting in honour of Florence Nightingale was reported by the *Manchester Guardian*:

The frank and joyous eye of the Duke was admired, but not much else of the Duke's face was visible—he was bearded "like the pard"—lip, cheek and chin being alike innocent of the razor. In a camp shaving is pursued under considerable disadvantages; and the Duke is no doubt right; but our young men at home, who can ring for their shaving water as usual on getting up in the morning, are beginning to make his royal highness the "glass of fashion and the mould of form", and are cultivating a beard in addition to a luxuriant moustache and whisker. Let Sheffield look to it, therefore, and pray for an early termination of the war.

Sheffield was to be disappointed; long after the war was over, the razors were still laid aside. The beard never became as ubiquitous, or *de rigueur*, as had been the wig, but was nevertheless formidable in its full flowering in the 'sixties, particularly in intellectual circles like that of Little Holland House. The seers of the age are almost to be recognised from differences in topiary work rather than in features. Although not the hall-mark of the Victorian innovation, the Grand Old Man (for the most famous of them, Gladstone himself, spurned it), the beard flourished on most of them, ranging in size from the Mephistophelian goat-tuft of Disraeli to the wiry entangle-ment of whisker and spectacle behind which Trollope's face was almost invisible under the bald crown.

Darwin's face, when melodramatically lit as in the well-known and regrettable portrait by Collier, the eyes glinting beneath overhanging eyebrows and over a white profuse beard, echoes curiously that of the ape in whom he found human origin; Morris gives off a nimbus of red hair like palpable energy; Watts' beard derives from the early Church fathers as represented by the Venetians; Clerk Maxwell's is professorial, Burne-Jones' is limp as that of W. G. Grace is energetic and

Plate 144 thirsty. But perhaps the most idiosyncratic beard of the nineteenth century is that of Charles James Napier, a beard that now, it may be feared, would be found almost mutinous by the War Office, but which, combined with the flash of naked spectacles under the topee as he rode into battle, no doubt facilitated in some degree the conquering of Sind.

Even those—as later did most of the younger men—who shaved their chins usually grew large side-whiskers, or a moustache, or both, and the variety of presentation was remarkable, including Dundreary, weeper and mutton-chop. In 1887, of the 700 odd Members of the Jubilee Year Parliament, just under a third had beards, but only about 30 were truly clean-shaven, the rest all having fringes of one kind or another. The bare-faced of the time included not only the *avant-garde* of intellectual and artistic fashion—the Wildes, Beardsleys and Beerbohms, but also some of the coming politicians, notably Grey and Asquith.

The reasons behind the cult of face-hair are difficult to demonstrate; it did not extend to the hair of the crown of the head, which was early macassared, and then became shorter and shorter, generally split by a white straight parting (though while Wilde shaved he let his top-hair grow). Fundamentally, it was probably but another outlet of the same male exuberance that had formerly expressed itself in coloured clothes. The Victorians were capable of splendid eccentricities of dress, particularly in check trousers and knickerbockers, but for business, daily wear, they subdued themselves steadily into the drab uniform of the City. The picturesque of Empire was paraded in the scarlet coats and feathered hats of the general officers who held the border marches in India and in Africa. The reflection of true imperial power is preserved in the *Plate 142* paintings of the statesmen, in mood very close to that of the sixteenth-century portraits by Mor and the Elizabethan painters; but now the frock-coat is sufficient as armour and as symbol. Individual virility decently expressed itself mainly in the top-hat and in face-hair (and perhaps, as with Joseph Chamberlain, for example, in the size and expense of the flower in the buttonhole, and other accessories—the massive gold chain across the waist-coat, the minutely opulent cravat-pin or cane-top). A haze of hair also lent mystery, and a beard, worn always by God the Father, is venerable. Its erotic possi-bilities were never, as far as I know, publicly discussed by an Englishman—that was left to de Maupassant.

Visually, the painters found Victorian sartorial fashions generally embarrassing and ugly; some, like Tissot, divined elegance in them, but none in England saw the black and grey drama, the possible heroic qualities in what Baudelaire, already in 1846, had called "the necessary garb of our suffering age, which bears the symbol of a perpetual mourning even upon its thin black shoulders...a uniform livery of affliction".[121] Manet and Guys each differently suggest this; in England, no one.

In formal portraiture, the Victorians sought for the dignity that becomes the public statue, a public composure of ex-pression that while allowing no direct appeal to the admiring spectators, yet broods on their behalf. Broadly handled, as by Watts and also by the much-maligned Millais at his best, such portraits might have a sincere dignity, but more often they were wrecked by a contradictory insistence on petty detail. Millais, when he abandoned his meticulous Pre-Raphaelite manner for his later, broader style, was probably justified, as far as portraiture was concerned; the verdict of the *Art Journal* in 1864 on Pre-Raphaelite portraiture (one of Holman Hunt's) would still be generally accepted:

Whoever would wish to study the topography of the human counten-ance, in its declivities and concavities, in its mountain ridges or its ravines cut by the course of time, let him pause here and take his lesson. The result is marvellous. We can scarcely add, agreeable.

319

Nor, indeed, coherent, particularly on a life-size scale; the genius that could blend such detail into coherence has been lost since Holbein.

The attempt was probably the indirect effect of photography upon the artists. That the camera had much effect on the composition of pictures before about 1880 is open to doubt (the so-called "snap-shot" angles, for example, might equally have been inspired by Japanese prints); that it had a profound effect on modes of perception is certain. In terms of light and shade the camera could record faithfully every strand of hair, every nook and cranny of the skin (even suggesting, as in some of Mrs. Cameron's photographs, a failure of the sitter to wash beforehand). It could seize relentlessly on every grace and every falter in the contour.

Therein lay its strength and its weakness; the public approved of the accuracy with which it rendered the graces and resented its cruelty to their weaknesses, and there too lay the terrible chance of the artists—to achieve a similar seeming-accuracy while actually ignoring the flaws. The dexterity of Ouless, of Cope, of Herkomer, in their various degrees achieved this, and Herkomer, a truly dreadful painter, acknowledged his art master in the shape of a camera obscura: "Nature is reflected and transcribed just as it ought to be painted."

It is in such terms that the presentation-committees and the general public preferred to have perpetuated those whom they honoured, and their preference, in spite of some flirtation with Sargent and his followers, remains still generally consistent. It is perhaps curious that life-size coloured photographs have not yet caught on, as they might be thought to offer (allowing for re-touching) all the advantages, besides being far cheaper, and more accurate. In fact, colour photography cannot yet quite rival oil painting in illusionism (and in durability and sheer physical presence), though that no doubt will come, but there are other more enduring reasons against it. There is a deeply-entrenched and natural snobbery, for which the sheer glamour of oil-paint and gold frame, of the name of the famous artist (who has also, as is well known, painted royalty), is necessary food; so too is great expense, ostentatious consumption. According to Sir Max Beerbohm, Lord Northcliffe's answer to the painter, who asked for comment on a suggested pose for Lady Northcliffe, was: "I don't care a damn, my good man, so long as you use the most expensive paints." Not to expend a great deal of money (at least as much as the subscribers have offered) would be to depreciate the sitter. And the paintings remain high-class, hand-made pieces of craftsmanship, often wonderfully skilful, and satisfying to the immemorial human delight in sleight-of-hand.

Chapter XIV

NOT BEAUTY
BUT CHARACTER

THIS BOOK has developed from a suggestion that an illustrated analysis of the Englishness of the English face was a subject worth the undertaking. I came to the conclusion that that aspect of the subject was outside my competence; it demands a trained ethnologist. It is in any event a theme, the illustration of which would be extremely difficult. Most people have some vague visual conception of an Englishman, an Irishman, a Welshman, a Scotsman, but if called upon to substantiate the images, the number of apt examples they could name amongst their acquaintances would be minute. And before one comes to assess a national face, one must have a clear realisation of the distinction between national and racial faces. Any Britisher owes the shape of his head to an ancestry, the elements of which include most of the known branches of the white race; the British nations are all of vividly mongrel stock.

The ethnologist can demonstrate the facial and cranial characteristics of any given race convincingly enough; thus the darker Keltish faces are often found in Wales and Cornwall, whither the Kelts, who had arrived on the island in the Iron Age, were ultimately pushed by the later Angles, Saxons and Jutes ("tall, heavy-boned, long-faced mesocephals"); black hair is relatively common in Cornwall and in Wales, but very rare on the east coast, where one may expect, and often does find, blonde men with clear light eyes, who would not be noticed in Denmark as foreigners. The variations through the country are great, and inconsistent, and the ethnologist, when asked what characterises the British face, has, like all of us, to fall back on a largely subjective gleaning of broad experience:

Although the British are quite variable in facial form, the features by which a foreigner would remember them would be a longness and narrowness of head and face, floridity, and a pinched prominence of the nose.[122]

That is the opinion of a distinguished American ethnologist, Professor Coon; it is, I should have thought, rather the sort of English face (one well known to Van Dyck) that can be recognised immediately abroad, even before one sights the G.B. plates on the car. But it is not a Scottish, nor a Welsh nor an Irish face—nor even, say, a Midlands face. Nor is it the face of John Bull—thick-set, wide-faced and long-nosed— which Professor Coon analyses with some preciseness as a derivation from the "larger brachycephalic element brought in by the Bronze Age invasion—a British form of the continental Borreby race".

But John Bull's history is relatively short; he was invented as a character by Arbuthnot early in the eighteenth century, but he did not settle into a fixed image until early in the nineteenth century (his image varies considerably in, for example, Gillray's cartoons).[123] About 1855 he was well consolidated and could be recognised by another American, Hawthorne, as "bulbous, long-bodied, short-legged, heavy-witted, material, and, in a word, too intensely English"; it is curious that he has less of the urban shopkeeper about him than of the tough roast-beef agriculturist. That he is an in-adequate symbol for Englishness is evident to the English if not to some of their critics and enemies. But the attempt to sum up the English face is vain; not long ago three British scientists[124] produced experimentally a typical English face, both male and female. They superimposed a large number of silhouettes of different men and women; and arrived at the result overleaf. To the layman this seems uninformative, except perhaps for use in support of Oscar Wilde's epigram on the English face—once seen, never remembered.

Fig. 3

The object, then, has rather been the more modest one of assembling a number of portraits from 1400 to 1900, from the beginnings, that is, of naturalistic portraiture in this country, and by my commentary to indicate how their relation-ship to the flesh and blood which they represent is controlled—by artistic and sartorial fashions, by the individualities of the sitter and the artist—and how through time this relationship alters. Every portrait is the result of a bargain between the sitter and the artist, and only in portraiture does the artist undertake a subject that can, and often does, answer back and argue; yet both are ineluctably of their time.

Plate 145   In a model, perhaps by Chinqua, a Chinese who was working in Madras about 1715, there is an unusual example of this compromise—a Chinese view of Western features. In Europe every national culture had its own view, constantly changing, of the ideal format of man and woman; thus in Lauderdale we saw an Anglo-Dutch, an Italian and an English view of a Scottish face (not that anyone would claim

Plates 59, 60,   Lauderdale's as a typical Scottish face), each strikingly different.
61

Not only did the artist compel his sitters into the rhythm of his style, but the sitter by dress, by constriction by corset, or by addition (at one time in the eighteenth century false stomachs were not unknown), by manipulation of the hair and by face-paint, built him or herself into the fashionable mould. It was the business of the artist to catch the individual within this common mould: Hoppner, according to his own testimony,

used to make as beautiful a face as he could, then give it a likeness to the sitter, working down from this beautiful state until the bystanders should cry out: "Oh, I see a likeness coming!" whereupon he stopped, and never ventured to make it more like.[125]

It is difficult to isolate any specifically English or British qualities that are constant through the ever-changing fashions of the beautiful in face and body. Stendhal, in 1817, located one with an attractive but doubtful precision: "The character-istic of the English beauty . . . is to have a very long neck."[126] Stendhal had perhaps been looking at portraits by Lawrence, but of most periods this seems fairly true. Although it was almost entirely obliterated by the ruff in the sixteenth century, women have generally favoured "the swan-straining, faire, rare stately neck" advocated by Herrick. The painters were well aware of its importance; thus the society pastel-portraitist Russell, in 1777: "As few necks are too long, it may be necessary to give some addition to the stem . . . nothing being more ungraceful than a short neck."[127] In the case of men, the importance is less certain. "Mr. Jorrocks was terribly thick about the throat—a sad sign of want of breeding", but many remarked admiringly of the colossal bulwark of Gladstone's neck. And anyway, neck, alone, is surely not enough. The ideal proportions of the face change continuously, but at any one time one may conform to the ideal standard and yet not be allowed beauty—and vice versa, as Hilliard already knew. When discussing the correct proportions, as laid down by many in this book), but it is not a statement of historical fact. And when dealing with portraits by great artists, the interpretation becomes even more ambivalent, for the great portrait-takers are really great portrait-makers, creators of characters whose unquestionable truth in the realm of imagination is not necessarily reconcilable with history: Charles I by Van Dyck exists in its own right just as Shakespeare's Richard III exists in its own right, and they are both images of such vitality that they have played a considerable part in the distortion, probably beyond hope of rectification, of the historical characters of Charles and Richard.

As in most historical quests, the search to reveal the man as he was from the wrappings supplied by his recording artists is beset with difficulties, and its end is uncertain. The great portrait-maker's genius enables him admittedly to create character, but we can never be sure how much of his creation is himself rather than his subject; for the average painter or sculptor of any conscience the problem must be maddening to despair. Here is Washington Allston, an average craftsman, recollecting in tranquillity his attempt to record Coleridge:

So far as I can judge of my own production the likeness is a true one. But it is Coleridge in repose, and though not unstirred by the perpetual groundswell of his ever-working intellect . . . it is not Coleridge in his highest state—the poetic mood. When in that state no face I ever saw was like his, it seemed almost spirit made visible, without a shadow of the visible upon it. . . . But it was beyond the reach of my art.[131]

Northcote, a better painter than Allston, once admitted resignedly that a portrait is only a little better memorial than the parings of the nails or a lock of hair; and Byron's cynicism—in his answer to the question, what is the end of fame?—that it was

> To have, when the original is dust,
> A name, a wretched picture and worse bust—[132]

was hardly to be entirely refuted by the quality of the recordings that artists were to leave of Byron. (The failure of great men to sit to the apposite painter is an endless source of regret.)

Yet even the most wretchedly executed portrait has generally some value, offering something that words cannot. Even the most incompetent or most mannered artist has had as starting-point a unique face; the body may be more often than not a symbol or a clothes-horse (and that is the reason why the emphasis in this book is on the face), but some attempt must have been made to catch the individuality of a face, each one unique. They hover dimly, the faces of the past, beneath the haze of time-darkened varnish, often shadowy as fish in neglected pools, in countless houses of Britain; thousands of them have lost their names, hundreds have acquired new and wrong names, yet each has its own mysterious identity. When the faces are of those well known to history, they add a new dimension to history. Words cannot convey more than a vague impression, different in every reader, of a character's physical displacement of time and space. It is the virtue of the portrait that it offers a definition, not a final one—and certainly not always a convenient one (it was, I think, Max Beerbohm who complained that so few people looked like themselves)—but nevertheless a positive and a measurable definition; it underlines its subject's humanity, the common heritage of perishable flesh. Through words the reader may become intimate with the whole range of an intellect, a character, a spirit, and in one sense the portrait may increase this intimacy, showing you the palpable shape of the man. In another sense, it may set up another and not unhealthy barrier between the reader and the man he seeks, for it places him in the long dead trappings and the differences of his age; it walls him in apartness, the invulnerable isolation of everyman in the fortress of his own body, that no love can entirely overcome. These faces still fight vainly, but not without hope, against oblivion, whether it be oblivion by statistics or the grave. They are not resigned, and they remind the historian, and all other seekers, simply of individual men and women, in the inextricable circumstance of time and place, of flesh and blood.

SHORT BIBLIOGRAPHY

A complete list of books consulted during the writing of this one would be both unprofitable and pretentious. The following brief list is therefore confined to the general works upon which I have leaned most heavily. Sources for most anecdotes and quotations are indicated in the list of references.

J. Brophy, *The Human Face*, 1945.

Sir J. Caw, *Scottish Portraits*, 1902.

C. W. Cunnington, *English Women's Clothing in the Nineteenth Century*, 1937.

C. W. and P. Cunnington, *Handbook of English Costume in the Sixteenth Century*, 1954.

C. W. and P. Cunnington, *Handbook of English Costume in the Seventeenth Century*, 1955.

R. Edwards, *Early Conversation Pictures*, 1954.

K. A. Esdaile, *English Monumental Sculpture since the Renaissance*, 1927.

K. A. Esdaile, *English Church Monuments 1510-1840*, 1946.

M. Florisoone, *Portraits Français*, 1946.

D. Frey, *Englisches Wesen in der bildenden Kunst*, 1942.

H. Gernsheim, *The History of Photography*, 1955.

R. Gunnis, *Dictionary of British Sculptors*, 1953.

A. Gwynne-Jones, *Portrait Painters*, 1950.

Sir H. M. Hake, *The English Historic Portrait, Document and Myth* (Henrietta Herz Lecture, British Academy), 1943.

B. Long, *British Miniaturists*, 1929.

H. Macdonald, *Portraits in Prose*, 1946.

G. Reynolds, *British Portrait Miniatures*, 1952.

G. Reynolds, *Painters of the Victorian Scene*, 1953.

S. Sitwell, *Conversation Pieces*, 1936.

G. Vertue, *Notebooks* (6 vols., Walpole Society Publications, 1930-1954).

SHORT BIBLIOGRAPHY

W. Waetzoldt, *Die Kunst des Porträts*, 1908.

E. K. Waterhouse, *Painting in Britain 1530-1790*, 1953.

W. T. Whitley, *Artists and their Friends in England 1700-1799*, 1928.

W. T. Whitley, *Art in England 1800-1820*, 1928.

W. T. Whitley, *Art in England 1800-1837*, 1930.

F. M. Wilson, *Strange Island*, 1955.

REFERENCES

1   See F. J. Mather, *The Portraits of Dante*, 1921.

2   B. M. Harl. Ms. 4866, f. 88.

3   See R. P. Howgrave-Graham in *Country Life*, CXI, 1952, 82 ff.

4   For the early English royal funeral effigies, see W. H. St. J. Hope in *Archaeologia*, LX, 523 ff.

5   See L. Stone, *Sculpture in Britain, The Middle Ages*, 1955, 193. A number of earlier sculptured portraits were probably also likenesses, but to what degree is problematic (see, e.g., J. Harvey, *The Plantagenets*, 1948).

6   M. Davies, *French School*, National Gallery, London, 1946, 46, and F. Wormald, 'The Wilton Diptych', in *Journal of the Warburg and Courtauld Institutes*, XVII, nos. 3-4, 1954.

7   *Official Correspondence of Thomas Bekynton*, ed. Williams, Rolls Series, 1872, II, 184.

8   F. H. Crossley, *English Church Monuments*, 1921, 31.

9   See J. Pope-Hennessy, *Paolo Uccello*, 1950, 142; the portrait of Grimston by Petrus is on loan from the Earl of Verulam to the National Gallery.

10 For the standard image of Henry VII, see Dr. P. Tudor-Craig's forthcoming catalogue of pictures in the Society of Antiquaries; for Sittow, see G. Glück, in the *Burlington Magazine*, LXIII, 1933, 100 ff.; for the funeral effigy, see Howgrave-Graham, *op. cit.*

11 A. F. Pollard, *Henry VIII*, 1951 ed., 31, 113.

12 Sir Walter Raleigh, *History of the World*, 1614, Introduction. For Holbein the most convenient handbook is P. Ganz, *The Paintings of Hans Holbein*, 1950. The folding twin portraits of Henry and Jane were perhaps the two now respectively in the Thyssen collection, Switzerland, and in the Mauritshuis at The Hague (the latter either a replica or studio work, the original is at Vienna); for Holbein's drawings, see K. T. Parker, *Holbein's Drawings at Windsor Castle*, 1950. The Whitehall painting was destroyed by fire, but is known from Holbein's cartoon for the left-hand half (at Chatsworth), and by a small copy by Leemput at Hampton Court.

13 G. P. Lomazzo, *Trattato dell'arte della pittura, etc.*, 1584 (trans.

333

48 C. F. Bell and R. Poole, *English 17th Century Portrait Drawings* (*Walpole Society*, XIV).

49 K. A. Esdaile, *J. Bushnell, Sculptor* (*Walpole Society*, XV, XXXI).

50 J. Elsum, *The Art of Painting*, 1703, 66.

51 J. Richardson, *Essay on the Theory of Painting*, 1715, 35/6, 175.

52 Shaftesbury (3rd Earl), *Second Characters* (ed. Rand, 1914), 134 ff.

53 J. B. le Blanc, *Letters on the English and French Nations*, 1747.

54 *Historical Mss Commission, Trelawney Papers* (1st Report), 510.

55 Walpole to Mann, 9th February, 1751.

56 G. Vertue, *Notebooks* (*Walpole Society*, XXII), 125/6.

57 Mme. du Bocage, *Letters concerning England, Holland, and Italy*, 1770.

58 Quoted by G. E. C., *The Complete Peerage*, under Darlington.

59 Walpole to Montagu, 23rd June 1750.

60 See M. I. Webb, *Michael Rysbrack, Sculptor*, 1954.

61 See K. A. Esdaile, *L. F. Roubiliac*, 1928.

62 A. P. Oppé, *The Drawings of William Hogarth*, 1948, 22. The most useful compendium on the paintings is R. B. Beckett, *Hogarth*, 1949; for the *Analysis of Beauty* (and the Auto/ biographical Notes) see Burke's edition, 1955, from which all quotations are taken.

63 See R. E. Moore, *Hogarth's Literary Relationships*, 1948.

64 Mary Granville (Delany), *Autobiography and Correspondence*, 1861, II, 72.

65 J. Stewart, *Plococosmos*, 1782, 203.

66 *Gentleman's Magazine*, XXXV, 1765, 95.

67 Captain Jesse, *Life of G. Brummel* (1893 ed.), 33.

68 For Reynolds, see E. K. Waterhouse, *Reynolds*, 1941 (with bibliography); E. Wind, *Vorträge der Bibliothek Warburg*, IX, 1930/31, 156 ff. For the *Discourses*, I have used R. Fry's edition, 1905.

69 F. W. Hilles, *The Literary Career of Sir J. Reynolds*, 1936, 161.

70 *Dr. Campbell's Diary, 1775*, ed. Clifford, 1947, 53; Boswell, *Tour to the Hebrides*, 1786; *Thraliana*, ed. K. C. Balderston, 1942.

71 W. Hayley, *Life of Romney*, 1809, 24.

72 For Gainsborough, see W. T. Whitley's biography, 1915; an adequate compendium will doubtless be provided at last by E. K. Waterhouse's forthcoming book on the artist.

73 Whitley, *op. cit.*, 73 ff.

74 *Conversations of J. Northcote with J. Ward*, ed. Fletcher, 1901, 160.

75 Hayley, *op. cit.*, 181.

76 Earl of Malmesbury, *Letters*, 1870, I, 299.

77 J. C. Lavater, *Essays on Physiognomy* (from the 17th English edition), 315. For a critical study, see C. Steinbrücker, *Lavaters Physiognomische Fragmente im Vorhältnis zur Bildenden Kunst,* 1915.

78 E. N. Jackson, *Silhouette*, 1938, contains much information, though not always reliable; see also R. L. Megroz, *Profile Art*, 1948.

79 Hazlitt, *Conversations with Northcote*, ed. Gosse, 1894, 89; the idea goes back at least as far as Fénelon's *Fables*.

80 Goldsmith, *Citizen of the World*, 1761, Letter 109.

81 Hayley, *op. cit.*, 204.

82 N. Karamzin, *Travels from Moscow*, 1803, III, 203, 217.

83 See K. Garlick, *Lawrence*, 1954; for biographical details, D. Goldring, *Regency Portrait Painter*, 1951.

84 Quoted by Goldring, *op. cit.*, 264.

85 E. George, *Life and Death of B. R. Haydon*, 1948, 209.

86 For Wilkie, see Cunningham's *Life*, 1843.

87 For Mulready, see F. G. Stephens' monograph, 1890.

88 See *Catalogue of Political and Personal Satires*, British Museum, 1870-1954, with invaluable introductions; F. D. Klingender, *Hogarth and English Caricature*, 1944.

89 Goldring, *op. cit.*, Chap. IX.

90 Chateaubriand, *Mémoires d'Outre-Tombe*, trans. de Metos, 1902, IV, 72.

91 Henry Fielding, *Enquiry into the Causes of the Late Increase of Robbers, etc.*, 1751, 156.

92 For visual records of urban and industrial workers, see F. D. Klingender, *Art and the Industrial Revolution*, 1947.

93 For photography, I am heavily indebted to H. and A. Gernsheim's standard *History of Photography*, 1955.

94 A. M. W. Stirling, *The Richmond Papers*, 1926, 123.

95 *Magazine of Art*, I, 1878, 49.

96 Stirling, *op. cit.*, 49.

97 Stirling, *op. cit.*, 60.

98 F. M. Hueffer, *Ford Madox Brown*, 1896, 100.

99 For the Pre-Raphaelites, see Holman Hunt, *Pre-Raphaelitism*, 1905; R. Ironside and J. Gere, *Pre-Raphaelite-Painters*, 1948; A. P. Oppé, "Art", in *Early Victorian England*, ed. G. M. Young, 1934.

100 See R. Barrington, *G. F. Watts, Reminiscences*, 1905; M. S. Watts, *G. F. Watts*, 1912; R. Chapman, *The Laurel and the Thorn*, 1945; D. Loshak, *G. F. Watts* (Exhibition Catalogue, Arts Council), 1955.

101 W. M. Rossetti, in Fraser's *Town and Country Magazine*, 1862, LXVI, 77.

102 See Myers & Co., *Catalogue No. 373*, 1952, no. 366. The generally adopted and highly developed use of cosmetics in the present century, by which women prepare a public face for almost all occasions, offers to some extent a defence against the camera.

103 H. Gernsheim, *Julia Margaret Cameron*, 1948.

104 W. B. Scott, *Autobiographical Notes*, 1892, I, 270.

105 W. Allingham, *Diary*, 1907, 209; cf. Carlyle's often-quoted remark that "the portrait was a small lighted candle by which the Biographies could for the first time be *read*, and some human interpretation be made of them. . . ."

106 A. Woolner, *Thomas Woolner, R.A.*, 1917.

107 Hueffer, *op. cit.*, 190, 165, 194.

108 D. A. Wilson and D. Wilson MacArthur, *Carlyle in Old Age*, 1934, 130; G. K. Chesterton, *G. F. Watts*, 1904, 69.

109 H. Gernsheim, *J. M. Cameron*, 1948, 78; D. A. Wilson, *Carlyle to Threescore Years and Ten*, 1929, 368.

110 Wilson and Wilson MacArthur, *op. cit.*, 371 ff.

111 Wilson and Wilson MacArthur, *op. cit.*, 405; for Millais, see J. G. Millais, *Life and Letters of Sir J. E. Millais*, 1899.

112 Wilson and Wilson MacArthur, *op. cit.*, 297 ff.

113 Wilson and Wilson MacArthur, *op. cit.*, 435.

114 E. Charteris, *John Sargent*, 1927; see also *Illustrations to the Sargent Exhibition*, Royal Academy, London, 1926.

115 T. Matthews, *Biography of J. Gibson*, 1911, 100.

116 I. McAllister, *Alfred Gilbert*, 1929, 105.

117 N. Hawthorne, *English Notebooks*, 1870, 19 February 1855.

118 Quoted by F. M. Wilson, *op. cit.*, 224.

119 For Tissot, see J. Laver, *Vulgar Society*, 1936.

120 Max O'Rell, *John Bull and His Island*, 1883.

121 Baudelaire, *The Mirror of Art* (trans. J. Mayne, 1955), 127.

122 C. S. Coon, *The Races of Europe*, 1939.

123 See D. George's introductions to the *Catalogue of . . . Satires*, British Museum, vols. V–IX.

124 McLearn, Morant and Pearson, in *Biometrika*, XXb, 1928-9.

125 *Conversations of J. Northcote with J. Ward*, ed. Fletcher, 1901, 190.

126 Stendhal, *Journal*, 9th August 1817.

127 J. Russell, *Elements of Painting with Crayons*, 1777, 35.

128 I have followed Sir H. Nicolson's outline, *Development of English Biography*, 1928.

129 Cf. Northcote, *Life of Reynolds*, 1819, II, 287. Lay-figures were also used, but the portrait of the body is normally a portrait of clothes; nude portraits are rare—they include Nell Gwyn's (see above, p. 128) and the lost portrait of Beckford (of *Vathek*) naked, painted by Mengs.

130 For the "character" and the mystique of the face, see J. Brophy, *op. cit.*; Max Picard, *The Human Face*, 1931; a remarkable passage on this subject is in Walter de la Mare's introduction to his anthology *Love*, 1943, lv–lxii.

131 Quoted by Whitley, *Art in England 1801-1820*, 1928, 236.

132 *Don Juan*, Canto I, ccxviii.

INDEX OF NAMES